STENT; R

A bespattered — ?

940

D1436176

Hertfordshire
COUNTY COUNCIL
Library Service

Hertfordshire
COUNTY COUNCIL
Community Information

A Bespattered Page?

RONALD STENT

A Bespattered Page?

*The Internment of His Majesty's
'most loyal enemy aliens'*

 ANDRE DEUTSCH

First published 1980 by
André Deutsch Limited
105 Great Russell Street London WC1
Copyright © 1980 by Ronald Stent

ISBN 0 233 97246 3

Printed in Great Britain by
Ebenezer Baylis and Son Limited
The Trinity Press, Worcester, and London

9.4. 5.P

'A bespattered page in our history'

Major Victor Cazalet
House of Commons
22 August 1940

'One only has to say the word Jew and certain members of this House lose all sense of reason. I sympathise with the Jews, but Germany has learnt to make skilful use of them. It is no good saying that because a person is a refugee or a Jew, he may not, nevertheless, be a danger to this country.'

Mavis Tate
House of Commons
10 July 1940

For Gabi Penelope

'A bespattered page in our history'

Major Victor Cazalet
House of Commons
22 August 1940

*'One only has to say the word Jew and certain members of this House lose
all sense of reason. I sympathise with the Jews, but Germany has learnt
to make skilful use of them. It is no good saying that because a person is
a refugee or a Jew, he may not, nevertheless, be a danger to this country.'*

Mavis Tate
House of Commons
10 July 1940

For Gabi Penelope

Contents

List of Illustrations

Plates 1–6 are from paintings by Wilhelm Jondorf
Plate 7 shows two paintings by Fred Uhlman
Figure 1 is from a sketch by Captain R. J. Thompson

Acknowledgements

I AM MOST GRATEFUL to the following people, who were all kind enough to give me very useful information:

Peter Beschizzi
Ruth Blunden
Sir Herman Bondi
W. Glanvill Brown
Dr Ruth Borchardt
H. J. Eysenck
M. H. Fisher
S. F. Hallgarten
Bruno Halpern
Walter Hughes
Peter Jacobsohn
Dr R. V. Jones
Dr Leo Kahn
Eric Koch
Helmut Koenigsberger
J. Layton
Heinz Lieser

Sir Claus Moser
Peter Moser
Siegmund Nissel
H. Piehler
William Powell
Margot Pottlitzer
Fred Rees
J. M. Ross
Victor Ross
G. Salinger
Michael Seyfarth
Peter Stadlen
Walter Stensch
Martin Sulzbacher
Fred Uhlman
Walter Wallich
Hans Wetzler

Many of them were fellow-internees; one of them managed to talk his way out of being arrested; others were concerned with internment from the 'other side of the fence'.

I must further thank the Imperial War Museum and, in particular, Mrs M. A. Brooks for making available to me some of the tapes on which they have recorded the recollections of a number of former internees; Walter Fliess, Dr K. Hinrichsen, Mrs Heller, Peter Johnson, Clive Teddern and Professor Helmut Weissenborn. The Museum also allowed me to consult the Sir Henry Tizzard papers. I would like to thank Robert Jondorf for allowing me to reproduce, both inside the book and on the jacket, paintings by his father, Wilhelm Jondorf. Wilhelm Jondorf ran a fine art publishing firm in Nuremberg; he came to Britain in 1938 and started a greeting card publishing

Acknowledgements

business on the Treforest Trading Estate in Wales, then a Government Development Area where many refugee industrialists were encouraged to settle. He was interned in May 1940 and spent almost a year, first at Prees Heath, and then on the Isle of Man. Though the author of many poems and songs, he only developed his talent as a water-colourist during his internment. He died in 1957. I also wish to record my thanks to the Home Office for letting me read the Paterson Report and other documents; to Bloomsbury House and to the Wiener Library for the help which they gave me and for letting me quote from the papers of Harry C. Schnur and C. Rosenberg; to the *Institut für Zeitgeschichte* in Munich for giving me access to the Alec Natan papers and to their Dr W. Roeder for his good advice; to Peter Henessey of *The Times* for publishing my request for sources; to my daughter Elizabeth Monica Howes for helping me with the script, and to my daughter and son-in-law Angela and Daniel Yergin, who encouraged me to embark on the project and whose editorial advice and suggestions were invaluable. Because the book is partly based on so many ex-internees' recollections of events which occurred almost forty years ago, not all the details, particularly the impressionistic ones, may be always entirely accurate. I have tried my best to obtain corroboration but it has not always been possible. But I hope that the flavour of the atmosphere in the various camps is right and that the overall picture is accurate.

Introduction

2 SEPTEMBER 1939. For two days bombs had been cascading on Poland. German armies were thrusting towards Warsaw, the future of Europe hung on a thin thread. Would the morrow bring general war? That evening most people in Britain were at home listening to the wireless, talking, arguing, worried about what was to happen and how it would affect their personal lives. None more so than the refugees from Germany and Austria who had found sanctuary in Britain from their Nazi persecutors. Many of them had but recently arrived. They were bewildered alien corn; uprooted, in a psychological as well as an economic limbo; hoping that after years of the locust at long last the British and French governments would stand up, fight, and crush the evil power which had unhinged their own lives. Yet, at the same time, deeply concerned how the war would affect them and how it might imperil the survival of those whom they had left behind.

The Radio Exhibition at Olympia in London's Hammersmith had been prematurely closed; the vast halls were empty. The windows had been painted black, the arc lights had been replaced by dimly glowing red bulbs. The whole cavernous place echoed to the occasional footsteps of a few workmen who were hastily converting the exhibition halls so that they could again serve a function which they had last fulfilled twenty-five years before, as a reception centre for interned enemy aliens. Internment was to begin that very evening, hours before the British ultimatum to Germany expired.

Some seventy-five thousand men, women and children whom the authorities considered to be of German nationality were living in Britain. Overnight they had become enemy aliens. They were a very mixed bunch of people. There was a relatively small number of long-time residents, apolitical businessmen, technicians, domestic servants, catering workers. Some had married British wives, others were British women who had become German by virtue of having married a German. There were temporary sojourners such as tourists and students, and there were some who were undoubtedly in the country for less innocent purposes. There was a somewhat larger number of political refugees from the Hitler régime: politicians and journalists of all shades from monarchist conservatives to communists; authors and artists; trade union officials; ex-members of the International Brigade in Spain; members of the Lutheran Confessional Church and of other religious bodies opposed to Nazism.

But the majority, perhaps some sixty thousand, were people who had been proscribed and persecuted in their native land for no other crime than origin; the people whom the Nazis had dubbed 'Non-Aryans', that is to say, confessing Jews, baptized Jews, people of Jewish or part-Jewish descent. They were of all ages and came from all walks of life, but the majority of them belonged to the middle classes and were of middle age or younger. Some of them had already achieved eminence in their native country and had significantly contributed to the material and spiritual wealth of Germany and Austria, as judges, senior civil servants, scientists, artists, bankers and businessmen. Others were on the threshold of brilliant careers, which later greatly benefited their country of adoption.

Some went on to become captains of industry and commerce such as Lords Schon and Plurenden, Daniel Prenn, Sir Alex Alexander and Ralph Ehrmann; others were to become prominent figures in the City such as Sir Siegmund Warburg, Ronald Grierson and Walter H. Solomon; some became, or were already, luminaries of academia, garnering Nobel prizes on the way, such as Sir Ernst Chain, Sir Francis Simon, Sir Hans Krebs, Sir Bernard Katz, Sir Rudolf Peierls, Dr Max Perutz, Professor Max Born. Professor Otto Frisch, the nuclear physicist and Louise Meitner's nephew, helped in the development of the atomic bomb. Sir Hans Kornberg became Professor of Biochemistry at Cambridge, Professor Herbert Fröhlich, Professor of Theoretical Physics at Liverpool and Professor Albrecht Fröhlich, Professor of Pure Mathematics at Kings College, London. Sir Hans Krebs eventually presented £100,000 to the British Academy as the refugees' contribution to the 'Thank-you Britain Fund' in recognition of the opportunity which Britain had given to them.

Some contributed to the advance of medical science, such as Sir Ludwig Gutmann of Stoke Mandeville fame; some became distinguished scientific civil servants, such as Sir Claus Moser and Sir Hermann Bondi; some founded great publishing houses, such as Lord Weidenfeld and Paul Hamlyn. Sir Ernst Gombrich became a leading art historian, Sir Otto Kahn-Freund a professor of comparative law, and Hilde Himmelweit a professor of social psychology at the London School of Economics; Professor Hans Eysenck is now well known as a psychologist; Geoffrey Elton, Professor of History at Cambridge, became Britain's foremost Tudor historian, whilst Professor Helmut Koenigsberger of King's College London is an authority on modern European history. Sir Heinz Koeppler, as warden of Wilton Park, Oxon, was responsible for many gatherings of the international intelligentsia. Sir Rudolf Bing was the prime post-war creator of Glyndebourne and the Edinburgh Festival; Ralph Koltai became one of the leading stage designers; the Amadeus Quartet have given enjoyment to thousands of music lovers. Sir Nicholas Pevsner is the great expert on English architecture; Sir Alan Richmond, the Principal of Stroud College is a leading educator. A number of former refugees are now sitting on the red benches of the House of Lords.

Others, and they were of course the great majority, were ordinary folk, engaged in the pursuit of clerical and manual jobs. Some had been in Britain since the early days of the Third Reich, but the majority had only arrived within the previous nine months. Of these, many were merely in transit, waiting for an opportunity to move on to the United States or to other more distant countries. Those who stayed did not become well known, but in their own way they also contributed to the variety of British life.

The refugees included people of all possible variations and permutations of age, temperament, social background, political and religious beliefs. What united them was their passionate hope that in the war, the inevitability of which they had been predicting to their disbelieving hosts for a long time, their old country's régime would be utterly routed, their new country of adoption or of transitory stay would be victorious, and that out of victory and defeat somehow a better world would arise. But whatever happened, few of them ever wanted to go back to the country which had treated them so abominably.

Even those who had close relatives left behind in Germany or Austria had no divided loyalties. They were anxious to do whatever was in their power to help Britain in the struggle to come. She had no more fiercely committed champions than the vast majority of these loyal enemy aliens. For them the issues were clear cut. At 11 o'clock the following morning, they, just as everybody else, heard on their wireless sets the sonorous voice of the Prime Minister, Neville Chamberlain. The refugees had never had much respect for him, they had been Churchillians all the way. Now Chamberlain was telling the nation that the ultimatum had expired and that Britain was at war with Germany. The news was received by them almost with a sense of relief, temporarily overshadowing worries and forebodings. The agony of indecision was at last over.

But for the Home Office and for the security services, who now had to tackle the problems of handling these seventy-five thousand enemy aliens and deciding their fate, the issues were anything but clear cut. What now follows is an attempt to focus these problems, to show how the authorities had prepared for the contingency, how, in the event, they handled or mishandled it, how the refugees fared and how they reacted to their treatment and what ultimately became of them. Over thirty thousand of them eventually found themselves behind barbed wire, incarcerated by their British friends, cheek by jowl with their Nazi enemies. A number of them were deported to distant parts of the Commonwealth; some of them lost their lives on the way to overseas internment; most of them stayed on the Isle of Man, some only for a few weeks, many others for more than a year; a few for the duration.

It is a story which redounds to the credit of many figures of British public life and of many ordinary British men and women; to the shame of others. A story of muddle and malfaisance; a story which shows how the refugees profited or suffered from their enforced isolation, often both at the same time; a story which brought out the best in some and the worst in others; a story which has its brutal as well as its bizarre elements, its humour as well as its tragedy. A story which it seems is worth recalling.

I   *Britain and her Refugees*

THE BRITISH ISLES, insulated by the sea, had, since the Norman Conquest, been relatively secure against invasion or unwanted immigration. The population had therefore preserved a largely homogenous character. Not many people from the continent ventured across the sea, except in certain emergency situations. The supervision of aliens, whether settlers or mere sojourners, had therefore never really been a serious problem, in contradistinction to the continental countries, where it could never really be effectively exercised.

The control of such foreigners, their admission, expulsion and imprisonment, has always been within the purviews of the royal prerogative exercised by the Council on behalf of the monarch, and until about two hundred years ago was not covered by any statutory law. In 1588 for instance, the Queen, in face of the threat of invasion, took severe measures against resident aliens. But in the seventeenth and eighteenth centuries the crown rarely exercised its prerogative, and control over the influx and residence of strangers by and large lapsed. The whole subject of nationality and national loyalty was never rigidly defined, but in 1697[1] a judge ruled that the state of war which then existed between Louis XIV's France and William's England, did not extend to the protestant refugees who had settled in England. This was the first judicial decision that political or religious refugees should be treated differently from other nationals of a country at war with England.

Until the outbreak of the French Revolution, there were virtually no restrictions on the entry of foreigners into the United Kingdom, and no control over them whilst they were resident. It was only the impact of the Revolution, the influx of agents as well as refugees, the fear of propaganda and, after 1798, of invasion, which caused the British government to become alarmed and to act. Pitt preferred not to rely on the royal prerogative, which had fallen into abeyance, but to exercise control by statute. The first Act for the control of aliens in war was passed on 1 January 1798, and was strengthened by an amending Act of 1 June of the same year.[2] This has a preamble relevant to this book:

> A just distinction may be made between persons who either really seek refuge and asylum from oppression and tyranny or are resident in this country for purposes only of commerce or other innocent purposes and persons who have come over or are in the country with hostile purposes and especially to favour and assist the execution of projects of the enemies of his Majesty, now openly declaring their intention to invade this Kingdom.

The preamble ends with words which could equally be applied to the situation 142 years on:

'*Salus populi suprema lex.*'

In 1803, when England was again threatened with invasion by Napoleon, a further Aliens Act was passed. It provided for aliens either to leave the country or face imprisonment. Their dwellings could be searched and householders were required to notify the authorities of the presence of foreign lodgers. Suspicious aliens could be detained during the King's pleasure, and the burden of proof of innocence rested on the detainee. These restrictions remained in force until after the Peace of Paris and the Congress of Vienna.

Throughout most of the nineteenth century, England remained what she had been for so much of her history, a haven and a refuge for the oppressed and the persecuted. Karl Marx, Mazzini, Kossuth, Napoleon III and Emile Zola are just a few of the political refugees who found shelter in Britain.

But when, during the first decade of the twentieth century, the possibility of a major war had to be seriously considered, the Committee of Imperial Defence formed a Sub-Committee on the Treatment of Aliens.[3] During its first meeting on 7 July 1910, the then Home Secretary, acting as the Committee's chairman, stated that on outbreak of war it would be relatively easy to deal with enemy aliens – all those of military age should be imprisoned and held as hostages. This was Winston Churchill. It would be interesting to know whether he remembered these words thirty years later.

As a result of the Committee's recommendations, a new Aliens Restriction Act was put on the statute book on the very first day of the Great War. It gave the Home Secretary full control over the movement of aliens and empowered him to arrest any suspected person without a special warrant. But it did not authorize him to order a general internment as happened in the following year. That in fact was carried out in both World Wars, not in pursuit of any specific statute or defence regulation, but under the royal prerogative.

The situation in August 1914 was very different from that in August

1939. Before 1914 there had been no proper controls over the entry and movement of foreigners. The Home Office kept no records of their numbers or their places of residence. Officials knew nothing about their antecedents or their political connections. But the Kaiser's war was perhaps the last of the old-fashioned wars, a war of nations against nations, fought for territorial objectives, in which patriotism, not ideas or ideologies, was the spur. It could therefore be reasonably presumed that most of the German and Austrian residents in Britain felt a primary loyalty towards their countries of origin. Again, this was significantly different in 1939.

By 9 September 1914, 50,633 Germans and 16,104 Austrians had registered with police; only those who were suspect were interned. As the war progressed, Parliament, the press, and eventually the public, became more and more concerned. Lord Charles Beresford complained in the House of Lords that aliens should not be treated with such flabby sentimentality, they should, without exception, be locked up. Very similar statements were made in July 1940 by such peers as Lords Elibank and Marchwood.

In the spring of 1915, tales of German atrocities and of espionage in Belgium and France, the sporadic Zeppelin raids and an intensified press campaign resulted in increasing violence, either by 'mob' or by a justly enraged populace, depending on which paper one read. There were riots against bakers' shops in Deptford which employed Germans; in Soho, windows of German restaurants were smashed and their staff manhandled; there was street violence in Liverpool. Finally on 12 May two members of Parliament presented a petition at the bar of the House, containing the signatures of over a quarter of a million women, asking for the immediate internment of all enemy aliens of military age.

This seems to have forced the Government's hand. In a complete change of policy the Prime Minister himself announced that the Government would proceed with the immediate internment of all enemy aliens between seventeen and fifty-five years of age and repatriate all over military age. In a subsequent debate, both sides of the House expressed broad approval of the steps, but one member advised caution and cited the case of Prince Louis Battenberg, the former First Sea Lord and Earl Mountbatten of Burma's father, who had rendered such distinguished service to his adopted country, but who had been hounded out of office by the popular press because of his German origins.

By the end of the year, 32,274 German and Austrian civilians had been interned. With some exceptions, they were not released until the end of the war.

Soon after the conclusion of the armistice the British establishment became alarmed that the unsettled conditions in Europe, and the human flotsam drifting about on the continent, might cause a large influx of aliens into this country. As a result in 1918 Parliament passed a series of amendments to the 1914 Act, which were finally replaced by the Aliens Order (1920), which gave the Home Secretary new and comprehensive powers to deal with aliens both in peace and war[4]. The new order authorized the Home Secretary to subject enemy aliens to whatever restrictions he considered necessary in the interests of national security. It enumerated the reasons which could induce the Home Secretary to order the internment of an alien in wartime, such as suspicion that the alien was an enemy agent, that he might yield to pressure and blackmail if he still had relatives or property in the enemy country, or that he might depress morale by defeatist talk or behaviour. Despite these comprehensive powers, the Home Secretary of the day made it quite clear in 1938 and 1939 that in the event of war, he would not rely on the Act, but on the royal prerogative; one reason for this may have been that invocation of the Act and pursuance of his statutory powers would allow challenges in open court, *habeas corpus* proceedings, etc., whereas the royal prerogative cannot be challenged. The 1920 Aliens Order remained the basic law concerning the treatment of aliens until the post-war years and the transformation of the British Empire, which threw up an entirely different set of problems, requiring different legislation.

* * *

Until 1933 the situation was relatively quiescent, and the influx and control of aliens were not amongst the problems which greatly troubled post-First World War Britain. This situation changed dramatically at the beginning of 1933. Hitler had been appointed Reich Chancellor on 30 January and the spectre of ostracisation and persecution of Jews – whether confessing or merely of Jewish or part-Jewish origin – and of political opponents, began to raise its head almost immediately. There was the first dramatic display of vilification and violence on 1 April, when Jewish shops were daubed and boycotted. The overt persecution abated for a while thereafter, but soon began to gather a steadily increasing momentum.

The British Government was aware of the problem from the very outset and so, of course, was the Jewish community in Britain. Immediately after the day of boycott the Foreign Office received a detailed dispatch from HM Ambassador in Berlin, Sir Horace Rumbold, showing to what extent the persecution had already started. The Cabinet decided[5] not to publish the report, so as to avoid public pressure at home and unfavourable reaction in Germany, which could only lead to increased discrimination against the Jews; they left it instead to the Foreign Secretary to show the dispatch privately to a few prominent British Jews, such as Lord Reading and Sir Herbert Samuel.

It was also decided during a meeting on 5 April[6] to set up a sub-committee, the Aliens Restriction Committee, to consider urgently to what extent the persecution might lead to an influx of refugees from Germany into Britain.

The Anglo-Jewish community had been alert to the crisis of German Jewry from the very beginning. At that time they were, like everybody else, quite unaware of the magnitude that this problem would assume during the next few years, but they got to work immediately to tackle it. A special organizing committee for the reception and care of refugees was set up. It submitted a memorandum to the Home Secretary, Sir John Gilmour, urging him to grant all refugees who sought shelter in this country permission to land until they could be found permanent homes elsewhere.[7] The committee undertook to maintain all such refugees at the expense of the Jewish community so that none would become a burden on the State. They estimated that over the next few years a total of three to four thousand might seek refuge in Britain. Although its estimate soon proved to be hopelessly inadequate, the Jewish community strictly kept this promise until after the outbreak of the war, when the sheer financial involvement under wartime conditions forced them to seek government assistance. Other bodies, such as the Church of England and the Society of Friends, also soon set up committees and organizations to care for the non-Jewish refugees, but their numbers were relatively small compared with the Jewish ones, and the main financial burden and responsibility fell on the Anglo-Jewish community, who rose to the occasion quite splendidly. Scientific and artistic organizations also arranged assistance for their fellow scientists and artists who had to flee from Germany. One organization in Britain which did rather less for their exiled German comrades was the TUC.

A week after the first meeting of the sub-committee, the Cabinet considered its report.[8] It endorsed the main recommendation that, despite the pleas and the guarantees of the Jewish community, the current policy of restricted immigration should be maintained for the time being, until the Cabinet saw how the political situation in Germany was developing. Only those people should continue to be admitted who could maintain themselves adequately without having to seek employment or become a burden on the public purse. However, a suggestion was accepted that a limited number of Jews who were prominent in the fields of pure and applied science, in music, the arts, or in industry should be admitted, even invited. That would create a favourable impression abroad. Anything beyond this would stir up hostile reaction at home and raise fears about displacing British workers at a time of high unemployment and when thousands of British-born migrants in the USA and elsewhere, who had acquired American or another nationality, were anxious to come back and were being prevented from doing so by the restrictions on aliens.

The Cabinet was therefore somewhat less than forthright when it instructed the Home Secretary to state, in reply to a question which Geoffrey Mander had raised in the Commons,[9] that, whilst the interests of the country had to remain predominant, the time-honoured traditions of asylum would be maintained and no unnecessary obstacles would be placed in the way of foreigners seeking admission.

In the event, the policy of HM Government in respect of the admission of refugees fleeing from Nazi oppression, whether for religious, racial, or political reasons, was much more generous than at first appeared. The influx, at first only a trickle, steadily grew as the Nazis tightened the screws and after the rape of Austria, and in particular after the *Kristallnacht* in November 1938, it grew to a broad river. In 1933 a total of 2,274 Germans were admitted to the United Kingdom for temporary residence; in 1934: 1,600; in 1935: 1,838; and in 1936: 6,865. By May 1937 a total of 21,322 Germans were registered with the police, but that figure included a number of resident, non-refugee, Germans.[10]

A year later, the Home Office reported that there were 12,800 *male* Germans and Austrians registered, of which seven thousand were refugees, and that they assumed this figure would rise by March 1939 to sixteen thousand male refugees.[11] The increase in immigration turned out, in fact, to be much steeper than the authorities had anticipated. During the period January to December 1938, twenty thousand refugees were registered with the Central Refugee Committee at Bloomsbury House.[12] In the next seven months, up to July 1939, a further twenty-seven thousand refugees registered. These figures do not include any children nor the substantial number of refugees who came over under their own steam, unaided, and who never troubled to register. In addition, up to July 1939, the Movement for the Care of Children from Germany brought over a total of 7,752 youngsters, of whom 5,673 were Jewish and the remainder either part-Jewish or baptized.[13]

Britain's record in this respect is an honourable one. At a time when all over the world frontiers were being closed to the German and Austrian Jews desperately seeking asylum, when the United States, vast, mighty and rich, refused to liberalize its strict immigration quota system in any way, or even to mortgage its quota ahead for a few years,* the admission of well over seventy thousand refugees (of whom more than half came during a span of nineteen months before the curtain of war fell), is in the best tradition of British compassion, and must always be borne in mind when one comes to consider the farcical internment tragedy which followed.

Amongst the chorus of liberal voices pleading for tolerance and generosity for the refugees, there were, of course, others who dissented and who, under the banner 'Britain First', demanded that all these foreigners should be kept out of Britain. They were not only members of the British Union of Fascists and such Nazi sympathizers as the Anglo-German Association or the Link, but also well-connected members of society and of the establishment. A typical instance is a report by the then Home Secretary, Sir Samuel Hoare (later Lord Templewood), in March 1938.[14] He had been told by MI5 that Germany was anxious to inundate Britain with Jews with a view to creating a Jewish problem in the United Kingdom. The Cabinet became sufficiently alarmed to appoint a committee of four to deal with the problem, 'bearing in mind the importance of adopting as humane an attitude as possible and at the same time of avoiding the creation of a Jewish problem in this country.' This is not the last time

---

* After the fall of France, in June 1940, Sir Herbert Emerson, the League of Nations 'High Commissioner for Refugees' pleaded with G. L. Warren, the Secretary of the Presidential Advisory Commission on Political Refugees in New York, to grant visas on the non-immigrant quota to certain ministers of religion and University teachers stranded in England, but was turned down. (Foreign Office file Gen 200/6/72.)

that we shall hear of the considered views of Military Intelligence on the Jewish refugees in Britain.

$$\star \quad \star \quad \star$$

Although the Munich Agreement was supposed officially to have brought 'peace in our time', the possibility of war with Germany in the foreseeable future had to be faced. It would find the United Kingdom with a considerable number of nominally enemy nationals at large within its shores. The number was very similar to that at the outbreak of the First World War, but the nature of the problem was totally different. This should – and must – have been obvious to the various authorities concerned with the question, but government preparations were, to a large extent, based on the precedents and the experiences of 1914–18, and were handicapped by bureaucratic rigidity and lack of foresight.

On 21 September 1938, the War Office issued its first set of Standing Instructions for the Administration of Internment Camps.[15] They ran to thirty-one typewritten foolscap pages and dealt primarily with such typically military concerns as reveille, lights-out, twice daily roll-calls, mealtimes, sick parades, discipline and punishments. None of the thirty-one pages gave any guidance or instructions on the real problems which the internment of a large number of 'refugees from Nazi oppression' (their eventual official accolade) would cause.

On 22 October the Home Office followed this up with a set of draft instructions which were to be inserted into the Standing Police War Instructions.[16] These stated that no general internment of male enemy aliens was contemplated at the outbreak of hostilities. If and when such an order were to be issued by the Secretary of State, the police would become responsible for arresting all persons affected by such an order and for their safe custody until they had been handed over to the military authority. The internees would be divided into two classes. Class 'A' was to include enemy subjects who had held commissioned ranks in the armed forces of that state or equivalent official positions in government service. In addition, such internees as might appear to Chief Officers of Police to be of good social and financial standing, and who were prepared to pay 4/6d per day, could also be sent to Class 'A' camps (the officers would get their special treatment free), the others would be accommodated in Class 'B' camps and fed on normal army rations. This somewhat snobbish discrimination was eventually put into effect in the first camps and continued to be practised there, so that some of the early internees who were suspected security risks received a much better treatment than the great majority of interned refugees.

The whole enemy alien problem was primarily one of security. The Committee of Imperial Defence therefore appointed a sub-committee on the control of aliens in war, just as it had done in 1910. It first met on 18 January 1939, and altogether held six meetings, the last being on 25 August, just a few days before the outbreak of hostilities.[17] During its first meeting the committee discussed the Home Office War Book, Section IX which dealt with the control of aliens in wartime. Chief officers of police were to keep lists of enemy aliens who were officials or members of certain organizations maintained by foreign powers and whose special qualifications would make them useful to an enemy in time of war. They would also have a list of suspected enemy aliens, supplied by MI5, who should all be arrested at, or immediately before, the outbreak of hostilities and put into prison until internment camps had been set up; some of them might also be deported.

It was not proposed to carry out a general internment of enemy aliens at the outbreak of war, but to confine it to agents, members of foreign organizations and persons with special qualifications, as well as enemy aliens found aboard ships or aircraft, when a security officer at the point of entry would decide on internment. Aliens' Registration Certificates would be endorsed so as to require the holder not to change his residence or be absent from it for more than twenty-four hours, except with local police permission. A travel permit would be required for journeys beyond ten miles and no motor cars, cameras, charts, firearms or explosives could be kept without a police permit. The Home Secretary had the power, under Article 91 of the Aliens Order (1920), to declare any part of the United Kingdom a protected area, with restrictions on the entry and residence of aliens. All naturalization proceedings would be suspended for the duration, except for special cases.

The committee also considered a report by the security services. MI5 expected that a total of 3,000 enemy agents and other suspected aliens would have to be arrested just before the actual outbreak of hostilities, of whom 1,300 would have to be picked up in London. But provisions should be made for an initial intake, within forty-eight hours, of 5,500 civilian internees.

Now, for the first time, the committee considered the question of the German and Austrian refugees, of which they estimated there would be some sixteen thousand males by the end of March 1939. They realized that most of them would be more favourably disposed towards the United Kingdom than to their own mother country and would wish to serve in some capacity. The War Office was not keen to invite them to join a labour battalion and the Lord Privy Seal's office was considering some other form of voluntary service for them. But whatever happened, it seemed likely that large numbers of refugees would have to be interned, if only for their own protection. As a Home Office official put it: 'The inflamed eye of the man in the street could not be expected to see them as other than German.' Here is the first of the many arguments which were later advanced to justify wholesale internment. Another argument put forward was that many aliens would become destitute as the result of the war, and would therefore have to be interned. Although there would no doubt be many refugees who would qualify for exemption, the only predictable course was to intern them first and give them the subsequent opportunity to appeal to a tribunal. If there was general internment of all male Germans, Austrians and Italians, the total number was estimated to reach eighteen thousand, of which batches of five thousand could be taken each week – figures which in the end proved to be much too low.

At the last meeting, held on 25 August, the MI5 representative again stressed that sufficient accommodation had to be available for all hostile enemy aliens on their lists, and that certain females who were suspect would also have to be arrested and accommodated somewhere. No enemy alien females should be employed as domestic servants by officers or senior government officials, and no civil servant should employ an alien without the consent of his Head of Department.

The committee also recommended that refugee aliens should be interned separately from hostile aliens. A Refugee Camps Committee should be set up with a view to appointing a Civilian Camps Commandant, to draw up regulations for rationing and accommodation and to make arrangements for the internees to engage in work of some kind. So, somewhat late in the day, the authorities concerned had woken up to the fact that they had problems on their hands which were quite different from those tackled in previous wars, and that the elaborate set of regulations which had been drawn up in the previous year were quite inadequate. In the event the chaff was not sorted from the wheat: refugees and pro-Nazis were not separated – at least, not in the early months of internment – and no really satisfactory means were ever found to organize productive work inside the camps.

Preparations for the setting up of internment camps started in the spring of 1939. On 4 June the Secretary of State for War (Leslie Hore-Belisha) reported to the Cabinet that staff and administrative arrangements to look after eighteen thousand internees were already in hand.[18] The camps would all be ready by the third week after outbreak of war at the latest, and would include provision for 3,500 young refugees who were to be accommodated at Richborough Camp on the Kent coast.[19] Richborough, or Kitchener, Camp near Sandwich had been a First World War transit camp for the BEF. It had lain empty during the inter-war years, but had recently been reactivated to provide accommodation for a substantial number of unaccompanied youngsters whom the refugee committees had managed to bring to England with a view to their ultimate transmigration to overseas countries.

On 25 August the Home Office issued its final Administrative Instructions for the internment.[20] In London, the central collection centre would, as in 1914, be at Olympia. Arrested aliens would be allowed to take with them as much luggage as they could carry in one hand. As before, they were to be divided into classes 'A' and 'B'. (These designations should not be confused with the subsequent tribunal classification of aliens into A, B and C categories.) It would be up to the arresting police officer to decide who was to be accommodated in A or B type camps. Females would be taken directly to women's prisons (Holloway in the majority of cases); their custody was no concern of the military.

Amongst the enemy aliens there would be a number who had been admitted to the United Kingdom for racial, religious, or political reasons.* If a general internment was ordered, it would probably be necessary to include them, partly because somebody who had been classified as a refugee might nevertheless be hostile to this country, and partly because the public would be unable to distinguish between a genuine refugee and a hostile alien; they would regard both with equal suspicion. This latter argument was advanced time and time again by various authorities and members of parliament, but there is no evidence that the general public, or even a small section of it, acted violently against any German or Austrian refugees, as had happened in the spring of 1915, until a press campaign was whipped up in the spring of 1940.

---

* 'A number' indeed: it was probably in excess of eighty per cent of all resident Germans and Austrians.

Even then there were no confirmed reports of any overt hostile actions against individual refugees.

Refugees should from the outset be housed and treated differently from the other internees, but, although they would eventually be administered and controlled by the Home Office, they would initially be looked after by the military in the same way as all other internees. But in order to simplify their eventual separation, the two sections should, from the beginning, be put into separate camps. A list of the proposed camps was appended, catering for a total of 17,950 internees. None of them were on the Isle of Man. Some of these camps were to be made ready at Z + forty-eight hours, some at Z + nine days, and others at Z + sixteen days. Amongst the camps to be readied within forty-eight hours were, significantly, four earmarked for refugees and having room for 2,500 inmates. Out of the six 'A' camps for 'officer status' internees, three were reserved for refugees. In actual fact, none of the refugees who were interned in 1940 ever enjoyed the privileges of these VIP camps; they were exclusively reserved for Nazi sympathizers or those whom the security services considered as such – which was by no means the same thing.

Various preparations and plans had thus been made to deal with the whole enemy alien problem the moment the dogs of war were unleashed, or even before. The errors and shortcomings of the First War were to be avoided.

* * *

On 3 September 1939 Britain finally went to war with Germany. However inexpert and insufficient the preparations had been for dealing with such a large number of enemy aliens in the country, they now had to be put into effect. One issue at least had been clearly defined beforehand: who was to be responsible for these aliens and for their possible internment. Subject to overall policy directions by the Cabinet, it was the Secretary of State for Home Affairs who made the decisions and who supervised the execution of such decisions. He in turn was guided and advised by the security services; his department had to work closely with the War Office who were to man and run the internment camps. A major responsibility, therefore, now devolved on the newly appointed Home Secretary, Sir John Anderson.

He had been a colonial servant, ending his administrative career as Governor of Bengal. In October 1938 he had been appointed Lord

Privy Seal in Chamberlain's Government and, when this was reconstructed at the beginning of the war, he was translated to the Home Office. He stayed there throughout the most critical phase of the war on the home front, the time when the threat of invasion was most imminent. In October 1940 Churchill made him Lord President of the Council in succession to Neville Chamberlain, who had resigned and who died shortly afterwards. Herbert Morrison, the former Labour boss of County Hall, London, took his place at the Home Office. It is difficult to imagine a greater contrast in background, training and experience than between the administrator of professional class origin and the working-class socialist politician (unless one thinks of the Foreign Secretary throughout most of the war, Anthony Eden, and his eventual successor, Ernest Bevin) but a former Home Office principal who served under both of them, says that they shared a common humanitarian outlook.

Though Anderson is best remembered for the corrugated iron backgarden shelters which bore his name, he had a multiplicity of responsibilities in connection with the home front. Yet it is doubtful whether any other caused him so much aggravation and so many awkward questions as the problem of how to deal effectively with the German and Austrian nationals resident in Britain.

According to his biographer, Sir John was determined at the outbreak of hostilities not to be stampeded into precipitate action or into oppressive measures by pressures from without.[21] He realized that the situation in 1939 was quite different from that which obtained in 1914. In particular, he was aware that most of the people admitted since 1933 to residence in the United Kingdom from Germany were refugees, opponents and victims of the Nazi régime, anxious to work and even to fight for the defeat of Nazism; all that was required was a winnowing process. Even when, early in 1940, the popular press began a campaign urging him to 'intern the lot', he wrote to his father: 'The newspapers are working up feelings about the aliens. I shall have to do something about it or we may be stampeded into an unnecessarily oppressive policy. It is very easy in wartime to start a scare.'[22] In a later letter, he added: 'There has been a lot of fuss in the papers about the aliens but I have seen no sign of real trouble in Parliament.'

After the invasions of Scandinavia and the Low Countries, the various pressures from military intelligence, the press and certain members of both Houses of Parliament substantially increased and Sir John gradually gave way to them, until, finally, in the second half of

June 1940, he yielded to what he had earlier termed 'a wartime scare', and ordered a general internment. But it must be emphasized that this was not his personal decision but one taken by the whole Cabinet, which had the full approval of the new Prime Minister. It was a decision which, when it became known, was applauded by almost the whole press and even by some voluntary aid organizations. It would, therefore, be unfair to blame him exclusively for it, if blame is to be attached to the decision at all.

According to a Home Office official, Anderson was known as *Yahveh* by his staff because of his detached attitude; it has been said of him that he looked on the refugees rather as he had looked on his Bengalis, and that he neither understood who the refugees really were, or what the war was all about. But there is no evidence for this assertion. One gets the impression that he found the whole action uncomfortable and unpleasant, albeit inescapable. This impression is even stronger in the case of his deputy at the Home Office, the Under-secretary of State, Osbert Peake, who had to face most of the critical attacks in the Commons, and who had the reputation of being a fair-minded humanitarian, pushed into an unenviable situation.

One of the aspects directly affecting the overall internment policy was the financial support needed to maintain all the refugees. Until 1939 they had been sustained by various charitable organizations, but primarily by the Anglo-Jewish community. In March 1939 however, the Central Committee for Refugees was forced to tell the Government that the influx had become so large that they were no longer able to shoulder the whole burden. Cabinet considered the situation in July 1939.[23] Sir Samuel Hoare, the then Home Secretary, reported that so far forty thousand refugees, mainly transmigrants, had been admitted. He then made the astonishing statement that the German government had offered to set up a trust fund of several millions to finance the emigration of Jews from Germany, provided other countries also joined in. Where the German contribution was to come from was not explained; perhaps from the funds confiscated from the German Jews! Whether the German offer was really serious and was perhaps meant as their early version of a Final Solution, events overtook any implementation of such an international scheme. Thus the outbreak of war found Britain with a large number of refugees, few of whom could be expected to be able to transmigrate in the foreseeable future, and many of whom would either have to be allowed to take employment or be financially maintained, whether within or outside internment camps.

As general internment was not to be adopted, other alternatives had to be explored.

A Cabinet sub-committee under the chairmanship of the Secretary of State for the Colonies, Malcolm MacDonald, was charged with investigating the problem. Their report was considered in Cabinet on 9 December 1939.[24] It stated that because of the general dislocation caused by the war, the Jewish community, who had been responsible for the support of eighty to ninety per cent of the refugees, had come to the end of its resources. The report suggested that the Exchequer should contribute for a period of six months, starting 1 January, a weekly sum of 8/- (40p) per person, provided that the voluntary organizations contributed the rest (which was to be another 8/-) and also guaranteed that no refugee would become a charge on Public Assistance.

The only dissent again came from the Minister of Labour, who was worried about the public reaction to the scheme, when there were so many British subjects out of work who did not qualify for assistance on a scale of 16/- per week. The Government decided, however, to adopt the scheme in principle, to approach the voluntary organizations, but not to publicize it, particularly not the proposed scale of government contributions. The arrangements were to run for an initial period of three months, with an overall ceiling of £27,000 per week, and they would then be reviewed. An additional grant of £100,000 would also be made in respect of expenses incurred during the first four months of the war.* The arrangements were in fact renewed until eventually almost every refugee, except for the old and infirm, had been absorbed in one way or another in the general war effort, and the call on public or charitable funds had become greatly diminished. Within six months of the outbreak of war, other, more harrowing problems, were crowding in on the situation of the German and Austrian refugees.†

---

* According to a statement by Peake in the House on 22 February 1940, the Jewish voluntary organizations were spending £60,000 a week in support of the refugees.

† In reply to a question, the Home Secretary, Herbert Morrison, announced on 27 November 1940, that from January 1940 to the end of November, a total of £857,526 had been handed over to the Central Council for Refugees which had defrayed seventy-five per cent of their administrative expenses and a hundred per cent of the grants made by the Assistance Board. The number of people requiring assistance was steadily declining. Ernest Bevin (Minister of Labour), added that eighty-five per cent of all the refugee males between sixteen and sixty-five years and of women between sixteen and fifty years, were now performing useful service for the country. The rest were unable to do so through no fault of their own.

2　The 'ABC' of Aliens

IN THE EARLY HOURS of 2 September, signals went out to all Chief Officers of Police to round up all aliens on MI5's special list. At that moment some seventy-five to eighty thousand Germans and Austrians, men, women and children, were in Britain. Of these, Military Intelligence only suspected some five hundred of being either active Nazi agents or sympathizers. Three hundred of them were to be arrested immediately; the rest were to be allowed to leave the country.*

The number of suspects seems surprisingly small. According to a memorandum by Sir John Anderson, there were a number of long-settled German residents such as businessmen, skilled workers, domestic servants and people with British spouses. No obstacle would be put in their way if they wanted to go, except for those who possessed special, sensitive skills. But even here it was preferable to risk adding to Germany's manpower reserves rather than to shoulder the burden of interning and feeding them.

Thus only the small number of security risks required immediate attention. Those who did not manage to skip the country were rounded up on D-Day minus one and were taken to the Olympia exhibition halls in the Hammersmith district of London. All of them were supposed to be overt Nazi sympathizers or covert Nazi agents, yet two detailed accounts which we have about these early arrests come from Jews – one a refugee who had come to Britain in 1933, and the other a very religious man who had been resident in England for over eighteen years. This second man, Eugen Spier, is a most unusual character. On the dustjacket of his book relating his internment experience, he claims that he settled in England in 1921 because he did not like the Prussian spirit which was reasserting itself in the new Weimar Republic.[1] He had established himself as a successful business-man, yet he made no attempt to obtain naturalization until 1938. His

---

* Memo by Sir John Anderson on: Control of Aliens. WP(G)(4)115. He told the House, however, on 1 February 1940, that the actual number of people interned at outbreak was 415.

application was refused, in itself rather unusual. He was a devout Jew and his book is peppered with quotations from the Old Testament.

After the advent of Hitler, Spier was one of the moving spirits in the founding of a remarkable, somewhat clandestine group of leading British politicians and industrialists who were greatly concerned about the rising German menace and Britain's unwillingness to face facts. This loosely woven group called itself the Focus for the Defence of Freedom and Peace. Its *guru* was Winston Churchill and amongst its members were people like Sir Robert Vansittart, Sir Austen Chamberlain, Duncan Sandys, Sir Archibald Sinclair, Wickam Steed, Sir Robert Mond and Lady Violet Bonham Carter. Spier seems to have been the only non-Britisher amongst them. They met at irregular intervals for lunchtime sessions at the Savoy Hotel, and it was that group who, unknown to the public, were behind the great Anti-Nazi rally in defence of freedom and peace, at the Albert Hall on 3 December 1936, which gave Churchill his platform to warn the country against complacency and appeasement. According to his own account, Spier regularly supplied Churchill and his fellow Focus members with intelligence on what was going on in Nazi Germany. Some of his prominent British colleagues vouched for him when at last he applied for naturalization, yet the Home Office turned him down.*

On the morning of 2 September, Spier went to the Home Office to offer his services to the government in the forthcoming struggle, in any capacity they chose. No sooner had he returned to his home, than two Scotland Yard officers came to arrest him. He was not even given the chance to appear before a tribunal. Lady Violet, in her preface to Spier's book on the Focus, says that it must be recorded to the country's shame that on the outbreak of war Spier was arrested and thrown into internment, where he spent the next two years. Such was the reward, she says, he received from a free country for his selfless service to the cause of freedom. It certainly is a strange story. What was it that Military Intelligence knew, or suspected, so that even the new First Lord of the Admiralty to whom Spier applied for help could not, or would not, help him?

---

* Eugen Spier: *Focus. A Footnote to the History of the Thirties.* London 1963. See also the footnote on page 862 in Volume V of Martin Gilbert's biography *Winston S. Churchill.* According to him, Spier helped to organize and finance 'Focus' from 1935 to 1939. Gilbert says that Spier was finally naturalized after the war and died in 1971.

The other account comes from Alec Natan, a sportsman well known in Germany, who shortly after the advent of Hitler came to the London School of Economics on a Rockefeller Foundation grant to study British constitutional history. His views were somewhat right-wing and conservative, and, according to his account, he was therefore unpopular with his left-wing fellow researchers at the LSE.*

Spier arrived at Olympia shortly before Natan: he was in fact the second man brought in and was designated prisoner number two; Natan became number seven. The vast halls were dark and empty. An Intelligence Officer took away their passports and police registration books and interrogated them briefly. They were allowed to keep everything else, including even Spier's dressing case with its silver brushes. These early, security risk, internees were in fact treated very much better than the thousands of refugees arrested in the following year.

They were soon joined by others, including 'Putzi' Hanfstaengel, Hitler's somewhat effeminate friend, with whom the Führer had later quarrelled. There was Captain Schiffer, the first head of the Prussian Secret Police, in which post he had preceded Himmler. He had established himself as an arms merchant in London and was believed to be the Gestapo chief in Britain. There was Count Albrecht Mont-gelas, a *bon viveur* and society lion, who at one time had been the London correspondent of a leading Weimar Republic democratic newspaper, and was now selling German beer; Baron Constantine von Pillar, London representative of the Nord Deutsche Lloyd, and, according to Spier, well known in better society for his anti-semitic views. There were also other 'non-Aryans' in that first batch: Dr Edgar Stern-Rubarth, former managing director of the leading German news agency, Wolf's Telegraphenbureau, and also friend and biographer of Stresemann; Dr Rosinsky, lecturer at the German military academy until dismissed by the Nazis.

The most surprising prisoner of all was Dr Bernhard Weiss, former deputy commissioner of the Berlin police force, a man who for years before 1932 had been a principal butt of Nazi hate propaganda. Goebbels had always referred to him as 'Isidor'. He had been sacked even before the Nazis seized power; he had fled to England where he was making a precarious living as a purveyor of office stationery. The

---

* He deposited an account of his internment at the Institut für Zeitgeschichte in Munich.

Nazis had put a price on his capture, yet here he was, thrown together with his enemies, amongst whom was the very man, Schiffer, whom Weiss had once arrested in the days of the Weimar Republic, and who, in turn, had signed the arrest warrant for Weiss, which he only escaped by fleeing to Britain.

Of this first batch, the notorious Nazi Hanfstaengel was, according to the *Daily Express* of 25 October, released again as a result of pressure by influential British friends and the decision of a special tribunal. Weiss, according to the *Daily Herald*, was only released on 6 November. Both were subsequently reinterned.*

By the evening of 3 September, forty men had arrived at Olympia and had been quartered in makeshift bunks in one corner of the vast Empire Hall. They were then paraded in front of the Colonel in charge, who told them that war had now been declared, that they had officially become enemy aliens and that they had better elect a leader or a spokesman. This request immediately showed up the cleavage amongst them; seventeen declared themselves to be anti-Nazis; a much smaller number expressed their open admiration for Hitler; the rest said that they were neutral. In the end, the candidate of the anti-Nazis, Dr Weiss, was elected as the leader. All that united that disparate group of men, Natan says, was their conviction that the war could not last long; the Nazis because they had faith in Hitler's *Blitzkrieg* machine; the 'antis' because Hitler was bound to be overthrown before long.

Later that night they were joined by thirty-seven sailors from the German merchantman *Polona*. They marched into the hall, with bellows of '*Heil Hitler*' that spelled the end of all pretence to genteel politeness between the two groups. Anti-semitic remarks soon revived the pro-Nazi sentiments which some of the first prisoners had so far hidden.

Gradually, more and more prisoners were brought in and the balance swung more and more towards the Nazis. After three days at Olympia, Spier, Natan and the rest of them were taken by train on a very circuitous route to Butlin's Holiday Camp at Clacton-on-Sea, one of the camps which had been programmed to be ready at Z + forty-eight hours. The camp had been left largely in the state it had been in when catering for its more usual summer guests. The internees were therefore quite comfortably housed and fed. The Nazis were

---

* See Leo Sievers: *Juden in Deutschland*, Hamburg 1977, for more of Weiss's career as 'Vi-Po-Prae' (Vice Police President).

A Bespattered Page?

boisterous and arrogant; the guards, Essex Territorials, distant and correct; only the refugees were depressed and suffering. More and more people were constantly arriving, including a Pastor Wehrhahn, padre of the German Embassy, and, unlike most of the other protestant clergymen, a particularly virulent Nazi. In his sermons at Sunday services, sometimes attended by British officers, he openly prayed for victory for German arms.

The first wave of MI5 priority suspects included more anti-Nazis and Jews than real Nazis. They were at first exceedingly polite and correct to each other as behoves people of breeding, but as more and more prisoners were brought in of different social backgrounds, the Nazis were soon in a majority and their arrogance asserted itself. Until about a year later, when they had finally settled down in internment camps in Canada, the Jews among this initial haul remained thrown together with Nazi civilians and captured merchant seamen, constantly subjected to intimidation, abuse, calumnies and even physical violence by young Nazi thugs. Their worst period of mental torture occurred during the dark days of the summer of 1940, when Germany was steamrollering through Europe and Britain seemed about to fall. The Nazis were cock-a-hoop, taunting their Jewish fellow prisoners that they would soon be the lords and masters and would string them all up. Raucous songs, such as the *Horst Wessel Lied* or the particularly reassuring 'When the blood of the Jews gushes forth from our knives, then everything goes twice as well', were intoned outside their huts, and the guards did little to stop it. Even those Germans who had not previously shown any marked Nazi tendencies – parsons, doctors, bankers and businessmen, were now cowed into silence and acquiescence. Time and again the Jews and other non-Nazis, amongst whom were some Lutheran clergymen as well as Catholic priests, protested and asked for separate fenced-off accommodation, but to no avail.

One can only speculate why Military Intelligence should have considered a man like Weiss to be a security risk. Perhaps it was because he had been an officer in the Kaiser's army (a feat difficult for an unbaptized Jew to achieve); perhaps because he had been such a conscientious and correct Prussian civil servant, that after his flight from Germany he had always refused to speak publicly or to engage in political activity in his new country.

Spier says that they were regularly supplied with newspapers – another privilege denied to the bulk of the refugees for weeks after

34

their internment. When he read in the newspapers that the alert authorities had been fortunate enough to round up the backbone of the Gestapo in Britain and had thus foiled the plans of the German Intelligence Services, and when he then looked around the scores of Jewish refugees and other anti-Nazis, he could not resist the conclusion that it might have been the Gestapo itself who in some cunning way had helped the British authorities to compile their list of suspects.

After the outbreak of war, the US Government had suggested to all the belligerents that they should refrain from indiscriminate internment of civilians.[2] The German Government promised that individual Britons would only be interned where, after a detailed examination of their case, it would be considered essential in the interests of security; they would have a right of appeal. All other British civilians against whom no criminal proceedings were pending could leave.[3] Britain had also promised the US on 24 November 1939, that she would adopt a policy of individual examination. However, the Germans later protested to the Americans, who at that time were looking after British interests in Germany, that Britain had in fact started to intern German men and women indiscriminately from 2 September. Germany had therefore decided to do likewise, but was willing to resume facilities for British subjects to leave the country as soon as the British Government gave proof that they were doing the same. The situation in the two countries was, of course, not the same. There was only a relatively small number of British subjects in Germany, whilst Britain harboured well over seventy thousand Germans and Austrians. The last thing which the great majority of them wanted was to be 'repatriated' to Germany.

At the outset, the government had decided on supplementing the information which they already had in Home Office files and police and MI5 records, by individual examinations of every German and Austrian, male and female, over the age of sixteen. The work was to be undertaken by local tribunals under legally experienced chairmen. These tribunals were asked to grade aliens into three categories. 'Security' was the decisive criterion:

Class 'A': Aliens about whose loyalty and reliability the tribunals had doubts and who might constitute a potential security risk. They were to be arrested on the spot for immediate internment.

Class 'B': Aliens about whose loyalty the tribunals were not absolutely certain and who for one reason or the other should be kept under a form of supervision. They were left at liberty but subjected to certain restrictions. They were not allowed to move further than five miles from their place of residence without prior police permission nor to be in possession of such articles as cameras, maps, field glasses, arms, etc.

Class 'C': All those about whom the tribunals were satisfied. They were free from restrictions other than those which had also applied to them in peacetime.

In the case of the Class 'C' aliens, the tribunals were also asked to make a further distinction between non-refugees and 'refugees from Nazi oppression', also sometimes referred to as 'friendly enemy aliens', or even in somewhat acrid jest as 'His Majesty's most loyal enemy aliens'. The instructions issued to the tribunal chairmen under the heading 'Guidance of Persons appointed by the Secretary of State to examine cases of Germans and Austrians', stressed that the onus of satisfying them that an alien should be exempted from internment or from special restrictions, was on him, and that there was no need for the police to produce prejudicial evidence. The normal tenet of Common Law, that the accused is innocent unless proved guilty, did not therefore apply. The decisions of the tribunals were not necessarily binding on the Home Secretary; he retained the right to order the immediate internment of any enemy alien, if a police or MI5 report indicated its advisability.

One hundred and six such tribunals were, with commendable speed, set up all over the country. They consisted of a legally qualified chairman, usually a county court judge or a well-known member of the Bar, assisted by a secretary, often a local police officer, who would also give evidence, a representative of one of the voluntary aid associations with whom the refugee had registered, and sometimes, but by no means always, a qualified interpreter. But the decision was the chairman's alone.*

A total of 62,244 German and 11,989 Austrian nationals of both

---

* Lord Newton complained in the House of Lords on 1 March that a harmless poet who spoke no English came before a chairman who spoke no German. No interpreter was present; in consequence, the poet was interned on the spot.

sexes had registered with the police, and of these a grand total of 73,355 were examined by the tribunals from November 1939 onwards.* They were graded as follows:

569 – Class 'A' or 'high security risks'
6,782 – Class 'B' or 'doubtful cases'
66,002 – Class 'C' or 'no security risks'

Of the 'C's' 55,457 were termed 'refugees from Nazi oppression' and their police registration books endorsed accordingly. This is approximately eighty-five per cent of all the enemy aliens who were examined. No statistics exist as to how many of these 'refugees from Nazi oppression' were of Jewish or part-Jewish origins, but, based on the records of Bloomsbury House it is reasonable to assume that at least eighty to ninety per cent of the 55,457 people belonged to that category. That overwhelming percentage was rarely mentioned in the subsequent parliamentary debates or in the press, but it should be kept in mind in the light of the events which followed.

The Home Office instructions proved inadequate to the purpose of enforcing any uniformity. The decisions made by the tribunals varied so widely that the fate of many refugees was determined more by where they lived and at what point their hearing took place than by the evidence offered. Some chairmen went so far as to create a sort of sub-category of their own devising which, while classing a refugee as a victim of Nazi oppression, also burdened him with the surveillance attaching to those who fell within the 'dubious' B category.

The Home Office tried to remedy the situation by issuing a further circular clarifying the basis for classification, and this had some effect. Those whose names began with letters later in the alphabetical sequence, and thus had not yet appeared before the tribunal, benefited. But there was no reconsideration of those cases which had already been heard, and many refugees who had been placed in the 'B' category, a

---

* According to a written answer by the Home Secretary on 1 March the rest of the people had been ill or had since left the country. These figures do not altogether tally with those given at other times by official spokesmen, but seem to be the latest and therefore presumably the most authentic. After the German invasion of Scandinavia, the Low Countries and France, further numbers of German and Austrian refugees managed to escape to England; others were taken off captured German or neutral ships, so that the total number of German and Austrian civilians with whom the Home Office had to deal at one time or other must have been in excess of eighty thousand.

status some chairmen awarded in the early stages to all who they did not actually intern,* would later suffer for this failure.

The opportunities for the expression of prejudice, ignorance or just plain stupidity on the part of the chairmen of the tribunals were obviously great, and there were many examples of blatant inequity. It is hard to follow the reasoning of the chairman who classed a protestant, half-Jewish, student – now on the staff of the LSE – as a 'B' category alien because he admitted that he was intermittently in contact with his non-Jewish mother via friends in Switzerland.†

Loyalty to the Allied cause was supposed to be the principal criterion, but many tribunals interpreted this as loyalty to the social or political prejudices of their chairman. With the Nazi–Soviet pact a bitter reality, there was some logic in treating communists with suspicion, but few tribunals had the ideological sophistication to distinguish between communism and socialism. Those who had been active in socialist politics or the trades union movements in their homelands, many of whom had also fought in the International Brigades, found themselves in categories 'A' or 'B' almost to a man. 'Judex' quotes one case in which a couple told their chairman that they had been supporters of the Weimar Republic and were curtly sent off to internment with the answer, 'Then you are Communists.'[4]

The *New Statesman* of 9 March 1940 quoted the case of R. R. Kuczynski, a well-known population statistician. The chairman asked him if he had any connection with 'that espionage system at Bloomsbury House', it was a strange description of the headquarters of the interdenominational organizations involved in refugee welfare, and clearly this chairman viewed all refugees with suspicion since he put the unfortunate Kuczynski in category 'B'. When Kuczynski protested that he was a lecturer at LSE he did nothing to improve his case: 'I know all about LSE,' replied the chairman, no doubt much reinforced in the correctness of his decision. For good measure Mrs Kuczynski was also

---

* See F. Lafitte: *The Internment of Enemy Aliens*, Penguin Books, 1941. The book created quite a sensation when it was published in white heat, but as it was written in October and November 1940, when internment was still in full swing, it obviously can only tell part of the story.
† This man later joined the Pioneer Corps, eventually transferred to the Parachute Brigade, was dropped over Normandy at H minus six, sixteen miles from the designated dropping zone; was captured and spent the rest of the war in various German POW camps without the Germans ever discovering that he was an Austrian refugee. His greatest worry was that because of his accent his British fellow prisoners might suspect him of being a German stool pigeon and denounce him to the camp authorities.

put in class 'B' since she was living under the subversive influence of her husband. Their son, Juergen, now one of the leading theoretical economists in the DDR, fared even worse. He was put into the 'A' category on the grounds that he had been involved in the Stepney Peace Council and had written some socialist pamphlets. The fact that he had, according to *Reynolds News*, also lectured widely on the dangers of Hitlerism, was of no avail.

Peter Jacobsohn, whose father founded the famous left-wing *Weltbuehne*, was classified 'B'; a few weeks later, having failed to tell the police of a change of address, he was made an 'A' and we shall meet him on the way to Canada. Sometimes the reasoning was even less explicable. One tribunal heard the case of a Jewish bookseller from Frankfurt who had attempted to smuggle money and valuables out of Germany in defiance of the Nazi decree that all Jews leaving the country must surrender all their belongings and wealth except for the sum of ten Reichmarks (16/–). The plan was detected by the Gestapo, though the bookseller escaped to Britain. He must have been puzzled by the mores of the English tribunal that told him he had behaved disgracefully in evading the laws of his native country and interned him instantly. He was later deported to Canada on board the ill-fated *Arandora Star*, saved from the wreck, re-deported to Australia on the *Dunera*, and only finally released in 1942.

Prejudice could operate the other way too; or at least that seems the best explanation of the ease with which a number of non-Jewish Germans whose political background was murky, but whose upper class credentials were impeccable, found themselves enjoying the freedom of Class 'C' aliens.

The behaviour of the tribunals, especially their widely differing decisions, soon caused questions to be raised in Parliament and in the press. After the second, clarifying, Home Office circular had been issued the Parliamentary Undersecretary for War, Lord Cobham, admitted in the House of Lords on 24 October that the tribunals had not worked uniformly.

On 23 November Eleanor Rathbone asked the Home Secretary in the House whether enemy aliens who had been put into category 'B' before the issue of the new circular, which discouraged the use of that category, could have their cases re-heard by the original tribunals or reviewed by the Home Office. Sir John refused to accept her suggestion. If a 'B' class alien should find the opportunity to be usefully employed without this being detrimental to the interests of a British worker, and if the place of work should be more than five miles from his place of residence, then the Home Office would grant him a special dispensation from the travel restrictions.

This is the first, but by no means the last, mention of the name Eleanor Rathbone. Not only did she take a prominent part in every debate on the subject of internment, but she also served on a number of government committees and voluntary aid bodies, and brought cheer and comfort to thousands of refugees. In fact, she was at one time dubbed as the 'Member for Refugees', more in derision by her opponents than in appreciation by her admirers.* Her fellow champion of the refugees was Colonel Josiah Wedgwood, Labour MP for Newcastle-under-Lyme, linear descendant of the eighteenth-century potter, radical maverick, initiator of a history of Parliament, champion of such diverse causes as land reform, Indian independence and Zionism.

As far as the 'A' class aliens were concerned, they were given the right of appeal to the Central Advisory Committee under Norman Birkett KC, which had originally been set up to deal with applications from those who had been interned at the outset. The Birkett Committee could only make recommendations to the Home Secretary; the decision was his. As a result of these hearings, a number of internees were again released, including those who had not been before a tribunal in the first instance.

In February 1940 the Government, under pressure from various interested parties, decided to set up a further twelve regional committees to review 'B' cases and any other case referred to them by the Home Secretary.[5]

The committees were to consider not only applications for reclassification by 'B' class aliens, but also any other cases which the Home Office thought merited reconsideration. For example, those of 'C' class aliens who might have been graded too leniently and should possibly be reclassified as 'A' and interned at once. The use of the 'B' classification was now officially discouraged.

The regional hearings only began in April and then did their work in a very slow manner. Moreover, they were not much publicized; many 'B' class aliens did not know that a procedure now existed to review their cases. By May only a small percentage of applications made by 'B' cases had been considered.

---

* For details of her life and of her many causes see Mary Stokes: *Eleanor Rathbone*, London 1949.

But the committees were not short of advice. Just one example should be quoted here. It emanated from Ferdinand Tuohy – a regular columnist of the *Daily Mail* – and is addressed to his brother-in-law, who was one of the committee chairmen. Tuohy wrote on 17 April:

> In France every male was interned without any tribunal. We can do with a spot more of French suspicion instead of carelessly working for Germany because aliens are such nice and inoffensive people. All that a Nazi agent has to do is to be attractive and well-behaved and to curse Hitler. Intelligent nobs are particularly good at falling for these people. If I were in your shoes, I would be ruthless.

A lot more such advice and such opinions will appear in the following chapter. It should always be borne in mind that when Tuohy and his brothers-in-spirit wrote about all these dangerous enemy aliens, they referred – and must have known that they did – to a group of which the overwhelming majority were Jews, who had been discriminated against and persecuted in the land of their birth. Many of them had been through one, or even several, concentration camps and practically all of them found at the end of the war that they had lost in the gas chambers those relatives who had not managed to get out in time.

The regional advisory committees did not operate for very long. By the time they started work the whole attitude towards the treatment of enemy aliens had materially changed. Instead of considering sympathetically cases of refugees who had been unfairly classified as 'B's', with a view to reclassifying them, the committees were now urged to get tough and intern as many as possible. A banner headline in the *Daily Mail* on 2 April 1940 reads: 'Aliens, Action at Last'. It went on: 'At long last the Home Office is taking vigorous action to deal with the enemy alien presence. Sir John Anderson has instructed the new committees: when in slightest doubt about an alien intern him.' The *Mail*'s stablemate, the *Evening News*, reported on the same day that the purpose of these committees was to review cases of enemy aliens who had been so far free of restrictions and either partially to restrict them or order their internment.

The dramatic changes in the fortunes of war of April, May and June 1940, imperilled the security of Britain, and with it the position of the refugees. The challenge to their freedom, and the press campaign which preceded it, must now be considered.

3   *The Watchdogs of Fleet Street*

FOR THE FIRST THREE MONTHS of the 'phoney war' period the problem of the 'alien corn in our midst' did not arouse much interest, either in Parliament or in the press. But at the beginning of 1940 there suddenly sprang up a propaganda campaign which appears to have been orchestrated from a central point and which rose to a full crescendo after the invasion of Scandinavia and the Low Countries.

The opening call was sounded on 23 November 1939 in the House of Lords, when Lord Hailsham* warned the House of the danger of only interning those aliens against whom a charge had been proven. If air raids should start in earnest, Germans at liberty could guide the enemy, start fires and sabotage the ARP services. Any minister responsible would lay himself open to grave criticism, even to public execration. Internment for refugees was much better than concentration camps and all those who were well disposed towards this country would cheerfully accept it. Whereupon Lord Newton interjected: 'They would prefer to remain at liberty.'

Most of the parliamentary questions in January and February came from members of the Commons sympathetic towards the refugees, such as Colonel Wedgwood, Miss Rathbone and Geoffrey Mander, who were concerned with the unsatisfactory work of some tribunals. But when Home Office spokesmen disclosed how relatively few people had actually been interned, other MPs, usually Tory die-hards, began to voice their apprehensions. On 21 January, Colonel Anstruther-Gay claimed that the enemy seemed to know a lot of what was going on: 'Have we been too lenient?' he asked. On 1 February Lieutenant-Colonel Acland Troyle asked whether a lot more should not have been interned.

There were not many such questions and they did not generate much heat in the House; for the time being the whole affair was being played in a low key. It was the press, and in particular the Kemsley and Rothermere papers, which were beginning to stir the pot in earnest.

---

* The former Douglas Hogg, father of Quintin, the present holder of the title.

The Beaverbrook papers, on the other hand, did not seem to have a coordinated policy dictated to them by the proprietor. The *Sunday Express*, and in particular its weekly commentator John Gordon, were undoubtedly part of the anti-aliens chorus whilst the *Evening Standard* took up a much more tolerant and compassionate stance, especially its columnist Michael Foot, who stood on the side of the angels. Some months later, after the collapse of France, he wrote:

> If we intern German anti-Nazis who fought Hitler for years, why not also intern de Gaulle? This war is not about national frontiers; it is on a scale not seen since the reformation. Instead of interning German political refugees we should use them as speakers to reach the hearts and minds of Germans and as underground fighters to spark off a revolution![1]

Simultaneously stories suddenly began to appear in various daily and Sunday papers reporting on, or implying, sundry nefarious activity by aliens. They were often mere insinuations, which looked as if they had been planted in order to arouse suspicion and disquiet. On 20 January, the *Daily Sketch* reported some mysterious explosions at the Royal Gunpowder Factory in Waltham Cross. As a result, the paper claimed, Scotland Yard were investigating the activities of Germans and Austrians whom Hitler might have sent over as spies in the guise of refugees. Three days later the *Daily Telegraph* claimed that Scotland Yard as well as Military Intelligence, were gravely concerned about the leniency shown towards aliens by the tribunals. In a number of cases, the paper claimed, Scotland Yard had submitted dossiers from the Special Branch and their Criminal Records Office; in others the Intelligence Department had shown proof that an alien had pro-Nazi connections and sympathies, yet the aliens in question had been left at large.

The *Sunday Express* of 21 January had a banner headline: 'Those Influential Friends of Dangerous Aliens'. The article below claimed that the officials whose duty it was to comb out and intern suspicious persons from the army of foreigners now in Britain, were 'gravely concerned' (that expression is repeated in almost every report in every paper) because of the difficulties put in their way by sentimental or foolish British people. These people rushed forward and vouched for people of whom they knew next to nothing and tried to interfere with steps taken solely in the interest of national security. Would a hostile Nazi really walk around, the paper asked, proclaiming himself to be a friend of Germany? The only safe rule was to intern everybody whose trustworthiness could not be proved beyond any question. The paper then alleged that a highly placed Jew, regarded here as an anti-Nazi, had been amongst the first to be rounded up. Prominent British Jews then pleaded on his behalf, but the police knew too much about him and his work. Many Gestapo agents were in fact rounded up amongst these so-called refugees. An unnamed official had told the *Sunday Express*: 'There are many refugees here with relations in Germany and Austria. They are not usually paid spies but will pass on information to Germany through neutral channels in order to save their relatives from the Gestapo.'

Similar stories continued to appear in the popular press. They were often mere innuendos and hints; rarely were any names or places given. As the *Contemporary Review* pointed out in August 1940, none of these insinuations were ever substantiated. In fact the Metropolitan Commissioner of Police issued an explicit denial on 23 January that there had been any proven or suspected cases of espionage or sabotage by any enemy alien. He issued a similar statement on 15 April.

In the forefront of the anti-alien agitation stood the *Sunday Pictorial*. On 28 January, its headline read: 'Arms Expert Loves a German'. It was a story about an Englishman in a key position in an armaments factory who had fallen in love with a beautiful German refugee girl. She very much wanted to marry him, but had told him that if there were difficulties in the way of their marriage this need not stop their companionship. Of course, added the paper, it might be a genuine romance; on the other hand it might not. Best to intern them all. The paper claimed that a great wave of uneasiness was sweeping across the country about those seventy thousand potential enemies at large. Sir Philip Game, the Metropolitan Commissioner, had denied that he was worried but the Secret Service certainly was. The kid-glove handling of enemy aliens had to stop, the paper claimed. There was a war on and we could not take any chances just for the sake of being polite.

At this stage the anti-refugee propaganda was only being waged by the press belonging to the ex-appeaser press lords, particularly the Kemsley and Rothermere families. For the moment the rest of the papers ignored the campaign of calumny or spoke out against it. The weekly *Spectator*, for instance, commented on 19 January that happily there was at that moment little of the conspicuous spyhunting on the part of the public which had been such an unpleasant feature in the opening months of the last war, and that the tens of thousands of refugees in Britain desired but one thing, our success in the war.

Incidents were now beginning to be reported of enemy aliens who had broken one or another of the war-time regulations, such as switching on lights during the nightly blackout without drawing the curtains. A more serious case was reported in the *Daily Mail* of 7 February. A small group of orthodox Jewish students had come over *en bloc* from a *Jeshiva* in Frankfurt together with their *Talmud* teacher just before the outbreak of war. They dressed in their traditional kaftans and led a spartan existence. Most of them were Poles and thus considered to be friendly aliens, but ten had German nationality. They all lived in the house of another rabbi who, unversed in such worldly affairs, had failed to notify the police of the presence of these enemy aliens. Both rabbis were summonsed and fined £50 each, later on appeal reduced to £5. There was nothing objectionable in the fine; the rabbis had, albeit unwittingly, broken the regulations. But what is one to make of the comments of the North London magistrate, Mr Basil Watson KC who, when told that the *Jeshiva* students were aged between seventeen and twenty-four, commented: 'Just a nice military age' and then added: 'I think it is a horrible state of affairs when men of this description [the two rabbis] can harbour the enemy in the centre of the biggest city in the world.'?

The *Hackney Gazette* on 7 February, published in what had been a focal district of the British Union of Fascists, went one better when commenting on the case: 'We are so trusting a people that we allow 60,000 of the enemies to be at large.' It coupled this with a report that details of a secret session of the House of Commons had been leaked to Germany and had been broadcast by Goebbels, as if somebody amongst those *Talmud* students or amongst the other fifty-five thousand class 'C' refugees had been responsible for the leak. Yet at that time Captain Ramsey, an MP* on the extreme right of the Conservatives, in reality a fascist, who was later interned as a security risk under regulation 18b, was still a member of the House of Commons and there were several members in both Houses who had been friends of Ribbentrop and other Nazis, as well as members of the Link or the Anglo-German Association.

The case which got the most publicity and led to a statement in the House by the Home Secretary, concerned a non-refugee, a student at Lincoln College Oxford, one Wilhelm Solf whose father had been German ambassador to Japan during the Weimar Republic. Solf was

---

* For Peebles (Indep. C).

living in Abingdon as a guest of the Controller of Machine Tools at the Ministry of Supply. He was well-connected and at his tribunal had been put in category 'B'. One night a German aeroplane had been shot down over a nearby RAF airfield. Solf had borrowed his host's camera (as a 'B' case he had had to surrender his own to the police), and had photographed the blazing wreck. For breaking war-time regulations he was sentenced to one month's imprisonment and, on release, was interned.

The Solf case also aroused attention in Germany, but the Ministry of Propaganda at their daily press conference in Berlin forbade any mention in the press of this or any other arrest. The Ministry spokesman said that they had no effective means of counteraction because the number of Englishmen in Germany was so very small.*

There were a number of questions in the Commons on the case, and the Home Secretary announced the setting up of the regional advisory committees to review all 'B' cases. But his statement did not satisfy the *Daily Mail*, which in four separate editorials used the case as a battering ram to drive home its viewpoint. On 27 February the paper said that every German was a German first and an ideologist afterwards. It was better to intern them all rather than run the risk of allowing any possible spies or saboteurs to go free. It claimed on 29 February that the public were now asking how many refugees like Solf were still at liberty. The police were asking how much longer they had to bear the enormous strain of keeping all those seventy thousand uninterned aliens under constant surveillance. At what point did the love of a country outweigh the hatred of that country's government? On 1 March the *Daily Mail* claimed that 'millions of relatives of the men in the fighting forces are perturbed at the latitude allowed to the aliens within our gates. The Home Office's childlike belief in the integrity of these people may imperil our safety. It is not good enough, Sir John.'

On the following day the paper claimed receipt of a large postbag on the question, all supporting the *Daily Mail*'s stance. One suggestion was: 'Put all the Germans and unfriendly aliens into a camp and have Poles as guards. I guess none would escape with their lives.'

Another letter, so the paper claimed, urged them to use their influence to have the whole crowd of seventy thousand refugees

---

* Bundesarchiv Koblenz, Saenger Papers Z Sg 102/22. Kingsley Martin (9 March in the *New Statesman* diary) pointed out that what Solf had done was certainly not espionage. It was just careless activity.

interned, many of them were living on the fat of the land, on food brought at their peril from overseas by gallant merchant mariners.

On 9 March, the *Daily Mail* quoted Air-Commodore Boyle, Director of Intelligence at the Air Ministry, as saying that careless talk might inadvertently pass on useful information to one of the seventy-three thousand uninterned aliens, which might go back to Germany. The same article also mentions that the suggestion to use Poles as guards had resulted in a German broadcast 'frothing with indignation'.

G. Ward Price, in his regular column, urged Britain to be tough and to wage an aggressive war, the same Ward Price who only a year or so before, together with his proprietor, had been a good friend of the Nazis and an arch apostle of appeasement, extolling the many virtues of the Third Reich at a time when many of those whom his paper was now branding as potential spies were languishing in German concentration camps.

On 23 March the *Daily Mail* published a letter from 'Brigadier Eastbourne', urging that all enemy aliens should henceforth be compelled to walk around with armlets showing their country of origin. The Brigadier no doubt got his idea from pictures of Jews walking around in Germany with yellow stars pinned to their breasts.

Who was that mysterious 'general public', those 'thousands of relatives of British fighting men' who were so deeply concerned about all the aliens roaming around unchecked and clamouring for their internment? Various Mass Observation polls conducted up to the end of April 1940 found no one who suspected refugees of espionage, or who suggested that they should all be interned.* It was only after the invasion of Holland that antagonism against them began to flare up. As for the general attitude towards refugees, Mass Observation found that anti-sentiments were strongest in the upper and upper-middle classes, where a concerted press campaign was making it the 'socially done thing'. But it was perhaps more than just the 'socially done thing', particularly for all those whose pre-war sentiments had been anything but anti-German and who had preferred a German to a Jew any day.†

---

* Mass Observation was one of the earliest pollster organizations, run by Tom Harrison.

† Yet a memorandum by the Home Policy Committee, dated 30 March, says that according to the MOI, there was evidence of a growth of public feeling against the refugees. HPC(40)69. For a somewhat more detailed report on this, issued a month later, see footnote (3).

The whole campaign at that time was only being waged in the popular press; the 'quality' papers adopted a much more reasonable attitude. Typical is a comment by a writer in the *Spectator* on 15 March: 'I would wager that if and when a spy is caught, he will not be found amongst the 73,353 enemy aliens examined by the tribunals.' Harold Nicholson took a similar attitude in the same journal on 26 April: 'It is most improbable that Germany would employ in key positions of its espionage network people of German origin. In almost every case in the last war the agents used by Germany in this country were either neutral citizens or British traitors.' Later in the year this point was repeated by many others. Their consensus was that the vast majority of refugees spoke poor English, were conspicuous in their speech, dress and manners and would stick out like a sore thumb if they tried to engage in espionage. There were many British sympathizers with Nazism, there were large numbers of German–Americans and citizens of neutral countries who could carry out such work less conspicuously.

Kingsley Martin in 'The Critic' column of the *New Statesman* mentioned on 6 January the word 'Refujew', which a BUF man had told him the Mosleyites had coined. The man had added: 'We have of course friends high up who may come in useful one day.'

* * *

It was the German assault on Norway in April 1940, and the emergence of a Fifth Column there, a Norwegian Nazi organization led by Major Quisling (who gave the English language a new generic term) which provided the anti-refugee campaign with a new impetus. In the Commons the agitation was still fairly muted. Sir Thomas Moore* asked on 23 April whether in the light of the revelations from Norway, all proper steps were being taken to ensure that the seventy-four thousand aliens in Britain did not constitute any danger to security, but Miss Rathbone pointed out that the danger in Norway had largely arisen from Norwegians and not from refugees.

The popular press, however, now had a cause which it exploited to the full. The *Sunday Chronicle* took the lead in the growing concert with its headline of 14 April: 'Intern Them All'. For the first time, 3,965 Hungarians and 47,664 Russians were also included in the catalogue of potential spies and saboteurs, but as yet no Italians. The

---

* MP for Ayr (C).

paper once again quoted the Solf case and also another case, again in Oxford, where an alien had been sentenced to three months' imprisonment for travelling outside his permitted area. This proved how British freedom was being abused. Many MPs, the paper said, were worried that we were not tough enough. The number of foreign-sounding names of people guilty of offences against wartime regulations showed how lax we were in dealing with this menace. There might be some genuine haters of our common enemy amongst our German and Austrian guests, but the only safe course was to intern the lot and then let those who wanted to be free again prove their innocence.

The most persistent and pernicious agitation against the refugees was being waged by the *Sunday Chronicle*'s regular columnist Beverley Nichols. Although memories are often short, he seems to have been conscious that his readers would remember his own immediate political past. So in his column of 21 April he prefaced his attack on the refugees by a personal explanation: nobody could accuse him of being a fanatical enemy of the German people. On the contrary:

> Many of us felt that by clinging desperately to such organisations as the Anglo-German Fellowship we might make the voice of sanity heard. I have no regrets. Today I wholeheartedly agree with the slogan 'Intern the Lot'. I know personally many Germans who found life under Hitler intolerable. You renounced your native land; in spirit you are as good Englishmen as anybody. For that reason you should be glad to be interned because you well know that not all are like you, that there are traitors amongst you and that only in whole-sale internment shall we find safety.

He then listed some examples of such 'traitorous' activity:

> Hardly a day passes without somebody being fined 5/- for a blackout offence. It is always the same story: the offender is a keen sympathizer of the allied cause. He lived lately in Berlin, but has now for personal reasons of health moved to the East Coast of Britain where for at least ten minutes the whole top floor of his house was ablaze with lights.

He ended his article: 'And even if we have no evidence (and we must assume there is evidence), why should Hitler neglect his most powerful weapon against his most powerful enemy?'

Similar stories appeared in other papers. But on 12 May, the *Sunday Chronicle* which did not often publish 'Letters to the Editor', was fair enough to print one from four people in Manchester. They asked how it was that the same stories got repeated in the same papers. Where was

Nichols' evidence about all these blackout offences and where was the evidence for other stories about well-dressed women pestering bus conductors and taxi drivers to death about details of our defence system? Had Nichols ever been pestered to death? What he advocated would cause misery to thousands of innocent people.

But the *Sunday Chronicle* was quite unrepentant. On the same day an editorial reiterated: 'Round up every enemy alien; every one of them is a potential fifth columnist, in plain words a traitor. However much he or she may profess to hate the Nazi régime the ties of the Fatherland may prove to be the temptation to betray us. Intern the lot – NOW!' From now on the words 'refugee' or Jew were rarely used. The seventy-four thousand people had simply all become dangerous enemy aliens.

The quality papers and periodicals at this stage were still distinguishing between a native Quisling and a refugee; the distinction became somewhat blurred in the following weeks. Lady Rhondda's *Time and Tide* provided a new argument in an article on 20 April, which was headed 'The Trojan Horse'. It recalled a conversation between Rauschning and Adolf Hitler.* In it Hitler had pointed out how easy it will be to undermine England from inside. Rauschning had no idea what opportunities existed in England, thanks to its 'good society'. Englishmen were psychologically so backward that they would find it difficult to believe in the possibility of an internal conspiracy.

Time and Tide commented that everyone knew about the fifth column on the Left; one only had to read the *Daily Worker*. But what about the one on the Right, where had they suddenly all disappeared to, all those who had been friends of Ribbentrop? They were the real Trojan Horse, they were the enemies who must be found and be made harmless. A week later, the journal again asked what had become of all the prominent members of the Link, an Anglo-German association with Nazi sympathies. Quislings should not be sought in the wrong quarters, such as amongst the communists, the pacifists, or aliens, but inside the Establishment, the Houses of Parliament, HM Forces, the City, etc.

Reynolds News was another paper whose views differed from Beverley Nichols and his confrères. On 9 June its columnist, J. B.

---

* Rauschning, the former Gauleiter in Danzig who later became disillusioned with the Führer, published these *Gespräche*.

Priestley, wrote that native Quislings and Mosleyites might admire and salute Hitler, but slandered the Einsteins and the Thomas Manns. There were far more really famous men with world-wide reputations living outside Germany than inside it. In fact the point was later made that if Albert Einstein and Thomas Mann had taken sanctuary here and not in America, and if Sigmund Freud had not died in Swiss Cottage just before the outbreak of war, they might have all found themselves interned on the Isle of Man. Freud's son Martin was in fact interned, and his grandson Walter deported abroad.[2]

Richard Crossman echoed J. B. Priestley when, in the same edition of *Reynolds News*, he said that if there was a fifth column at large in the country it would be found amongst 'the rich and the respected of the land. I can only explain the arrest of Social Democrats from Nazi concentration camps as a hysterical attempt to convince public opinion that something is being done about a fifth column. It arouses my suspicion.'

The Ministry of Information circulated a confidential memorandum on 27 April about the problem of a fifth column and the refugees.[3] It stated that the present press campaign was concentrating on the aliens as the chief potential menace, replacing the communists, fascists, Left Book Club members, Moral Rearmament and Peace Pledge Union. There was so far no evidence that the press campaign was causing a parallel intensity amongst the general public.* However, the memorandum said, the Citizens' Advice Bureaux were concerned about a growing anti-alien feeling. In Manchester and Liverpool it was becoming identified with anti-semitism. The refugee committees were growing anxious about the whole situation. The sympathy for the refugees had partly evaporated and suspicion about their loyalty had taken its place.

The most significant part of this report is undoubtedly the observation about anti-semitism. The Jews whom Hitler, from the first moment of his political activity to the last, had vowed to fight and eradicate, whom he never tired of proclaiming as his public enemy number one, were now being suspected as potential Nazi spies and

---

* However, it seems to have had a deleterious effect on some Conservative MPs. According to the *Daily Sketch* of 25 April, Sir John Anderson indicated to a crowded meeting of the 1922 Committee of backbenchers the strong measures which he was about to take against fifth columnists, including enemy aliens. 'The MPs left the meeting reassured.' In the light of Sir John's views expressed at that time in various Cabinet memoranda, the report of the *Daily Sketch* seems suspect.

A Bespattered Page?

collaborators. It was an Alice in Wonderland situation, which only confirms the residual strength of anti-semitic sentiments which existed amongst certain sections of the population, and which some of the newspapers had never been slow to exploit.

4 *The Enemy at the Gates*

AFTER SEVEN MONTHS of phoney war, the sitting-on-the-fence came to an end. The invasion of Denmark and Norway ushered in a period of ten weeks that shook the world and completely changed the face of Europe. The refugee problem now took on entirely new dimensions. As Norway fell, some German refugees who had earlier fled to Norway managed to escape again to England; they were immediately interned. Herbert Frahm, who became Willy Brandt, had stayed behind. Had he managed to escape he would no doubt have also been interned.

The new regional committees had begun at a leisurely pace to examine some of the 'B' category cases. By 2 May, 605 people had been heard, of whom thirty-two had been interned.[1] The popular press was preoccupied with the momentous events in Scandinavia and for a week or two the refugees were left alone. As a postscript to the events in Norway, Dingle Foot wrote in the *Spectator* of 3 May:

> The animus displayed against the aliens is quite the most unpleasant feature of the present outcry. It would be tragedy if the victims of Nazi terrorism, who have passed under the scrutiny of a tribunal, should now be regarded as Hitler's aiders and abettors. The spy fever which has been so sedulously worked up during the last few days might easily lead to stupid cruelty. On the whole the Home Office attitude so far has been reasonable and humane. It is hoped they will not allow themselves to be stampeded.

A week later everything had changed. The disgraced Chamberlain Government resigned. On the same day Hitler launched his *Blitzkrieg* against the Low Countries and against France. Within a very few days wild stories about treachery in Holland came flooding across the North Sea. With that, views on the German and Austrian refugees in Whitehall, in Parliament, in the press, and in major sectors of public opinion changed almost overnight.

Two months earlier, at a meeting of the Deputy Chiefs of Staff, the Home Secretary, Sir John Anderson, had rendered a detailed review of the steps taken to control the aliens in wartime Britain. He had again rejected wholesale internment. He pointed out that the risk of sabotage did not only arise from foreigners but also came from Irish extremists, British fascists, communists and naturalized Britishers. Moreover, agents sent over by the enemy were more likely to be found amongst non-enemy aliens than amongst Germans and Austrians. Therefore to intern every German and Austrian would be of no real help.[2]

Despite the pressure exerted on him, Sir John stuck to his policy. Even after the invasion of Holland, he refused to heed the panicky advice given to him from virtually every quarter, including his new Prime Minister. 'There should be a very large round-up of enemy aliens and of suspected persons in this country', Churchill told Cabinet on 15 May.[3] 'It would be much better that all these persons should be put behind barbed wire and internment would be much safer for all the Germans.' When Germany began air attacks on Britain, Churchill warned: 'public temper in the country would be such that such persons would be in great danger if at liberty.'

The cause of much of the alarm was the dispatches from Sir Nevile Bland, the British ambassador at the Hague, who painted a sensational picture of extensive cooperation between German parachutists and a fifth column in Holland. German maidservants who had worked there until the outbreak of the war were alleged to have been dropped, together with male parachutists, sometimes directly into the grounds of the houses where they had previously worked. At the Cabinet meeting, the Chief of the Air Staff said that there had been several reports during the previous night of landings of parachutists in the UK. None had been substantiated, he added, but the reports were indicative of the nervous state of the public. Churchill then requested Clement Attlee (Lord Privy Seal) and Arthur Greenwood (Minister without Portfolio), the only two Labour members of the new Cabinet, to study the whole problem urgently.

The Home Secretary submitted a memorandum outlining a new policy, which received Cabinet approval.[4] Sir John wrote that he had indeed received information from the Dutch Government that the German invasion forces had received valuable assistance from German residents there, but the Dutch had no evidence implicating any refugees. Moreover, he said, the situation was in any case entirely different in the United Kingdom. Holland had an open border with its neighbour, and as a result some one hundred thousand Germans, many of them undoubtedly Nazi sympathizers, had settled there. Out of seventy-three thousand Germans and Austrians in this country, over sixty-four thousand had been individually examined and the great majority classified as refugees from Nazi oppression. The intelligence services had no evidence at all that plans existed for resident Germans or Austrians in Britain to help any invading forces.

Having thus argued at some length that the country stood in no danger from the refugees, he then announced the following steps which were to be taken immediately:

(1) all male Germans and Austrians between the ages of sixteen and sixty, regardless of their categorization, who were resident in areas of possible military operations (such as the East and South coasts) were to be immediately interned.

(2) all male Germans and Austrians between the ages of sixteen and sixty in category 'B' were also to be interned regardless of where they lived.

(3) he would issue individual internment orders against anybody who gave ground for suspicion.*

Sir John correctly anticipated the reaction of public opinion against wholesale internment. It would perhaps be accepted at this stage, even welcomed by some. But before long there would be the inevitable popular reaction against it. If thousands of women, including pregnant ones, or those with young children, were subjected to barrack room life in camps it would cause an outcry, particularly amongst all those British subjects who had befriended the refugees. To intern thousands of useful people would also be detrimental to the war effort. It was a view which Sir John was not long able to sustain in the face of pressure from many quarters.

Official pressure to proceed with internment at this and subsequent stages seems to have come mainly from the War Office and, within it, from the security branch. A Foreign Office memo clearly states that the instructions which the Home Secretary was about to send out were being issued at the behest of the Secretary of State for War.[5] Telegrams were sent to the Chief Constables and to the Metropolitan

---

* The first Statutory Rule in respect of the 'Aliens in Protected Areas' No 468 was issued on 29 March 1940. It defined the limits of the coastal belt. Subsequent orders Nos 857, 869, 931 and 988 issued on 31 May, 2 June, 6 June and 14 June respectively, extended these limits further and further inland. The last one covered some of the outskirts of London where sensitive military installations were located, such as the Naval Headquarters in Northwood and the airfield at Northolt.

Commissioner, advising them which areas were being declared as 'protected'. In a series of Orders-in-Council the areas were bit by bit enlarged until they encompassed the whole of the coastal belt and eventually also all those inland areas which contained military installations. Any enemy alien found within an area so designated was immediately arrested, even if he happened to be spending a day at the seaside when the order was issued. Non-enemy aliens were required to leave the area immediately unless they were given special permission to stay. This led to criticism from friendly governments such as the Polish, Dutch or American ones.

The Foreign Office was very much concerned about this and asked for a much more discriminating policy towards friendly and neutral aliens. 'The instructions will be carried out by local constables whose intelligence is limited', replied the Home Office on 11 May. 'In view of the great risks involved they cannot be given any discretion beyond not interfering with any Frenchmen' (the French were exempt). In the end, however, the Home Office also relaxed the restrictions in respect of US citizens. A former Home Office principal remembers that around that time Sir Frank Newsam, head of Department B3, summoned the Chief Constables to a conference at which he explained to them the reasons for internment. The security services, he said, considered that in the event of an invasion ancestral blood would be stronger than any political convictions.

Internment of male 'B' aliens began on 15 May. As the total only amounted to 2,181 people the arrests were quickly completed. This figure is considerably smaller than the original number of aliens classified as 'B'. A few had afterwards been reclassified by a regional committee; others had emigrated. Amongst those who had been classified as 'B', as a possible suspect, by his tribunal was the Austro–Jewish author Stefan Zweig. He had meanwhile moved on to Brazil and thus avoided internment. Not long afterwards he committed suicide.

Internment for the 'B' refugees came quite unexpectedly. Two police officers in mufti usually called at the alien's home or boarding house in the early hours of the morning. But the tactics of arrest varied from one police station to another. In some areas the aliens were told that they were about to be interned and allowed, sometimes even encouraged, to pack a suitcase with essentials, including winter wear (this was May). In others they were told that they were merely wanted for questioning at the local police station and would probably be back again before the morning was out. They were discouraged, in some instances even forbidden, to take any luggage with them. For some of those it took weeks before they could get a change of clothing. Some of those arrested at the coast were elderly people spending a few days in a private hotel at the seaside; others were youngsters living in boarding schools.

When the Home Secretary belatedly announced the new policy on 23 May, he encountered quite a hostile reception in the House. He had not gone far enough in the view of many MPs. Sir Thomas Moore objected that only men had been rounded up. 'Is the female of any species not generally more dangerous than the male?', he asked. In a debate on the same day in the Lords, Viscount Elibank objected to the age limits of sixteen to sixty as being much too narrow. The upper limit was an insult as many members of the Government and of Parliament were over sixty years old. These limits implied that they were no longer capable of action. Similar sentiments were being expressed in the other chamber: 'Our Prime Minister is 65 and what a danger he is to the Germans!', said F. S. Cocks, a Labour member.*

Viscount Elibank also criticized the fact that general internment was restricted to the coastal belt only; German parachutists were not bound by Home Office regulations. Lord Marchwood also warned that women spies were much more dangerous than men: 'We are fighting for our lives', he said, 'and we should immediately put out of harm's way all the aliens together with communists, fascists and pacifists.' Viscount Elibank was convinced that the information which Lord Haw-Haw† was broadcasting was all obtained from German nationals in this country. None of them could be trusted, he said. But when Reginald Sorensen‡ asked on 29 May what percentage of refugees from Nazi oppression were known to have committed hostile acts and how did that number compare with similar acts by friendly aliens, Osbert Peake had to admit that so far there had not been a single hostile act by any enemy alien proved by any court of law. Sorensen hoped that this fact would be made public to counter the extravagant anti-refugee agitation.

But now, for the first time, the public was becoming seriously

---

* MP for Broxtowe.
† Originally the name given to Baillie-Stewart, it was then transferred to the Irishman William Joyce who was regularly broadcasting propaganda from Germany. After the war he was hanged as a traitor.
‡ MP for Layton West (Labour).

rattled. The Germans seemed to possess an invincible, unstoppable war machine. The stories coming out of Holland of parachutists raining down on Rotterdam, disguised as priests and nuns, were splashed across the front pages. The unexpectedly quick collapse of both the Netherlands and Belgium was generally attributed to deceit, treachery and internal collapse. A Mass Observation report of 14 May paints a picture very different from the earlier ones. Although people were not expressing their sentiments very loudly in public, the news from Holland was engendering a growing anti-alien, and sometimes anti-semitic, feeling.[6]

Sir Neville Bland, the British Ambassador to the Netherlands, had contributed to this growth of anti-refugee feeling. 'Be careful at this moment how you put complete trust in any person of German or Austrian connection', he warned on 30 May in a widely reported broadcast. 'If you know people of this kind, who are at large, keep an eye on them.'[7] For the record, it should be stressed that several members of the Dutch Government-in-exile later denied that they knew of a single case where a refugee had aided or abetted the invaders.*

The King had received a report from Prince Bernhard about the activities of the Dutch Nazis after the German invasion and had relayed the confidential information to the Home Secretary. The stress was on Dutch Nazis – the followers of Mussert – and not on German nationals, let alone refugees. It was perhaps this information which induced Sir John to amend Defence Regulations 18b by an Order-in-Council, preparatory to the internment of several prominent British fascists and friends of Nazi Germany. George Darling in the *Reynolds News* of 19 May, had named several well-known members of the Anglo-German Association and of the Link, such as Sir Barrie Domville, Professor Sir Raymond Beazley and Lords Redesdale and Sempill. The Associations had now been dissolved, but, asked the paper, had the men changed their spots? The German Ministry of Propaganda had a list of prominent Britishers who had shown sympathy to Germany. Already, the paper claimed, swastikas had appeared on public buildings in London and in other towns. 'The danger is real,

---

* This is also confirmed by a letter from the Chaplain to the British Embassy in The Hague, in *Time and Tide* of 8 June 1940: 'It seems to me particularly childish to regard refugees as a particularly important part of the fifth column for that was not the way it actually happened in Holland.' A Mr Erasmus Herder wrote in the *Manchester Guardian* of 11 October 1940, that Sir Neville had told him that he could not give chapter and verse of a single case where a German disguised as a refugee acted as a fifth columnist in Holland.

the Nazi poison must be cleansed from the British body.' The un-proven linking of prominent right-wing figures with the daubing of swastikas is, of course, just as reprehensible as the linking of the two rabbis, who had been fined for a breach of police regulations, with the broadcasting by Germany of the contents of a Commons secret session.

In fact the German and Austrian refugees in Holland, who did not manage to escape or to go underground with the help of Dutch friends, were almost all gassed by the Nazis. The fate of Anne Frank typifies what happened to them. As the *New Statesman* pointed out on 25 May: one of the first orders which the new Nazi commissar for Holland, Seiss-Inquart, issued concerned the confiscation of all property belonging to refugees who had settled in the Netherlands since 1933 and their incarceration in camps. But in May 1940 Anne Frank was an unknown Jewish girl, hiding in an attic in Amsterdam, and the Kemsley and Rothermere papers were having a field day in their anti-refugee campaign.

On 13 May, the *Daily Mail* called the three thousand arrested 'B' class aliens, all real or potential fifth columnists and on the following day said that they could look forward to a life of luxury on the Isle of Man. Thirty large hotels and boarding houses on the sea promenade, north of Ramsey, had been ordered to eject all their guests and be ready to take internees by the next Saturday. 'There the aliens can be sure to have hot and cold water in their bedrooms, electric or gas fires, comfortable armchairs and good furniture.' On 18 May it enlarged its description of this pampered existence in an article headed 'Luxury War for Aliens', which described the pleasures to which the arrested refugees could look forward, including such amenities as a private golf course, private seabathing, cinema shows and perfect mountain and sea air. They would not have to cook their own meals nor make their own beds; the owner of a miniature golf course had been told to clear out but to leave behind all his clubs and balls.

The paper followed this up with a report on 21 May, by a reporter who had seen hundreds of enemy aliens marching through Liverpool on their way to the seaside, each carrying a suitcase or a haversack. Here and there he saw a boy waving his schoolcap. All were in good spirits and joked as they walked along between files of soldiers with fixed bayonets. The following day the paper mentions Huyton Camp as if this too was a most desirable holiday spot. 'A well-known film producer interned there is already looking for talents to provide

A Bespattered Page?

entertainment.' It was almost certainly Huyton which was again instanced when an MP referred in the House on 30 May to enemy aliens being interned on a brand new housing estate, whilst many members of the British working class continue to live in slum conditions.

Almost every day the *Daily Mail* complained that the measures taken did not go far enough and that everybody should be interned. Ward Price reported on 24 May that the Head of a Balkan State had told him: 'In Britain you fail to realize that every German is an agent.' On the same day the Home Secretary at last proceeded against the British Union of Fascists. The *Daily Mail* reported the arrest of Sir Oswald, Captain Ramsey MP, and eight other leading fascists. But Ward Price had no comment on this.

Not all the alarm came from journalists and newspaper proprietors with axes to grind. On 25 May, the *Daily Mail* reported a remark by the Registrar of Oxford University, Douglas Veale: 'All aliens are a potential menace and should be interned. That is the general opinion of the university.' A detective constable in the Oxfordshire constabulary reported to his Chief Constable that Sir Robert Robinson FRS had expressed to him his concern that three refugee scientists named Strauss, Weiler and Gruenfeld were working in university research laboratories where they could do enormous damage 'if they were evilly disposed; and who knows?'[8] Sir Robert thought it much better to put them all out of harm's way. Of all the British universities, Oxford had given the most refugee scholars shelter. The University had a world-wide reputation for tolerance, yet at this stage the anti-alien phobia seems to have been more widespread there – amongst gown and town – than elsewhere. That is perhaps a measure of how far the press propaganda had succeeded.

A. J. P. Taylor, in his *English History 1914–1945*, relates how refugee scientists were excluded from working on radar. They were thus able to continue research into nuclear physics, which at that stage was not considered critical for the war. This work, and indeed many of the scientists themselves, were later vital to the Manhattan project.[9]

Under the auspices of Sir Henry Tizard, the Scientific Adviser to the Air Ministry, a small committee was formed in January 1940 to find suitable employment for refugee scientists, with Dr Reginald Jones acting as its Liaison Officer to the Air Ministry. Dr Chaim Weizmann, later the first President of Israel, was one of its members; so was Simon Marks (of Marks & Spencer) who provided the funds for the committee. Its original object was to harness the knowledge and expertise of many distinguished refugee scientists and industrialists to the prosecution of the war, by giving these men suitable appointments. In addition they also provided most useful information on the location of certain key plants in Germany, and on the general state of research in Germany, including nuclear fission (or as it was then called, the 'uranium bomb'), and bacteriological warfare. This committee, and Sir Henry in particular, later on made strenuous efforts to keep these refugee scientists out of internment camps, and to get those who had been interned released as quickly as possible.[10]

At this stage there were still a number of publications which had managed to escape the rampant anti-refugee paranoia. Harold Nicholson, in the *Spectator* of 26 April, pointed out that it was most improbable that Germany would employ in its espionage network people of German origin who had taken refuge in England. In almost every case in the last war, the agents and middlemen used by Germany in this country had been neutral citizens or British traitors, often enjoying the reputation of being fanatical anti-German. Kingsley Martin, a month later, went further in his condemnation of 'all that hysteria regarding refugees' by pointing his accusing finger in a different direction. It may well have been whipped up, he said, by comfortably placed Nazi sympathizers to 'direct attention away from the real fifth columnists'.[11] Similar suspicions had been voiced by *Reynolds News* on 7 April: 'The outcry for internment is coming from all the old appeasers, the friends of Franco, the members of the Economic League, from all those trying to direct attention from themselves.'

But the pressures on the Home Office from certain sections of the press, from some Members of Parliament, and, what was much more effective, from inside the War Office, to extend internment beyond the existing two classes, increased as the military situation continued to deteriorate. On 23 May the Duke of Devonshire, who answered for the Home Office in the Lords, asked their Lordships not to join in the stampede to 'Intern the Lot'. This would not only be unjust and cruel, but would also be a waste of effort and of manpower. But he added that the whole subject was under constant review; it would be inadvisable to announce in advance any further steps which the Government might take.

The Home Secretary had told Cabinet on 18 May that the extent of any danger from women refugees was open to argument, but that he was prepared to intern 'B' class women as soon as possible.[12] Six days later, Neville Chamberlain – just two weeks in his new office as Lord President of the Council – told a Cabinet meeting that the War Office had requested the previous night the immediate internment of all enemy aliens regardless of classification.[13] Sir John disagreed. He warned that to intern them all forthwith would cause a breakdown of machinery and would not really be effective, since the danger from neutral aliens was just as serious as from enemy aliens. However, he had decided to intern all 'B' class women between sixteen and sixty years of age on the Isle of Man and to impose special restrictions on all others.

On the same day Sir John's Permanent Undersecretary, Alexander Maxwell, sent a secret memorandum to all Chief Constables.[14] He advised the police authorities that internment of all 'B' women between the ages of sixteen and sixty, would most likely take place on Monday 27 May at 7 am, but that they should take action only after receipt of a telegram:

> Operate German and Austrian women scheme at 7 am on
> (date)

The Women's Voluntary Services would help the police in the arrests. The premises of any arrested female should be searched and any incriminating material (such as plans for assisting the enemy) should at once be reported to MI5. The only women exempt would be those who were infirm, who were in an advanced state of pregnancy or who were mothers of dangerously ill children. As to those to be arrested, nothing was said as to what was to happen to their babies and infants. In the event there was confusion about this; some women were allowed to take them with them, others were refused permission but their children were allowed to join them later.

The wife of a well-known Jewish shipowner from Hamburg, who had come to England in 1938 together with a cargo boat, two seagoing tugs and six Jewish seamen (the husband had himself been interned a few days before), was allowed to take her five months old baby (now the wife of a QC and herself the mother of four children) with her to Holloway prison where most of the women were incarcerated. They were put into the prison hospital but, when the bed was needed for a sick case, the baby was taken to its grandmother and the mother transferred to an ordinary cell. The child was eventually restored to her at Euston Station, when she and the other Holloway prisoners were about to board a train for Liverpool on their way to the Isle of Man. As the train was about to start up her own mother thrust the baby into her arms at the last minute, together with a basket full of baby food and clothing.

At this stage the Home Secretary was still determined not to order indiscriminate wholesale internment. In his memorandum to the War Cabinet, he pointed out what a formidable task and what a waste of manpower it would be to intern the sixty-four thousand 'C' class enemy aliens, how it would immobilize military personnel for guard duties and deprive the country of the services of thousands of refugees who were well disposed towards it.[15] An even more compelling reason was that there should be no discrimination between these refugees and the rest of the alien population:

> I have (he said) in my files considerable information about every man and woman who has been interviewed at a tribunal and I know much more about them than about all other foreign nationals. But as men and women should be treated equally and as I have already ordered the internment of all male 'B' aliens, it is only logical to intern also the 'B' women.

His logic must have temporarily deserted him when he later ordered the internment of all the 'C' men, but left the 'C' women at liberty.

Who in fact were these category 'B' women and men who had now been put into prison or behind barbed wire? In a memorandum to the Foreign Office dated 24 May, Douglas Philips – described by the FO as a 'well-known solicitor' – had pointed out that at the beginning of the war, the Home Office had intended to ask the various organizations caring for the refugees to recommend to them a panel of reliable refugees to assist the authorities in the weeding out of undesirables.[16] The suggestion was later dropped and chaos had resulted. Many people who had been put into category 'B' and now been interned were a hundred per cent genuine refugees from Nazi oppression. County Court judges in Bromley, Beckenham and Chistlehurst had, for instance, simply put everybody into category 'B'. In addition, class 'C' pupils in boarding schools located on the coast, and old men who had spent a weekend in Brighton or Bournemouth, had now been interned. In the interests of justice as much as of public safety, all those now interned should be urgently re-examined. Philips pointed out that the only person who could really tell whether somebody was a genuine refugee was another refugee. Why not appoint a panel of twenty absolutely reliable, well-known refugees from various parts of Germany, and of various professions, to advise the Home Secretary?

The situation was somewhat different for women. Amongst them there were a number of non-refugee girls who in pre-war days had come to England as domestic servants. At their tribunals most of them had been put into category 'B'. Although there were probably very few, if any, planted agents amongst them, there is no doubt that a number of them were proud of being Germans, sympathized with the Nazis, and in the event of an invasion would have become a security risk. It was sensible to intern them; they should, in fact, have been put into category 'A' and interned immediately. A refugee lady imprisoned with them at Holloway, recollects that some servant women were secretly sewing swastika flags in their cells to be ready for the day when the conquering Nazis came to liberate them.

Stories now began to appear in the newspapers about how the arrest of the aliens had been effected and who had been interned.

The *Daily Mail* reported on 17 and 20 May how the Yard chiefs had been up all night preparing to swoop at 8 am in hundreds of police cars on the 1,500 enemy aliens to be taken in London. Many others had still been in bed and had been ordered to dress at once. Armed soldiers had been on duty at all stages of the journey from the various assembly centres in Kensington and North-West London to the internment camps. Amongst those arrested was the former leader of the Vienna Municipal Orchestra, now in Leeds, many businessmen in Glasgow, and, at Gordonstoun, six masters and eleven senior pupils, aged sixteen and seventeen, of whom ten were German Jewish refugees. Dr Kurt Hahn, the founder of the school, was in no danger because he had been naturalized before the war. A prominent German arrested a few days later was Captain Von Rintelen, the master spy of the First World War, although he was over the age limit.*

Another non-refugee German who was interned at that time was Prince Frederick of Prussia, a grandson of the Kaiser and great-grandson of Queen Victoria. During his period of internment he was known as Count Lingen. He had consistently expressed anti-Nazi feelings and was living in voluntary exile. He was subsequently shipped to Canada and returned to England in April 1941. He is the only

---

* *Daily Mail* 28 May. He is the author of the book *The Dark Invader*. He had lived in England for a number of years.

internee whose individual fate merited discussion at Cabinet level, where it was decided that it would look bad if, as a Hohenzollern, he was treated differently from the rest. He should be released but only for work on the land or in forestry. According to the *Daily Mail* of 1 January 1941, he was then actually working with a pick and shovel in a demolition gang, which was cleaning up London's debris. The paper says that whilst in Canada Prince Frederick had acquitted himself well scrubbing floors, but that he had been anxious to return to England.

John Gordon's *Sunday Express* could not resist the opportunity to put in its anti-semitic oar. To be sure, the word 'Jew' was never mentioned but the implication was clear.* Under the heading: 'How The Old Place Has Changed', it reported with glee how the shop-keepers in Hampstead and Golders Green suddenly had very few customers. For the first time one heard only English spoken. A shop-keeper had told the paper: 'They rounded up 2,000 aliens in this area and that has killed our trade.' The chairman of the Hampstead Chamber of Commerce was reported as saying that British people had refused to remain next door to these refugees who had taken over whole streets, and traders who had been in business in Hampstead for many years had been forced to close.

Beverley Nichols, naturally, was not satisfied with the steps taken by the Home Office. In his *Sunday Chronicle* column of 26 May, he again reassured his readers that he had many German friends, but he now wanted to 'see them all, yes all, behind bars'. The letters which readers were sending to the paper about all the Germans running free in their district 'would make your hair stand on end. Some of the letters refer to German women, some pretty and not above offering their charms to any young man, particularly if he works in a munition factory or in a public works.' Nowhere does he advocate any protective steps to be taken against his former friends – if indeed they were 'former' – in the BUF or in the various pro-Nazi Anglo-German associations to which he once belonged.

*   *   *

The refugee problem had assumed much bigger proportions by the

---

* For an investigation of the phenomenon of pre-war anti-semitism in the British Press see: Andrew Sharf's *Nazi Racialism and the British Press*, London 1963, particularly pp 14 ff.

end of May 1940 and became much more complex. Large numbers of people had managed to cross the seas to find sanctuary in Britain, some from Norway, but very many more from Holland and Belgium. After the collapse of France came another civilian invasion. Most of these refugees were nationals of the allied countries, not only Norwegians, Dutch, Belgians and French, but also Poles and Czechs who had previously found refuge in those countries. Amongst them was also a small number of German and Austrian refugees who, under considerable difficulties, had been allowed to board the various crafts ferrying civilians across the North Sea. On one of the smaller cargo boats were a number of German Jews – seventy-two adults and sixty-five, mostly orphaned, children. By sheer persistence and some good fortune, they had managed to board the vessel, which proved to be the last ship to leave Holland. On arrival at Dover they were separated from the other passengers who were mainly Dutch refugees, and were shut up in the hold of the ship with hardly any food or blankets. They were first taken to Falmouth and then to Liverpool, where, without any prior warning, the men were separated from their wives and children and taken to Huyton internment camp.*

The interest which the US Government was taking in Britain's treatment of the German and Austrian refugees, the impression this treatment was creating in neutral countries, as well as the way in which the Nazis were trying to exploit it, all now brought the Foreign Office increasingly into the picture.

Because the Foreign Office was not directly involved in the day-to-day control of aliens and in the problems which their internment was causing, in the way the Home Office or War Office were, the FO officials were able to take a much more detached and balanced view. Their comments show that these civil servants had not only a very much better grasp of the issues at stake and a much better knowledge of the kind of people who were being put behind barbed wire, but that they also had a rather poor opinion of their colleagues at the Home Office and at Military Intelligence. But whilst the Foreign Office people understood the situation better, they had much less influence than the other Departments of State concerned with the problem.

One case which aroused some quite unfavourable comments in the USA was the temporary detention of Arthur Koestler. At the outbreak

---

* A detailed account of their harrowing journey has been deposited in the Wiener Library by Harry C. Schnur.

of war Koestler had been interned in France; he was released and joined the Foreign Legion and was serving in North Africa when France surrendered. On 6 November 1940 he landed at Bristol from Casablanca. He was promptly refused permission to land, lodged in Pentonville Prison, and only released on 13 December. 'We managed to get Koestler, a Hungarian, who had been the *Daily Telegraph*'s correspondent in Spain out of Franco's prison where he had been sentenced to death', noted a senior Foreign Office man. 'He has just published a new book *Darkness at Noon*, a biting indictment of totalitarianism. It is just like the Home Office to refuse him a visa. They probably don't read books.'[17]

The various organizations responsible for the welfare of refugees were now getting increasingly concerned about the situation, and were slowly succumbing to the general change in climate. On 23 May a Joint Consultative Committee meeting was held at Bloomsbury House, which was attended by the various bodies engaged in the care of refugees, such as the Church of England, Society of Friends, Catholic and Jewish organizations, the High Commissioner for Refugees, the Society for the Protection of Science and Learning, the Save the Children Fund, and the TUC. Lionel Cohen, representing the Central Council for Jewish Refugees, stressed that they were not concerned with matters of general policy, those, he said, were solely for Government to decide. The Council would accept whatever decisions the Government took without question. Their job was merely to alleviate hardships.[18]

The Jewish community had become anxious that the refugees should present as low a profile as possible in public. The Board of Deputies had appointed a lady Public Relations Officer. Her main job now became to monitor and, if necessary, to correct the public behaviour of refugees in London.[19] She approached people in the street who spoke German too loudly. She remonstrated with café owners who displayed German language newspapers and she arranged for vigilante committees to be formed by the Jewish communities in the provincial centres to keep watch on their refugees. Before the war, Bloomsbury House had issued a pamphlet 'Do's and Don'ts for Refugees', written in English and German, containing a code of behaviour, which had been handed to every refugee as he first registered. This pamphlet was now reissued. Newspapers were carefully scrutinized for reports of any refugee who had drawn unfavourable comments. When, for instance, the *Oxford Times* reported on 21 June that a Fritz Meyer had been sent for trial on charges unspecified, the Secretary to the Board of Deputies asked Bloomsbury House whether this man was registered with them as a refugee. The answer was: 'We have eighteen different Fritz Meyers registered with us!' Like all the other bodies concerned with the welfare of the refugees, the Jewish organizations had at this stage decided not to oppose, either publicly or privately, the Government's internment policy. All they too were interested in was the alleviation of hardships.

By the end of May, the military situation on the continent was turning into a catastrophe. The evacuation of Dunkirk began on 27 May and was completed on 3 June. Over three hundred thousand men were brought back to England, but all their equipment was lost. By the middle of June invasion of Britain seemed a distinct possibility. On 18 June, Churchill in his famous 'This was their finest hour' speech, warned that an attack was imminent. The nation geared itself for a last stand. To fight the Germans on the landing grounds and on the beaches now became the supreme task, the only one that mattered, the one to which all others had to be bent. In the almost desperate climate then prevailing, internment of all the German and Austrian refugees, the greatest number of whom were still at liberty, became almost inevitable.

5 'Interning the Lot'

'And as I was left there in the darkened house
Listening for the fat clink of the softly shut door,
Looking for the oiled glint and ghost of light,
Sliding soundlessly along the wall towards me,
Knowing that round me they were mobilising
Their old implacable forces slowly,
I shouted. No one answered, one by one
My listening hopes crept back to me
Out of that dead place, mine was a lighted face.
Looking into the darkness, seen but seeing nothing.
(A poem entitled: 'The Interned Refugees'
by W. R. Rodgers, printed in the New Statesman on
12 December 1940).

JUNE 1940 IS A MONTH which those who lived through it in Southern England are not likely to forget. It had an air of unreality about it, as if one existed on two levels of consciousness. There was the appalling news on the radio and in the press. The unimaginable was happening; the Germans had reached the other side of the Channel. Nothing and nobody seemed able to stop them; invasion appeared imminent. It looked as if a thousand years of an historical continuum was about to crumble; values, standards, traditions, a whole civilized way of life might any day be destroyed. Yet the weather was perfect; blue, cloudless skies, green fields, flower-filled gardens, the English countryside at its best; a picture of pastoral peace which even the few planes in the sky, trailing their whispy vapour, could not really disturb. The mind simply refused to accept that death and destruction were rampant on the other side of the Channel.

For the refugees from Germany and Austria, the situation was twice as poignant and twice as unreal. Uprooted, precariously exposed, in a vacuum, it was almost impossible for them to grasp the full import of what was happening around them. At best, they faced the prospect of internment and of indefinite separation from their families; at worst, capture and concentration camps for them all – the end of a long road. Yet many of them would not or could not really comprehend what a successful invasion would mean: the destruction of their idealized image of Britain's traditions, and of Britain's invincible might, and, with it, the destruction of their own lives. They could not entirely share in the *sangfroid*, in the grin-and-bear-it attitude which singled out the people of Britain for the next few years and evoked so much admiration everywhere. But the majority of them also tried to shut out fear and despondency from their minds and to tackle whatever personal problems their daily life threw up. On the whole they were less successful in this – they were too greatly concerned, had experienced too much, had too few anchors left. It was in such a state of mind, where fear of the morrow was suffused with a traumatic escape into unreality, that the refugees were facing the crisis days.

* * *

Until now the pressures on the Government to 'intern the lot' had been coming primarily from certain sections of the press and from some Members of Parliament. Now a much more powerful body joined the chorus – the military establishment. The Chiefs of Staff met on 27 May to consider home security arrangements. They submitted an urgent memorandum to the War Cabinet recommending that:

> the most ruthless action should be taken to eliminate any chance of fifth column activities, including the internment of all enemy aliens and of all members of subversive organizations. Alien refugees are a most dangerous source of subversive activity. The number of new refugees admitted to Britain must be cut to the minimum and those admitted must be kept under closest surveillance.[1]

The Chiefs pointed out that internment on the British Isles was no longer sufficiently secure and recommended the removal of all refugees to Canada. This was the first time that overseas deportation was officially recommended.*

The reports on fifth column activities continued to be confused. Early in June the Civil Defence Authority submitted a memorandum stating that whilst they had received many reports about suspected

---

* Concern about, or prejudice against enemy aliens was not the exclusive preserve of the Top Brass. According to his security officer, the Group Captain commanding the RAF group at Benson, was disturbed that he had serving under him Acting Pilot Officer Robert Kronfeld, who despite his German nationality had got his commission through 'high influence'. (FO 371 25/97.) Kronfeld, an Austrian Jew, had been the man who had pioneered gliding in Germany and in pre-Nazi days had been Germany's best known glider pilot.

espionage and fifth column activities, most of them had been found groundless.[2] But during a discussion at a Chiefs of Staff meeting on 9 June, the Chief of the Imperial General Staff promised that he would raise the whole matter at the next meeting of the Home Defence Committee of the Cabinet, under the chairmanship of the Prime Minister, and, provided the right decision was being taken, he would then disclose to the Home Defence (Security) Executive all the evidence on fifth column activity which they had accumulated. At a subsequent meeting of the Chiefs, Military Intelligence reported that they had received numerous reports about light signals having been fired from the ground near aerodromes, but that military and RAF units had so far failed to catch anybody.[3] On the evidence available, the MI representative claimed, there seemed, however, to be no doubt that fifth column activity of this sort was in fact going on. He offered no evidence to link any of these acts of sabotage to refugees.

The Home Defence Committee of the Cabinet met on 11 June.[4] Mussolini had just declared war and Churchill instructed Sir John to intern immediately all male Italians. As to the Germans and Austrians, Churchill said, they should also be interned as quickly as possible so as to put them out of harm's way. Individual cases could subsequently be examined and then those found to be well-disposed could be released. Even in these circumstances, Sir John Anderson still resisted wholesale internment. 'Experience has shown us,' Sir John said, 'that once large numbers have been collected in concentration camps, a serious danger arises that aliens previously well-disposed to this country will be disaffected by contact with more dangerous characters.' For the moment the Home Secretary had his way.

Churchill's attitude towards the refugees from Germany was ambivalent throughout. This can perhaps be explained on the one hand by his singlemindedness in subordinating everything to the one over-whelming purpose of fighting off invasion and crushing Germany, and on the other hand by his longstanding hatred of the Nazis, and his even older sympathies with the Jewish aspirations in Palestine. He told the Cabinet on 24 May that:

> The proper method by which Germans opposed to the Nazi regime could contribute to the common cause was by work in the factories, fields and, best of all, under the discipline of the Pioneer Corps. German techniques in the occupation of the Low Countries have exposed weaknesses, I am there-fore strongly in favour of removing all internees out of the United Kingdom.

On 11 June Churchill urged that everybody should be interned, but ten days later he asked the War Office to consider raising a Foreign Legion:

> Many enemy aliens have a great hatred of the Nazi regime; it will be unjust to treat our friends as if they were our foes. As things stand at the moment we may not have enough arms and equipment for such a force but they can be found in due course. Meanwhile it will be just as well to have them under military discipline. They could for instance be used immediately in Iceland.[5]

Suggestions to raise a Foreign Legion of alien volunteers or a specifically Jewish Legion to fight under British command, continued to be made from all quarters, including American Jewry, but they all foundered in the face of determined resistance by the War Office.

Meanwhile the authorities pursued the possibility of deporting internees overseas. At the Cabinet meeting on 11 June the Lord President of the Council, Neville Chamberlain, reported that Canada had now agreed to take the three thousand prisoners-of-war and four thousand civilian internees, of which 2,500 were to be Germans, and 1,500 Italians. 'That would be enough to put all the really dangerous characters out of harm's way,' he said. During a Cabinet meeting on 22 June, the Minister of Shipping, R. H. Cross, was asked to explain to the Dominion Governments that the transportation of prisoners-of-war and of internees now had to take priority over the evacuation of British children to North America.[6] The Secretary of State for Dominion Affairs, Lord Caldecote, reported that the Canadian Government did not wish to take any more prisoners or internees than they had originally agreed to take. He was instructed to ask the Australian and New Zealand Governments whether they were willing to accept them and in what numbers. The ships in which the deportees were to be sent could be used as troopships on their return journeys.

On 22 June Lord Caldecote told Cabinet that Australia had signified its willingness to take as many prisoners-of-war and internees as the Government cared to send.[7] Newfoundland, which had also been approached, was willing to take up to one thousand people. In the event, none were sent to either New Zealand or Newfoundland; Australia received only one cargo of civilian internees, the infamous *Dunera* contingent. Only Canada got both civilian internees and prisoners-of-war.

★   ★   ★

By the middle of June, despite the propaganda and the pressures from every quarter, the great majority of German and Austrian refugees were still with their families, uninterned. The constant enlargement of the protected areas had driven a number of them away from their homes; many were living with packed suitcases, waiting for the morning knock at the door, yet hoping that internment might somehow pass them by. 'Public opinion favours internment of enemy aliens,' said a memorandum submitted to the War Cabinet by Clement Attlee on 17 June. 'Security Services fear that in the event of an invasion a considerable number of such aliens, even those genuinely well-disposed towards the United Kingdom would in virtue of their nationality help the enemy. Thus there exists even from the refugees from Nazi oppression a present potential danger.'[8]

What finally decided the issue was the mounting pressure from the military authorities which Sir John could no longer afford to resist. On 19 June the Chiefs of Staff followed up the sombre warning to the Cabinet of 27 May with a further plea which was headed: 'Urgent measures to meet an attack'.[9] 'We must regard the threat of an invasion as immediate' the Chiefs warned. They had been advised by the Home Office that out of a total of approximately seventy-six thousand male and female Germans, only about twelve thousand had so far been interned, and out of fifteen thousand Italians, only 4,500. In view of possible fifth column activities:

> to leave such a considerable proportion of enemy aliens at large at a time like this seems to us to be taking unwarranted risks. From a purely military point of view we consider that *all* (underlined in the text) should be detained forthwith on the understanding that those who can be proved beyond all doubt to be harmless could be released subsequently.

The Chiefs acknowledged the problems of administration and accommodation of such a large number at such short notice and suggested that the majority should be sent to Canada. Large liners, they understood, were available for that purpose.

There was a rumour in later years that the Chiefs had called on Churchill late one night and warned him that they could no longer be held responsible for the safety of the country if all enemy aliens were not interned immediately. Whether that particular story is true or not, the 'Urgent measures' document is sufficiently forthright to have made it impossible for any Prime Minister or Secretary of State to fly in the face of the recommendation, bearing in mind the parlous situation of the country. The Home Policy Committee of the Cabinet therefore decided to commence immediate internment of all male 'C' class aliens between the ages of sixteen and seventy.

On 21 June an urgent circular was sent to all Chief Officers of Police, advising them that HM Government had decided to intern all male Germans and Austrians, subject to certain exceptions. But as sufficient accommodation was not immediately available for the approximately twenty-five thousand people involved in the operation, they would have to proceed in stages.[10] These were as follows:

Stage I: All those who had been classified as non-refugees, except for those who had been resident in the country since 31 December 1919; also all, including refugees and long-term residents, who were unemployed.

II: All residents outside Metropolitan and City districts.

III: The remainder.

For the moment only enemy aliens in Stage I were to be arrested, and their internment should commence on 25 June.*

The following people were to be exempted:

(1) persons under sixteen and over seventy years of age.

(2) persons under eighteen years resident with British families or in residential educational establishments.

(3) invalids and infirm persons.

(4) people engaged in work of national importance who had permits from the Aliens War Service Department.

(5) people granted permission to remain in protected areas because engaged in key work of national importance.

(6) people released from internment since 15 May.

The exemptions were also not properly observed and many people were interned who fell under one or the other of these exemptive clauses.

The premises of the arrested persons were to be thoroughly searched,

---

* No other amending or additional instructions have been traced. Yet when internment commenced four days later, the circular was ignored. The writer of this who fell within stage II was interned on day one; many Jews who had been living in England since before World War One, and who according to the circular should never have been interned at all, were taken at the outset as were people of all three stages.

all incriminatory material was to be seized and sent to MI5. The circular emphasized that under no circumstances should it be made known that this was merely a first step and that HM Government had decided to intern all the other aliens at some later date.

These instructions were dated 21 June; internment was to commence in the early hours of 25 June. Yet already on 21 June the Home Secretary reported to the Cabinet that enemy aliens were being locked up as fast as accommodation could be provided.[11] Any accommodation vacated by internees who had been sent overseas was immediately filled up by fresh intakes. Reliable aliens would be combed out but he expected this to result in only a limited number of releases.*

The Refugee Section of the General Department of the Foreign Office was kept informed as the decisions were taken. The comments of the officials in this section must be mentioned in some detail, particularly those of Mr R. E. Latham, a fellow of All Souls College and temporary Civil Servant, because he showed an unprejudiced grasp of the situation at a time when almost everybody else had succumbed to the panic atmosphere.[12]

The Home Office, Latham observed, which normally had quite humane sentiments, had yielded to military pressure and adopted a pathetic policy of general internment. However, it might, even at this late hour, still have been possible to introduce some discrimination, humanity and common sense into the treatment of the refugees if a strong interdepartmental committee had been formed, consisting of representatives of the Foreign, Home and War Offices, and also of Military Intelligence, but the committee would have had to be presided over by somebody of senior ministerial rank – unless Sir Robert Vansittart† were persuaded to undertake the chairmanship, vested with the necessary authority.

MI5, the department of the security services responsible for the examination of the loyalty of the refugees, Latham said, under the

---

* 'Argus', in the *Contemporary Review* of January 1941, claimed that Sir John Anderson did not bring the whole internment issue to Cabinet but decided on it on his own as a result of military pressure. He cites as evidence that several ministers were shocked when they heard that some of their friends and people whom they considered vital for the war effort, had been interned and tried in vain to get them released again. The columnist thinks that indiscriminate internment would never have taken place if the whole matter had been discussed in Cabinet. In the light of the Cabinet minutes and memoranda now available at the Public Record Office, this supposition is plainly incorrect.

† Permanent Undersecretary at the Foreign Office – the foremost pre-war anti-appeaser in the Establishment.

stress of recent currents in public opinion and under the influence of 'a high authority in the War Office', had adopted a rule of thumb that any foreigner was presumed (almost irrefuttably presumed) to be hostile, whilst any person of British nationality was presumed to be loyal. This, in his opinion, was tantamount to failure, for, after all, MI5 existed for no other purpose than the examination and judgement of individual cases. He suspected that the real object of the propaganda disseminated by the 'actual fifth column' in Britain, had been to convince public opinion as well as the military authorities, that the real fifth column did not consist of themselves, but of refugees from Nazi oppression. The whole Home Office machinery originally set up to classify persons of enemy nationality into friendly, doubtful or hostile categories, had *de facto* broken down; it was faulty from the start. But some effort had to be made to put all this right, particularly now that Britain was fighting alone, if she wanted to rebut the charge that the war was not really for the liberation of other people, but merely for British interests.

Latham's references to a 'high authority in the War Office' and to the 'actual fifth column' are significant, and they seem to convey a hint of a treasonable conspiracy somewhere high up the ladder. It is unlikely that the deputy head of a Foreign Office section would commit to paper such a remark, even in a confidential office memorandum, unless he thought that he had some solid grounds for suspicion.★

Two days later he suggested to the Foreign Secretary, Lord Halifax, that we might send abroad as many prominent and exposed Germans as possible; Australia or some of the colonies might be willing to accept them. Lord Halifax minuted that he was in favour if it could be arranged, and so would be the Home Office. The suggestion obviously referred to a voluntary evacuation rather than to a compulsory deportation and internment, but Snow, Latham's superior officer, disagreed. He saw no reason why 'in the event of a successful invasion these people should not go down in the common ruin'.†

As far as is known, none of the German and Austrian politicians, journalists and trade unionists who were on the Nazi blacklist, had

---

★ See also *Hitler's Table Talks 1941–1944*, London 1953, page 203. Hitler said that Mosley had nine thousand supporters and some of them belonged to the best English families.

† T. M. Snow, Head of the Refugee Section FO 379/25253. Lord Halifax annotated this correspondence: 'There might be serious objections by the public if the refugees are taken to safety whilst British prominent politicians are left to face the threat of invasion.'

asked to be taken to safety overseas. All they had always wanted to do was to share in the fate of the common people and play an active part in the struggle. It was only when they were frustrated, first by mistrust and then by internment, that some of them accepted the chance to move on to the United States.

One case was that of Rudolf Olden. He had been the political editor of the *Berliner Tageblatt*, one of the foremost liberal papers in pre-Nazi Germany; he had found sanctuary in England in 1934 and had published an authoritative book on Hitler. At the outbreak of war he was living in a house put at his disposal by Gilbert Murray. He had repeatedly tried to put his intimate knowledge of Nazi Germany at the disposal of the British authorities, but as a 'C' class alien had now been interned. Whilst on the Isle of Man his friends had obtained a professorship for him at the recently established New School for Social Research at New York University.

He was one of the first people to be released again from a camp on the Isle of Man (Hutchinson) where he had been a pillar of strength and inspiration to his fellow inmates. He, his wife and many evacuated British children were drowned shortly afterwards when the *City of Benares* was torpedoed in the Atlantic.

When Bruening, the last Chancellor of the Weimar Republic proper, then teaching at Harvard, heard about Olden's fate, he commented that Olden's death was the heaviest blow which post-war German politics could have suffered. Olden's brother told Prince Hubertus zu Loewenstein, a prominent Roman Catholic refugee living in New York, that his brother had been shocked by the treatment which he had received from the hands of the British authorities and that even his farewell from England had been soured by the fact that his police registration book had been endorsed with an abundance of red ink: 'No permission to return to England.' Loewenstein says that when he saw a Mr Malcolm at the Embassy in Washington to plead for Olden's release, he was told: 'Any German in England ought to be locked up in a concentration camp.' Whereupon the Prince replied: 'Look here, whilst Olden and others whom you have now interned, were fighting Hitler you were still flirting with him.' Loewenstein also told Peter Olden that he had heard from H. G. Wells that fascist elements in the British Government had been responsible for the internment of political refugees.[13]

In a further memorandum to the Foreign Secretary, Latham suggested, following up an initiative by Sir Robert Vansittart, that much better use could be made of the German refugees by, for instance, employing them in the preparation of widespread revolts in Nazi-occupied Europe and by converting the unarmed Alien companies of the Pioneer Corps into a fighting Foreign Legion under British command. He again warned that the real fifth columnists were trying hard to divert the attention of the public as well as of the military, from themselves to the victims of Nazi oppression.[14]

*   *   *

During June, whilst the Home Secretary was gradually yielding to pressure from the War Office, Parliament continued to air the refugee issue, with the advocates of 'interning the lot' now clearly dominating the field. In Sir John Wardlaw Milne's* view, there was great public resentment on the Isle of Man about all the alien women living in hotels and boarding houses at a cost of 21/– a week, with their own swimming baths, tennis courts and golf links, whilst the wives of the ordinary private soldiers had to do with 17/– allowance a week, plus the 7/– docked from their husbands' pay. Could these women not be made to do some useful work? The Home Secretary replied that these camps had been selected for security and not because of any amenities. The payment to the landladies whose premises had been requisitioned included food at standard rations. Sir Annerley Somerville echoed Sir J. Wardlaw Milne in complaining about the luxurious life of the interned women which was causing a great deal of feeling, particularly amongst the thousands of women on war work.† Eleanor Rathbone objected: these people were not being kept in luxury and idleness. They were longing for nothing so much as to be allowed to do some active work, in or out of internment. Sir Annerley's insinuations were a cruel insult to them. But during those days she was rather a lonely voice.

On 13 June, the Home Secretary told F. S. Cocks‡ that a total of 10,869 enemy aliens had so far been interned. This figure included all the 'B' women and men as well as the 'C' men who had been caught in the protected areas. When Cocks asked what further measures were contemplated to reduce the large number still at liberty, Sir John told him that it would not be in the public interest to disclose any in

---

* MP for Kidderminster (C) on 6 June 1940.
† MP for Windsor (C) on 6 June 1940.
‡ MP for Broxtowe (Lab).

advance. On 27 June Cocks asked again that all enemy aliens should be interned except those who could be trusted and who could be of positive service to the country and to its defence. This was two days after general internment had begun, but it had, of course, not been made public. Sir John told him that certain further measures were at present being taken, but that he had to defer a statement on their character and scope.

In view of the awesome events taking place day after day, the popular press was preoccupied by the military problems of the moment, and their attacks on the refugees abated to a large extent. In fact from now on it was the quality dailies and weeklies which were becoming increasingly concerned with the whole question of internment. The *Manchester Guardian*, in particular, became the great champion of the refugees. Up to the end of 1940 it published over fifty-four editorials and articles and printed more than 110 letters, all concerned with the fate of the internees. Presumably the paper received many more letters on the subject than it could publish. Of those correspondents whose letters the paper published, only two were critical of the refugees and were pro-internment.

The *Sunday Express* was one of the few popular papers which kept up its interest. On 9 June under the headline: 'Our Gauleiters-to-be-Interned', it claimed that the authorities had in their hands a list of all the fifth columnists in this country, as well as of the men who had been selected as Gauleiters once the invasion had been successful. It claimed that police raids on the headquarters of the British Union of Fascists had provided lots of useful information. In the same article the paper reported that ten thousand aliens had already been interned. A month later at a time when general internment was already in full swing, the paper in a stirring call to the government to prepare the people against invasion, warned that it was useless to fiddle about with the alien problem any longer. Every one of them between the ages of fifteen and seventy, male and female, should be interned immediately. Why, one might have asked, should every alien be interned immediately if, according to the *Sunday Express*, the security services knew exactly who was a fifth columnist and who was a security risk?

Whilst the press and the House of Commons were concerned for the time being with the altogether more critical issues of the moment, the House of Lords on 12 June devoted a major debate to the refugee problem. This was the first occasion on which the third champion of the refugees, alongside Colonel Wedgwood and Miss Rathbone, spoke at length on their behalf. George Bell, Bishop of Chichester, had from the outset of the Nazi régime taken a leading part against the persecution of the confessing Lutheran Church in Germany, and had also ceaselessly worked on behalf of all the religious, racial and political refugees. Of all the bishops in the Church of England, he had been most maligned by the Nazi propaganda machine. According to his biographer, he felt it an outrage that those refugees, in particular the German pastors, whom he had helped to escape, should now languish behind barbed wire, separated from their families.[15]

At a time when no decision about interning the lot had been taken, but when there were many clear signs of the way the wind was blowing, his speech in the Lords encompassed most of the arguments which were articulated from July onwards in many parliamentary debates and in the press. At the time, he was attacked by some of his fellow peers such as Lords Elibank and Marchwood, who warned the 'Right Reverend Prelate that this was a war and not a picnic'. What he was saying endangered 'the very lives of our people'. Not only should every alien regardless of sex and age be interned, but the BBC should be purged of all aliens, communists, pacifists and conscientious objectors. By contrast, Lords Noel-Buxton and Cecil of Chelwood supported Dr Bell. When fighting on behalf of liberty, Viscount Cecil said, 'we must not diminish that very liberty which we have all enjoyed for so many centuries and which is now menaced by this crushing system of dictatorship.'

Dr Bell forcefully argued that the internment of all aliens of German and Austrian origin, irrespective of their character, their attitude towards the Nazi régime and their devotion to the cause of this country, was neither demanded by national security nor by justice. The refugees had been driven to Britain as a result of persecution and regarded the Nazi régime with horror. Many had been in concentration camps; all had been treated as outcasts because of race or strong political opinions.

> If Hitler achieved victory in this country it would be terrible for us all, but it would be triply terrible for them. Yet many are now victims of an internment policy which started on Whit Sunday. What sense is there in putting men and women who were rescued from Hitlerism and who were full of gratitude to this country behind barbed wire?

Dr Bell assured the noble Lords that he personally knew of over thirty scholars of great eminence whose loyalty was beyond any doubt and who had been doing work of great national importance; now they had been made utterly useless. Internment, Bell said, was playing straight into Hitler's hands. People of indubitable integrity and loyalty must be released. But if it could not be done quickly enough, then at least the conditions in the camps must be improved.

The Duke of Devonshire replied for the Government. In his view the Bishop's speech would probably command more sympathies after the war than at that time. The Duke knew that the vast majority of all these unhappy people were genuine refugees from Hitler. 'But there may be a few who are not,' said the Duke, 'and one cannot always prove a man's *bona fides*. We must also consider that were we to be subjected to heavy bombing, this might engender a violent exacerbation of public feeling against Germans at large.' He cited the case of a religious farming community in the West Country – all pacifists, living on the produce of their own land, wearing long brown robes.

> Many of them are Germans who speak little English, obviously the last persons whom German Intelligence would wish to employ. Yet there is so much suspicion in the district that these unhappy brothers had asked to be interned for their own safety. If we do it, then we lose a valuable agricultural production asset; if we don't we might expose them to calumny and possible violence.

Towards the end of June it became known that the government had decided on the internment of all 'C' class aliens. The critics of the whole internment policy had no choice but to accept this as a fact of life, and thus for a while concentrated their efforts on improvements in the conditions in the camps rather than continuing their attacks against the whole principle. Later on both objectives – speedy releases as well as better internment conditions – were again simultaneously pursued with increasing vigour.

On 24 June, as general internment was about to commence, a deputation consisting of various members of the Parliamentary Committee on Refugees and of representatives of the refugee organizations, met Oswald Peake, Undersecretary at the Home Office, together with General Hunter, the Director of Prisoner-of-War Camps at the War Office.* Peake did not disclose the new action to them,

---

* Memorandum at Bloomsbury House. The committee had requested to see the Home Secretary himself, but he was fully busy with more urgent matters. The chairman of this committee was Captain Victor Cazalet; the secretary Miss Rathbone, and the two vice-chairmen were David Grenfell and Sir Arthur Salter. Amongst other members of the delegation were Sir Herbert Emerson, the League High Commissioner for Refugees, and Blanche Dugdale, the niece of Arthur Balfour.

but hinted that the nature of the emergency made it impossible to give any advance warning of further internments or of any further designation of protected areas. But he assured them that only dangerous aliens would be transported overseas, that there would be a strict separation between proper prisoners-of-war and interned civilians and that as far as possible families would be interned together. Just how dangerous the majority of the civilian deportees were; to what extent the Dominion Governments were made aware of the separation required; and just when a family camp was finally set up on the Isle of Man, will be shown.

Thus, as France was succumbing, and as the British people were bracing themselves for the supreme test, thousands of refugees were taken away into an unknown future. They were joining those who had been interned at the outbreak of the war as immediate security risks; those who had followed them in November 1939 after 'A' classification by the tribunals, and all those who had been arrested after the fall of Holland just six weeks earlier. They went to camps all over England, Scotland and the Isle of Man; some were carried much farther afield to Canada and to Australia.

The point has now been reached in our narrative where we must begin to look at life in the internment camps. For this we must go back again to the early days of the war.

6   The First Camps

'*La sciate ogni speranza voi ch'entrate*'. A category 'A' internee, one of the misclassified Jewish refugees, thinks that Dante's exhortation would have been a suitable inscription to be chiselled into the gates of his internment camp. Yet in some respects the catchment centres for internees who were considered to be genuine security risks were much superior to those into which the category 'B' and 'C' refugees were herded later on. This was irrelevant, of course, for the refugees amongst them who, regardless of the better material conditions, constantly suffered mental anguish.

These early prisoners had been given the choice of either going to a VIP place, Dixon's Holiday Camp in Paignton and paying 4/6 a day for extra privileges, or going to a run-of-the-mill camp, Warners at Seaton. The majority chose not to pay extra (not many could have afforded it anyhow) and by the middle of November 1939 some five to six hundred internees had been accommodated in Seaton.[1] The holiday chalets there were in a somewhat dilapidated state, bare of everything but beds, with broken taps and ceilings full of holes and leaking, with the wind whistling through doors and windows. The camp, a few miles from the sea, was surrounded by two barbed wire barricades, with watchtowers and searchlights. The internees had been issued with one blanket each. According to the Jewish sportsman Alec Natan, who was one of those arrested on D-Day minus one, they were suffering badly from the cold. The camp leader was the ex-correspondent and Lager salesman Count Montegelas, who had also been rounded up at the very beginning. By now he had identified himself completely with the more aggressive Nazi element. With the help of a Baron von Richthofen, a relative of the First World War air ace, Natan tried to organize an anti-Nazi group, but the Count accused them of marxist sympathies and forbade any further activity. An anonymous note, addressed to Natan and signed 'Black Hand' threatened him with a beating-up.

In time the original group was joined by others whom the tribunals had classified 'A' for immediate internment. Amongst them were a further number of refugees, so that by May 1940 the camp housed some eighty Jews plus a number of international seamen and other 'politicals'.[2] By then some of the most rabid Nazis had been transferred to Swanwick Camp, exclusively reserved for persons of that ilk. The new camp father was a 'non-aryan' solicitor from Hamburg, then a director of the Calor Gas Company. They were joined by a growing number of Germans arrested in various British colonies and shipped to Britain for internment and possible eventual repatriation to Germany. Amongst them were engineers, businessmen, university teachers, all well-bred and well-educated, but many of them, all the same, imbued with a virulent, chauvinistic Nazism. One of the most unpleasant of them was a man of God, a protestant Prebendary, who had been pastor to the German community in Windhoek. After his repatriation in April 1940, he complained to the German Foreign Office that the commandant had been a '*Kaltschnaeuziger Deutschenhasser*' that the 'Jew' Eichenberg, the camp father, was his creature who employed a great number of spies to find out who was a Nazi. It had been dreadful to be together with all these Jews; all their applications to be separated from them had landed in the commandant's wastepaper basket. He believed there were two Scotland Yard officers in the camp, masquerading as refugees and spying on them.[3]

It is interesting to compare the Prebendary's complaints about the 'arrogant hater of Germans' with a report by a Swiss diplomat, relayed to Berlin via the German Embassy in Berne.* He had regularly visited these camps and was of the opinion that the class 'A' internees were being treated much better than those in category 'B' and 'C' elsewhere.

He thinks the different treatment is due to the fact that the British were afraid of countermeasures against their nationals stranded in Germany if they did not treat the 'aryan' Germans well. They were less bothered about the refugees. The Swiss official also declared that British officers often had a higher opinion of people who stuck to their beliefs regardless of consequences. This latter observation is quite shrewd and fits well with the comments of some of the tribunal chairmen, who showed no sympathy towards people whom they considered traitors to their own country, never mind who they were or how badly their country had treated them.

---

* Dated 7 February 1941 (RX II ZV 190). The Swiss official is Herr Preisswerk who was the liaison officer at the Swiss Legation in London for internment and POW camps.

In accordance with the provisions of the Geneva Convention, the War Office had handed to the Swiss photocopies of the camp registration forms of all the internees at Seaton, Paignton and Lingfield. Despite repeated assurances in parliament that under no circumstances would Germany receive the name or other particulars of any interned refugee, these batches of forms handed to the Swiss and forwarded by them to Berlin, contain dozens which quite unmistakably refer to 'non-aryans'.* One man describes himself as 'banker-German Jew'; another as 'Jew-Orthodox'; another shows his nationality as 'stateless'; many show their second forename as 'Israel', which the Nazis had compulsorily awarded to all 'non-Aryans'; others with 'suspicious' names had their cards endorsed by somebody in Berlin with the word '*Jude*'. All this on British forms which the internees had completed because they had been assured that they would only be used as internal records.

The German Embassy in Berne also told their Foreign Office that the head of the special division in the Swiss Legation in London had repeatedly asked the War Office and the Foreign Office for lists of all the people interned in England, Canada and Australia, but in vain.[4] The Swiss did not think that this failure was the result of any deliberate obstruction, but that the disorganization existing in British ministries was simply unbelievable. Records had been dispersed all over the country; files could never be found, and if found were always incomplete; what a contrast, he flatters them, to German office efficiency. The German diplomat in Berne adds that he is quite ready to believe the Swiss official's impressions; they should be a useful guide to how effectively other British Government departments are organized for the war effort. Knowing now the critical views of some of the Foreign Office mandarins about the whole internment policy, one wonders whether the tale of the missing files was not a deliberate obfuscation after all.

Compared with all the other camps, Dixons in Paignton was sheer luxury. At first it contained only forty or fifty pensioners; by May 1940 the number had risen to 120 to 150. Amongst them were some of the more recent arrivals from South-West Africa, including the Prebendary, for whom the accommodation at Seaton had not been good enough, and who were gladly paying the extra 4/6 a day.

---

* Photocopies preserved in the *Auswaertige Amt* Archive. See also the Duke of Devonshire's statement in the Lords on 9 September 1940.

According to his report he obtained a well-furnished accommodation in heated huts and more than adequate comestibles, prepared by professional chefs and served by experienced waiters. He says the service was up to good hotel class standard. At Christmas hired entertainers put on a cabaret, including a troupe of female dancers. They offended the clergyman's sensibilities because they wore 'unbelievably few clothes'. What also shocked him was the fact that the comedian of the show cracked a lot of jokes at the expense of British Ministers and of wartime conditions in Britain. He again complains that more than half the inmates at Paignton were 'Jews and Refugees', but according to the Rabbi who visited the camp, there were only ten Jewish internees at Paignton.

One of the Jews wrote on 31 May 1940 to the Board of Deputies thanking them for 'the means to celebrate Passover in our present plight. It was more consoling to us than in previous years to be able to hold a Seder and observe its traditions.' No doubt, when they held that Seder evening the internees thought of the deliverance and exodus from Egypt. Eugen Spier, the 'Focus' man, then at Seaton, wrote a few days earlier also expressing his thanks to the Board for enabling them to commemorate their festival which 'never fails to renew our faith and hope'.[5]

Both Seaton and Paignton were closed down after most of the class 'A' internees had been shipped overseas, but Lingfield remained open much longer, changing its purpose several times. At first it serviced the early 'A' class internees, joined later by captured merchant sailors. When indiscriminate internment was ordered, it became for a while a transit camp for those destined for shipment overseas; later it was used again for transit but for internees travelling in the opposite direction. They were people about to receive their US visas or due to emigrate to other parts of the world, of which at that stage of the war there were very few still open, or were people called back from the Isle of Man for a special purpose.

The first fifty internees transferred from Seaton to the newly opened camp on the Lingfield racecourse, were a mixed batch of refugees and others. They were quite comfortably housed in horse boxes. They got on reasonably well with each other until they were joined by the crews of three captured merchantmen, when the inevitable tension arose and the educated 'decent' Germans tacitly acquiesced in the constant harassment of the refugees. In a way, these internment camps produced microcosms of the pattern which had grown up in Germany since 1933. The bully boys held sway and the 'decent' Germans were too scared or too little concerned to intervene.

Amongst these sailors, Natan claims, were some who had worked as Gestapo agents overseas. All of them were put up in the main Tote building, in front of which they put up a big poster with the legend: 'No entry for Jews'. The authorities did nothing to have it taken down. They were later joined by a group of intellectuals who had been captured on a neutral boat returning from South Africa. They soon helped in spreading Nazi culture through the camp including propagation of its racial myths. Natan claims that some of them were friendly with or related to leading members of British society who lavishly provided them with food, books and tobacco. They now supplemented the strong-arm tactics of some of the sailors with a more subtle mental torture of the refugees.

On Winter Solstice night, 21 December 1939, a pagan celebration was held on the racecourse. Huge baulks of timber were piled high and set ablaze. Putzi Hanfstaengel, Hitler's former friend, presided over the ceremony and read passages of the nordic *Edda*.* Runes were cast, followed by the chanting of the Horst Wessel song. British officers watched what Natan calls a 'monstrous revival of paganism' and Spier 'a mockery of christianity'. The officers made no attempt to interfere whilst the rest of the internees looked on with disgust from the members' box on the grandstand. The good Prebendary was also at Lingfield at that time. In his report to the German Foreign Office he makes no mention of this heathen exhibition. If he looked on he was no doubt able somehow to square in his theological conscience, these crude rites with the Sermon on the Mount.

Spier records that they had been joined by the fee-paying internees from Paignton, who were again given much more luxurious sleeping quarters. They had a daily delivery of newspapers and messed in their separate dining-room on superior food. They also had a special tea-room in which twice a week internees were allowed to receive outside

---

* Hanfstaengel is something of an enigma. He had quarrelled with Hitler and had gone into exile. His name is on the famous Gestapo *'Fahndungsliste'* of people to be arrested as soon as invasion had been accomplished. An intelligence officer at Lingfield has told the author that when invasion appeared imminent, Hanfstaengel pleaded to be taken overseas as he was afeared of his life. Yet Hanfstaengel was never released. After British Intelligence had interrogated him he was taken to the USA for a similar purpose, then returned to Britain and reinterned. Those refugees who met him in internment say he was an arrogant and unrepentant Nazi.

visitors. It should always be remembered that the majority of these privileged prisoners were either genuine security risks or dubious customers. The treatment has to be compared with that meted out to people like the grandson of Sigmund Freud, who a few weeks later was deported on the *Dunera*, under somewhat less luxurious conditions.

On one occasion Spier was permitted to entertain his own wife in the tea-room. An elaborate chocolate gâteau had been baked for the occasion. It so happened that Mrs Spier did not fancy such rich food, and preferred some plain sandwiches. After her departure Spier gave the cake to some of his Nazi stable mates. All of them became violently sick. A fanatical Nazi pastry cook had mixed soapflakes into the dough after he had heard that the cake was destined for a Jewess. Spier calls the incident poetic justice.

During May Lingfield became the temporary home for eleven boys from Scotland. Among them was a lad of sixteen, later to become a handicrafts teacher in a London school. He was a 'C' case, a refugee from Nazi oppression. When Scotland became a protected area in May 1940, he and ten other boys were arrested straight from school and taken to Lingfield because the camp was supposed to be the only one with facilities for further education. In fact, neither they nor any of the other youngsters had any proper tuition. On their way south they were joined by thirty-four other youngsters. They had come from Wittinghame in Ayrshire, an estate owned by Lord Balfour (of the 'Balfour Declaration') which had been turned into an agricultural training camp for Palestine (a 'hachsharah').

The Wittinghame lads were kept at Lingfield until over a year later, when they were returned to Scotland to continue to grow food for Britain. In the camp they were popular with both the older internees and the camp staff, helping out wherever they could and acting as general handymen and errand boys. An Intelligence Officer became their patron saint because he insisted that they should be separated from some Hitler Youth with whom they were having constant fights. When they finally left they gave him as a token of their gratitude, a book about the birds of Britain. Its dedication, subscribed by thirty-four very German–Jewish sounding names, reads: 'Lang may your lum reek'.

Lingfield was the only UK internment camp where there was a genuine and almost successful attempt to escape. A tunnel was dug beyond the perimeter fence, its exit well concealed behind a clump of bushes. Electric light and a water pump were installed; a sailing vessel, chartered by outside accomplices, was waiting for the escapers in a nearby harbour. A date was set for fifty of the Nazis to escape when at the last moment the whole enterprise was betrayed by a German communist. At least, this is how the Prebendary reported the incident to the German authorities.

Spier's account is a different one. He claims that the object of the tunnel was not to facilitate permanent escape, but to provide a temporary exit. Against a fee of 1/– payable to the tunnel constructors, internees would be able to use this means of egress to pay nocturnal visits to girlfriends in nearby East Grinstead, on the promise that they would be back before the morning roll-call. He too says that the enterprise was blown at the last moment by an anti-Nazi whose life was afterwards threatened and who had to be transferred to another camp. The Prebendary's version sounds the more plausible one.

Amongst the earlier camp leaders was Albert Lieven, the film actor, who portrayed thoroughly nasty ss officers in countless post-war films, and Dr Gustav Lachmann, chief aeronautics designer with the Handley Page company. Whilst interned he was frequently visited by Sir Frederick Handley Page, who tried his utmost to get his key engineer released. Lachmann became well known after the war as the designer of the Viking civil airliner.

In the middle of June Lingfield was being emptied of its original category 'A' visitors, who were then transported to the docks in Liverpool for embarkation to Canada or Australia. Like another racecourse, at Kempton Park, Lingfield now became a temporary home for class 'C' aliens who were being rounded up outside.

Swanwick Camp in Derbyshire was the place where the more rabid Nazis had been concentrated. Not surprisingly it seems to have been much superior to the dilapidated holiday chalets, race tracks, disused cotton mills and encampments under canvas which were being used for the refugee internees. One of the Nazis said that of all the camps in which he had been, Swanwick was by far the best.[6] It was an old manor, the Hayes, which had been used pre-war as a conference centre. The stately home, with its own chapel, was situated in the middle of a park, surrounded by flower beds, with its own kitchen garden and greenhouses. Each older internee had his own room; the youngsters shared the big hall. There was central heating in every room and the bathroom facilities were most adequate. Natan, who had not been there himself, heard from others that the place was run on strict party lines, and had its own underground connection with Germany, perhaps by wireless. People who did not conform were beaten up. When someone complained, the British commandant is supposed to have replied: 'Don't get excited; it is just as in one of our Public Schools, where newcomers always get a thrashing as a sort of initiation.' *Reynolds News* of 7 April 1941, quoted a question to the Prime Minister by D. L. Lipson,* alleging that the camp leader at Swanwick censored all outgoing letters before they ever reached the British censor, and that everybody there was forced to join in the singing of the *Horst Wessel Lied*, the rousing anthem extolling the slain Berlin pimp whom the Nazis had turned into their great hero.

The Oratory School in Chelsea was used to house those appearing before the Birkett Committee which had, in November 1939, begun to hear appeals of people who had been interned at the outbreak of war, and also of those whom the tribunals had put into category 'A'. Natan, internee number seven, was there altogether three weeks. His comments are not complimentary. The internees spent most of the time locked in a filthy cellar; their only exercise was once a day in a yard forty by ten yards. He describes the sanitary arrangements as antediluvian. He and his peers spent most of their time rehearsing endlessly what they would say at their hearings. On 12 December, he was summoned, without notice, to meet the Advisory Committee sitting in the Royal Academy, consisting of the chairman, Norman Birkett KC, Professor Collinson, and, as he recalls, either Margaret Bondfield or Ellen Wilkinson, both prominent Labour politicians. On 9 February 1940 he was told that his appeal had been unsuccessful.

The most mysterious camp of them all was Latchmere House on Ham Common. A. Schuetz, an Austrian refugee who during the First World War had been an Intelligence Officer and cryptographer in the Austro–Hungarian Army, spent some time as a prisoner in this building. Like Spier, he had been active before the war in warning influential Britishers about the dangers from Nazi megalomania. Like him, he had been interned for his troubles and also like Spier he has recorded his adventures.[7] The main purpose of his memoirs is to prove that the British Secret Service, who grilled him at Latchmere House, was not only grossly inefficient, but also extremely rude to him; he is equally scathing about all the other national Intelligence Services. His book is emotionally supercharged and vituperative, and his details must

---

* MP for Cheltenham (C).

be taken with a certain amount of scepticism despite a very complimentary introduction by Wickham Steed; the very vehemence of his views is counterproductive. He describes Latchmere House (he does not actually name it, but the hints are unmistakable) as a 'horrible, filthy building, surrounded by barbed wire and a phalanx of Irish Guards, where the prisoners are locked all day in single cells and treated most discourteously'.

Little was known about the purpose of the place, and the Government was obviously obfuscating the issue. Richard Stokes complained in the House on 19 September 1940 that after having been examined by an advisory committee, internees were kept there under strict military guard in solitary confinement. Osbert Peake replied that those who were taken to Latchmere House, usually only for a short period pending further investigation, were people who claimed or who were thought to have information of interest or value to HM Government. On 9 October, Stokes quizzed the Home Office again. Peake again stressed that the internees were never kept there for more than a month and in isolation only for a few days. The main purpose of the place was to provide temporary accommodation for civilians from many countries and for that reason unlimited association between them was impossible; a somewhat different explanation from the one given before.

However, the minutes of the First Meeting on Internal Security, held by the Home Defence (Security Executive), disclose a somewhat different *raison d'être* for the secret place.[8] It had been established as a separate camp for internees who had to be segregated from the rest for several reasons. Some had volunteered for Special Operations, had been recruited by SIS or SOE, or were in possession of special knowledge which had subsequently been found unsuitable for special employment. Some of these could eventually be returned to an ordinary internment camp, or even be released once the information which they possessed had become obsolete; others had to be kept segregated until the end of the war. Rejects from SIS were usually aliens, from SOE usually British subjects. Some were illegal immigrants who could not be set free. Others might be suspected resident aliens who had at first been interned in ordinary camps and then taken to Latchmere House for interrogation and whose presence in internment had become known to their respective governments. Such people could not be returned to the Isle of Man because any contact they had with visitors endangered the secrecy of their information. Such contacts included charitable organizations and representatives of protective powers. In fact, the War Office had recently refused a request by the Swiss Minister to visit Latchmere House. The Committee discussed whether it would not be better to transfer these internees to Stafford gaol, where their presence could be more effectively concealed from the outside world.

* * *

The German Government naturally was most interested in the location of the various internment camps, both from the point of view of the aerial bombardment of the British Isles and of Operation *'Seelöwe'*. Because new camps were being opened all the time and old ones being closed, they had great difficulty in ascertaining how many there were and pinpointing their location. On 28 May 1940, the German Foreign Office forwarded to *Luftwaffe* HQ an *Abwehr* map, showing the location of all the camps known to them.* The same map was also sent to the High Command of the Armed Forces, with the comment that the British were constantly changing the names of their internment camps so as to confuse them, but the Foreign Office was fairly certain that the same eight camps still existed in the same places.[9] A month later they issued another list, this time only containing seven names: Donaldson School, Swanwick, Bertram Mills Winter Quarters near Ascot, Taunton School Southampton, Seaton, Paignton, and a 'Women's Camp on the Isle of Man'. They seem to have had no knowledge of the existence of Kempton Park, Lingfield, Huyton, Warth Mill and Prees Heath, all of which were by then in business, and which will be described later. The question of Germany's knowledge of what camps there were and where they were situated, had a double-edged significance. The Nazi internees favoured it because it would assist their aircraft to avoid dropping any bombs on them and after a successful invasion they could be liberated that much quicker. They therefore did not object to the camps being brilliantly illuminated at night against a blacked-out background. The refugees in due course interned on the Isle of Man, did not like it at all, because they were

---

* RX II ZV 57. The *Abwehr* under Admiral Canaris, was the military German Intelligence Service, combining both espionage and internal security. It ran alongside and competed with the *Reichssicherheitshauptamt*, the Party police organization, until the latter swallowed up the former. For further details see David Kahn: *Hitler's Spies*, London 1978.

afraid the Germans might select the camps, into which their enemies had so conveniently been concentrated, for special attention. As it was, no camp either on the mainland or on the Isle of Man ever received a direct hit.

In every camp, whether in Britain, Canada or Australia, where refugees had to live cheek by jowl with Nazi Germans, they had to endure taunts, insults and occasional physical assaults. From the very outset they and their sympathizers in Parliament and in the press agitated for a physical separation of these two totally disparate elements; yet it took many weeks before their grievance was remedied. But the pressure for separation did not only come from the refugees and their champions. The dyed-in-the-wool Nazis seem to have equally resented cohabitation with the Jews. The files of the German Foreign Office are full of letters of complaints from internees or repatriated party faithfuls about the ignominy of having to consort with 'Jews, Communists and the like' and the German Government repeatedly requested the Swiss to press the British authorities for a change.*

On the Isle of Man such a separation presented difficulties. Two Swiss representatives visited the island from 8 November to 11 November 1940.[10] The officer commanding all the camps told them that he now had 18,980 internees in his custody, of whom 3,960 were women. He admitted that the mixing of 'aryan' Germans and Jews was creating a lot of difficulties, but it was hard to know who was who. The Swiss could convince themselves of these difficulties when they visited the camps the next day and talked to many internees. Some of these 'aryan' Germans had lived in England a long time and had no objections to being together with Jews. Others were afraid to put their name down for an intended all-aryan camp because they suspected it would be on the mainland where they would be exposed to greater danger and could no longer visit their wives, also interned on the island. Curiously none of the Swiss reports ever mention the not inconsiderable number of 'aryan' trades unionists and other political refugees, perhaps because they, like the Jews, had refused to acknowledge the Swiss as their protectors.

From the beginning of the war, efforts had been made by both the German and British governments to ease the burden of looking after

---

* See, for example, a letter dated 30 January 1941 from the German Embassy in Berne to the *Auswaertige Amt*, stating that once again they had requested the Swiss to insist on a separation of the Germans from the Jews. (RX 11 ZV 175.)

civilian internees. In consequence, repatriation had been going on almost from the beginning of the war. Due to the pressure of events it was suspended during the most critical phases of the war, but then resumed so that on 12 July 1944 Anthony Eden could declare in the House that a general exchange of civilian prisoners and internees had been arranged with the exception of those who did not want to be repatriated or could not be for security reasons. His opposite number, Joachim von Ribbentrop, had originally objected to the idea of individual exchanges on a tit-for-tat basis because Germany held fewer Britons in custody than vice-versa, but finally an overall exchange via Sweden and Portugal was arranged.

But of course, the great majority of the German and Austrian nationals in British hands had no desire to be 'repatriated'. In fact, they dreaded nothing more; Germany had ceased to be their *patria*. They wanted to help Britain wherever they could in her war effort, but for the moment a different fate awaited them: internment for many; overseas deportation for some.

7   Towards Canada

'A DISASTER DATE in the annals of British justice.' This is how a senior British civil servant characterized the deportation of internees to Canada, adding that it was 'impossible to discern any principle underlying their selection, ranging from sixteen to seventy years, robust to moribund, university professors to mentally deficient pedlars; brothers, fathers and sons, friends separated at random.'[1]

The official, Alexander Paterson, one of HM Inspectors of Prisons had, in response to persistent questionings in both Parliament and the press, been dispatched by Sir John Anderson to Canada to investigate complaints about the treatment of internees during their passage to the Dominion and their sojourn in the camps there. He spent several months in Canada, but by the time he submitted his report in September 1941, over a year after the deportations had taken place, Herbert Morrison had become Home Secretary. Morrison rightly described Paterson's monumental report as 'a great humanistic document and also a great state paper' and congratulated Paterson on the way he had 'overcome so many obstacles and had been able to infuse into what could have become a too soulless and rigid administration a humanitarian spirit.' Morrison realized that the report could not possibly be puslished at that stage, but hoped it would be done after the war when it should be prefaced by an explanation of the dramatic circumstances of the time and the difficulties of the hurried operation.

The report in fact has never been published. It is indeed an outstandingly compassionate and understanding document, a great credit to the man and, it must be said, also to a Home Secretary and to a government which at a time of great national peril did not attempt to sweep the disquiet and the complaints under the carpet, but sent Paterson to Canada and gave him virtual *carte blanche*, in cooperation with the Canadian Government, to put right what he could.

The idea of transporting internees and prisoners-of-war overseas had been hatched in the War Office and was supported by a minister, Lord Swinton, who on behalf of the Home Defence (Security) Executive, warned the Cabinet about the danger of retaining aliens in the United Kingdom in view of the help which they might render to invading forces.[2] It had the keen approval of the Prime Minister. On 30 May, the High Commissioner for Canada cabled Ottawa to ask whether the Canadian Government was prepared to come to the assistance of the UK Government, which was sorely pressed by the threat of invasion, by receiving as many aliens as possible, all of whom were potentially dangerous persons. Other dominion governments were similarly approached. After initial hesitation, the Canadian authorities cabled their consent, and the transportation of interned men and boys was underway within three weeks of the suggestion first being raised. Canada agreed to a limited number, Australia's commitment was open ended.

It was made clear to both governments that they were merely expected to provide the camps, the military guards and the provender; the UK Government retained sole responsibility for transportation and release.

Between 30 June and 10 July 1940 four ships left for Canada, and one ship for Australia. Altogether 7,715 persons were dispatched to Canada (not all of them arrived there), and 2,732 persons to Australia, made up as follows:[3]

CANADA

	Sailed		
Duchess of York	21 June	2,102	'A' class internees of whom 1,697 were seamen.
		500	POWs.
Arandora Star	30 June	479	'A' class Germans and seamen.
		734	Italians.
Ettrick	3 July	1,307	'B' and 'C' class Germans.
		1,348	German POWs.
		407	Italians.
Sobieski	7 July	405	Single Italians.
		983	'B' and 'C' Germans.
		450	German POWs.
		———	
		8,115	

AUSTRALIA
Dunera   10 July   244   'A' class Germans.
                                 200   Italians.
                               2,288   'B' and 'C' Germans.

      Grand Total: 11,447* People

Although the whole deportation procedure was kept a military secret, the US Government had got wind of it; perhaps had even been officially notified. On 28 June, seven days after the *Duchess of York* set sail, the US Ambassador to the Court of St James wrote to Lord Halifax recalling that the British Government had protested through him about the treatment of British nationals stranded in Denmark after the occupation, and warning him that any compulsory transfer of German internees would lead to retaliation by Germany.[4] The US Ambassador in Rome issued a similar warning in respect of Italian internees. By then of course it was too late to stop the action. Germany did not resort to any retaliation. They were in no position to do so because of the small number of British civilians in their hands.

The civilians, shipped on the first transport, the 20,000-ton *Duchess of York* of the Canadian Pacific Steamship Company, were mainly people who on outbreak of war had been interned immediately as security risks, as well as German merchant seamen.† They had been drawn from various camps in England, the last one of which had been on Lingfield Race Course near East Grinstead. They were joined on board by sundry prisoners-of-war, mainly young and cocky *Luftwaffe* officers, who had been shot down in various theatres of war, including the Home Counties. Amongst these 'security risks' was Eugen Spier, who is one of our main sources of information for the passage of the *Duchess of York*.[5] We also have the remarkable testimony of the young teacher, who, together with the other ten youths – all, it

---

* The total number of deportees is actually only 11,003 because 244 'A' class Germans and 200 Italians on the *Dunera* were survivors from the *Arandora Star*. Altogether 226 Italians and 303 Germans had been saved (FO 371/25210). Some of these could not be immediately redeported because they had been injured. The figures in the Foreign Office memo do not tally with those in the Paterson report. Where there are discrepancies the Paterson statistics have been taken.
† The seamen were presumed to have all been Nazis, but a number of them were in fact members of the International Seamen's Union, a socialist trade union, proscribed in Germany. They had been removed from non-German ships. Nearly two hundred of the rest, all stigmatized as Nazis, were refugees (see Paterson report).

should be remembered, classed as 'refugees from Nazi oppression' – had been thrown in with much older, cock-a-hoop Nazis.

When the internees at Lingfield heard that they were once again being moved, they expected to be taken to one of the newly established camps on the Isle of Man, where some of them were hoping to be reunited with their wives and children. After leaving the camp and marching through the peaceful village to the local railway station, the Nazi majority amongst them raucously sang their anti-British and anti-Jewish songs, such as '*und wir fahren gegen Engeland*' or '*Heute gehört uns Deutschland; morgen gehört uns die ganze Welt*' and the particularly nasty one, already cited: '*Wenn das Judenblut vom Messer spritzt*'.

The internees had been without any news for several days. When the kindly disposed escort sergeant slipped a newspaper into the hands of one of the Nazis, the news about the capitulation of France soon spread. It caused thrill and excitement amongst the Nazis, dismay and gloom amongst the small contingent of refugees. They were entrained for Liverpool and then marched to the quayside. When they saw the huge size of the *Duchess of York*, they realized immediately that she was much too big for the Isle of Man traffic. Their hearts sank. As Spier puts it: 'If a Leviathan or any other sea monster had jumped out of the sea, it could not have frightened or distressed us more.'

The ship was very overcrowded; people were lying all over the decks. Spier found his allotted berth at the bottom of the ship. He describes it as a filthy little place where forty people were lying in a small cabin, half naked, on palliasses. The heat, the heavy perspiration of the men, the nauseating smell of oil from the adjacent engine room, created an atmosphere which Spier found intolerable. He tore up his berth ticket and tried to bed down in the dining-room where Nazi officers and some German consular officials were swaggering about, clicking their heels, '*Heil Hitler*ing' each other and pouring ridicule on the British, who, they claimed, would soon be licked and then punished for what, in defiance of all international conventions, they were doing to these German heroes by deporting them overseas through mine-infested waters. One particularly noisy Nazi was sure that a British submarine would in due course send the ship to the bottom of the sea. The British would thus get rid of them all and then blame it all on the wicked Germans.

The eleven young refugees had not been allocated any sleeping berths and had nowhere to go. They were bullied around by the Nazis who had taken control of the ship. They slept the first night on the floor of the dining-room, but were chased out at five am when the room had to be prepared for breakfast. Some of the German civilians threatened to throw the boys overboard if they did not make themselves scarce, and would do so in any case as soon as Britain had surrendered, which was bound to happen any day. The lads tried to make themselves as inconspicuous as possible. They got little sleep and even less food. Until now internment had been for them a bit of an exciting adventure, rather like a scout camp, but now they were exposed to a taste of Nazidom.

The seamen and *Luftwaffe* officers on board outnumbered the British escort troops, who were armed only with ancient rifles. Spier overheard several of the German officers openly discussing the chances of disarming the guards, seizing the ship and sailing it to Hamburg. The few British officers on board obviously had realized how exposed their position was, and were nervous and irritable. The Nazis saw this and sneered and jeered whenever a British officer, hand on his holster, passed them. But when, during a disturbance on deck, the guards opened fire and one of the obstreperous prisoners was killed, the atmosphere on board quietened down and Spier heard no more talk about taking the ship over.

Amongst the Germans was Captain O. Scharf, pre-war Commodore of the *Norddeutsche Lloyd*. Scharf, well known to transatlantic passengers, had been captured off Narvik. Spier and the teacher both speak well of him. Later, after repatriation, Scharf submitted a report to the German Foreign Office. In this he claimed 'an officer told us to clear the deck, but we did not move fast enough for his liking. He gave orders to fire. One German seaman was killed, several others were injured.'[6] Scharf says he was later told that the British officer concerned was subsequently relieved of his post. When he wrote his report Scharf himself was under investigation by the Gestapo because of his alleged friendliness towards Jewish co-internees whilst camp leader in a Canadian internment camp. His whole report is an obvious attempt to please his masters.

Spier was mercilessly teased by the Nazis. One of them, pretending that his comrades had smuggled aboard a radio receiver, told Spier hair-raising stories of how panic-stricken England was on the point of collapse; that the Nazi conquest of Britain had begun; how the British Empire was disintegrating and how the Americans and the Arabs were veering more and more towards Nazi Germany.

For the first few days of the journey the prisoners could only speculate on their destination. But when they entered a zone full of icefloes they realized that they were bound for Canada. These POWs and early internees were treated much better than the refugees who were transported on later ships, those aboard the *Duchess of York* had the freedom of the ship.

As the boat was sailing towards Quebec, passing the Chateau Frontenac, the Nazis were in great spirits, singing: 'Join the British and see the world', cock-a-hoop that they would soon all be back in Germany, feted as heroes. The Jews, the ex-members of the International Brigade and the rest of the non-Nazis aboard were silent, apprehensive about the immediate future. There was a delay just before they were allowed to disembark. They were all puzzled as to the reason until a high ranking *Luftwaffe* officer told them: 'The ship is going to sail straight back to Hamburg; Great Britain has surrendered; King George has abdicated; Churchill has fled to Canada!' Shortly afterwards they were taken off the ship and marched into internment camps.

*   *   *

The next ship to set sail was the *Arandora Star*. She never reached Canada and her tragic fate attracted, at the time, great attention. She was a ship of 15,500 tons, built in 1927. In pre-war days she had been used on the luxury traffic to South America.[7] She was a fast vessel and did not sail in convoy.

Her complement of internees consisted of Italians and captured German merchant seamen and of 'A' class German and Austrian internees. The 734 Italians aboard had been rounded up on the morrow of Italy's entry into the war. Many of them were long-term residents in Britain who had been employed in the traditional Italian occupations in Soho, Glasgow and elsewhere. Very few of them had any political interests or affiliations. Amongst them was an eighteen-year-old boy, who, with his parents, had come to England ten years before. He recorded his internment adventures on a roll of government-issue toilet paper with a stump of a pencil. It is a vivid and exact log which he has preserved until this day.

Together with 1,600 compatriots, the boy had been kept at Warth Mill near Bury in Lancashire. During a roll call on 20 June, about half the Italians were told that they would be moved to an unspecified destination. In many cases the move involved the splitting up of fathers and sons, of brothers and of friends. Last minute substitutions occurred. In a scene of general confusion no proper records were kept of these changes. Nobody in the end knew who had been put into which group.

The first contingent left Warth Mill the following morning, immediately after roll call. They did not travel further than the Isle of Man, where they stayed put. The remainder left by train in the afternoon for Liverpool. Just as Spier and his fellow prisoners had done a few days before, the Italians realized that the liner which was waiting for them at the dockside was much too big for the Isle of Man services. They had heard rumours before that deportations to Canada were about to take place and correctly guessed their destination.

The young man, like Spier on the *Duchess of York*, found the accommodation below deck so crammed and stifling that he appropriated for himself a shelter on the promenade deck. He put down his mattress and his blanket, which he had been given on boarding. Wandering around the deck he came across a lad from his native region of Italy, whose father was somewhere deep down in the bowels of the ship. He invited the younger boy to share his shelter. All the internees had been left entirely to themselves. They had received some food and lifevests, but there had been no boat drill, no instructions on what to do in any emergency, no information of any kind. The two lads sat down in their shelter somewhat apprehensively.

The 'A' category internees boarded last. Amongst them were a number of mislabelled refugees, including the Jewish antiquarian bookseller and young Peter Jacobsohn. Jacobsohn did not like his below-deck quarters. He found himself an empty bathroom, hung up a sign outside which read 'Private – No Entry', locked the door, turned on the taps, and for the first time in many months allowed himself to luxuriate in a hot bath. Whilst immersed in his tub he heard a peremptory knock at the door. A ship's officer told him in no uncertain terms to clear off. Jacobsohn found himself a shelter on the boat deck amongst a number of Italians.

The ship set sail in the early hours of 1 July. At first the sea was smooth but after lunch the weather changed and the ship began to pitch and toss. During the following night when she was some 200 to 250 miles off the north-west of Ireland, it began to rain quite hard. The young Italian was awakened at six am by drops of rain splashing down on his legs through chinks in the wooden roof of the shelter. At around six-forty am he heard a muffled explosion; then there was a sudden shudder which jerked him into an upright position. He and his companion got up and tied each others lifejackets. The other boy left to look for his father down below; neither he nor his father were ever seen again.

The *Arandora Star* had been ploughing through relatively smooth seas at a speed of some eight knots, when the torpedo struck her. Although nobody knew what was happening, there was no immediate panic on deck. People were milling around everywhere; some were trying to lower the few lifeboats from the top deck, others to prise loose life rafts which had been tied to the side of the ship. But they had no tools and were unable to cut the wire ropes. The Italians, the German seamen and the German and Jewish internees had originally been segregated, but now they were all moving around, few of them knowing what they should do. The British soldiers were equally clueless; there were very few British sailors in evidence. The escort troops tried to lower the boats, but the davits were rusty and the ropes would not move easily. One of the soldiers cut a rope as a boat was nearing the water's edge; it crashed into the sea, drowning some of those who were swimming around in the water. Another soldier was standing on guard with his bayonet fixed; the Italian advised him to drop the rifle and try to save himself. He never saw the soldier again.

When after a few minutes the list of the ship increased and it seemed as if it might sink very shortly, the Italian decided that it was time to get off. He spotted a rope ladder hanging on the side and ran towards it, just as a German refugee reached it from the other side. After some: 'after you, no, after you', both climbed into the water. The Italian had buttoned his mackintosh over the lifevest which was now billowing in the water like a collapsed sail. He grabbed a piece of flotsam which was floating past him and with the other hand began to swim away. Suddenly there was a hissing sound and the *Arandora Star* slid under with many people still aboard. Amongst them was her British captain and the senior German merchant marine officer. They had been joined on the bridge by an Italian padre who blessed them all as they went down. A couple of guns that had been lashed to the deck broke loose as the ship was tilting and crashed into the sea. It was exactly 7.25 am when the *Arandora Star* finally disappeared. The Italian boy was still swimming when he noticed a largish piece of wood floating by, which looked like the side of the hut which he had used as a shelter on board. On it were five people. He swam towards it, but they waved him away. But he saw there was still room on it and hoisted himself on with the help of an old British sailor. He had swallowed a lot of oil and seawater and sank back exhausted and feeling sick. When he came to again he saw that there were now eight people aboard the raft, five Italians, two Germans and the British sailor. Suddenly the old man began to mumble and moan; he got up, staggered about a bit and fell over the side of the raft. The Italian pulled him aboard again but when he looked at his ash white face and closed eyes he knew the sailor was dead. He could not bring himself to push the dead man back into the sea and held on to him. It was hard not to fall asleep.

They had been all alone but after some time a man with a pipe stuck in his mouth, sitting on a barrel, floated past looking just like Popeye the Sailorman. He told them not to despair; they were bound to be rescued soon. Sure enough, around noon they spotted a speck in the sky which gradually came nearer and grew bigger. It was a Sunderland flying boat. It swooped over them for a while and dropped something, but they were not able to pick it up.

The captured German sailors had first been put into a large messdeck, but, according to one of them, were later told to exchange their quarters with 'some Italians and Jews' because the Nazis were a 'tidier lot and better organized'. They were in fact given first-class cabins. All of them had been provided with life-jackets. After the torpedo had struck, they tried to reach the lifeboats but were unable to get anywhere near them. They decided to jump into the water, surrounded, as witness reported, by 'crying and praying humans'. The water was covered by a thick film of oil with pieces of cork, wood and canisters floating around. Whilst he was still trying to get hold of some of this flotsam, the ship started to slip. Everything on board, anchors, chains, guns, crashed into the sea, people were howling and shrieking until, suddenly, all went deadly silent. This German eventually found a broken mast to which several British soldiers were clinging. He grabbed hold of it and as they were drifting away from the maelstrom, one after the other of the exhausted soldiers dropped off and drowned. Only a few of them were eventually saved.[8]

Peter Jacobsohn had been asleep amongst the Italians when the torpedo struck. The ship began to tilt gently; there was a slight panic amongst the Italians, many of whom fell on their knees, praying to the Virgin Mary to save them. He fastened his lifevest and moved off. He passed the ship's dining-room where silverware and crockery were sliding from the tables and clattering to the floor. Eventually he met up with some German seamen who, under command, and with discipline, were one after the other jumping into the water. He followed them. Several lifeboats and rafts passed by but they were either too far away or filled to over-capacity. He tried to hoist himself atop a floating bench, but always fell back again. After a while a solitary man, an Austrian refugee still immaculately dressed, floated by on a small plank. The Austrian called to him: 'Good morning Mr Jacobsohn' and then drifted off. After about four hours he spotted a raft, clearly marked 'Maximum five persons'. Ten people were on it. He tried to reach it but they waved him away shouting that the raft was full. In the centre of the raft he saw a familiar figure, sitting cross-legged and looking like a serene *Buddha*. It was the Jewish bookseller and antiquarian. This man, although then in his forties, was a strong swimmer and had been able to hoist himself aboard the raft some time after it had been launched. He was a deeply religious man and when he saw that the other man was in such obvious straits, he remonstrated with his fellow passengers on the raft that they were all God's children and that it was their bounden duty to save him, which they eventually did. The raft contained a mixture of survivors. There was a cabin boy from a German merchantman, a British sailor who had once before been torpedoed at Narvik, and there were some more refugees. One of them was totally naked, having been blown out of his bunk by the explosion. Our man, who was dressed in his pyjamas tore off the trouser leg so that this fellow could at least cover up his private parts. They too saw the flying boat, but by that time they were already waist-deep in water; the raft might sink at any moment. There had been an earlier discussion whether in order to keep the raft afloat it might be necessary to push one of them overboard. They fancied the cabin boy, the only 'proper' German amongst them, but once again the bookseller insisted that God would not allow it.

All the people still afloat in the water were eventually rescued by HM Canadian ship *St Laurent*, which had been sent to pick up survivors. They lowered lifeboats and soon the Italians and Germans were able to clamber aboard the destroyer. They were left to find their own shelter in driving rain and a bitter cold. The Canadian sailors gave them a tot of rum and a hot drink, and some even gave their own clothes, but there were not enough to go round so most had to stay in their soaking wet clothes. They were given some food, but the Italian was unable to eat anything because the oil which he had swallowed had seared the roof of his mouth. Four of the rescued Italians died from exhaustion during the night. The remaining Italians and Germans were landed the next morning at Greenock, where they were temporarily housed in a disused factory. Their most immediate request was to be allowed to let their families know that they had been saved, but it was only after several days that they were given postcards which simply said: 'I am safe!' However, a Scottish priest who visited them broke regulations and wrote to as many families as possible that he had seen their men and that they were hale and hearty. The Italians and the Germans were after a few days moved to different camps, but they did not stay in Scotland for very long. Within a week they again found themselves aboard a liner, bound for another part of the Empire. Of the 734 Italian civilians aboard the ship, 486 lost their lives. Out of 479 Germans only 175 drowned. This disproportion later led to accusations in parliament and in the press, that the Germans at the height of the panic had brutally pushed the Italians aside to save their own skins. All those interviewed, including several German Jews, deny this.

Within a few days of the sinking of the *Arandora Star* and the news becoming public, the War and Home Offices were besieged for information by anxious relatives of the internees. But substitutions and switches had occurred among both the Italian and the German internees, sometimes with and sometimes without the knowledge and approval of the camp officers. Thus nobody knew exactly who had been shipped, who had been lost and who saved. Wives were told that husbands who had never set foot on the ill-fated ship had been drowned; parents were told that their sons were safe when in fact they had lost their lives. The only roll of internees had gone down with the ship, and that had been inaccurate anyhow. Similar substitutions also occurred during the subsequent transportations to Canada, and the embarkation lists handed to the Canadian authorities were also quite inaccurate. It was later alleged that all these switches had been effected without the knowledge of the camp authorities, that they had been done for monetary compensation and that a number of known Gestapo agents had thus avoided being sent out of harm's way. But the internees all agree that in the majority of cases the camp officials had allowed these changes and merely failed to keep proper records of them. It was mostly a case of an unattached and adventurously inclined youngster agreeing to take the place of a married and worried older man.

A Bespattered Page?

Herbert Morrison, who had just taken over as Home Secretary, had to admit in the House on 8 October, in answer to several questions, that the Government had no accurate record of who had been aboard the ship because of the general muddle due to the emergency.

The sinking of the *Arandora Star* was for a while a topic of attention and discussion. The press took up the incident immediately and Parliament did not lag behind. On 9 July, George Strauss* asked why the ship had not been travelling in convoy. Had there been enough lifeboats aboard? How many of the Germans had been Nazis and how many refugees? Reginald Sorensen wanted to know whether any class 'B' and 'C' refugees had been aboard and had they been compelled to go? Cross, the Minister of Shipping, replied that fast ships did not normally sail in convoy; there had been enough lifeboats and rafts, and that the War Office had told him that all the Germans had been Nazi sympathizers.

Sir H. Morris-Jones† claimed that there was a general feeling in the country that the lives of British sailors should not be sacrificed to save the skins of enemy aliens. Mr Logan† complained that ships' officers had been handing lifebelts to some of the internees, whilst some of the crew had to do without them. During the long adjournment debate on 10 July, the statement that all the Germans aboard had been Nazi sympathizers was challenged. Graham White‡ claimed that at least two hundred of them had been refugees. Amongst those drowned were two prominent German trade union leaders, Valentin Witte and Louis Weber. Another prominent politician drowned was Karl Olbrich. He had been a social democrat member of the *Reichstag*, had been arrested as soon as the Nazis had come to power, had spent three years in a penitentiary and another year in a German concentration camp before he had been allowed to come to Britain. According to Lord Farringdon there was not the slightest doubt about his loyalty and whoever was responsible for his internment was now answerable for his death.[9]

Twenty-one other prominent socialists, including the Austrian ex-deputy Kurt Regner, had been saved. Colonel Wedgwood alleged that the Nazis aboard the *Arandora Star* had put up a swastika flag in

---

* MP for Lambeth North (Lab).
† MPs respectively for Denbigh (Nat-Lib) and the Scotland Division of Liverpool (Lab).
‡ MP for Birkenhead East (L).

the wardroom and had forced the non-Nazis to salute it.* Despite all the evidence now coming to light, the Secretary of State for War, Anthony Eden, again maintained on 16 July, in reply to various questioners, that all the people aboard the *Arandora Star* had been Italian Fascists and German Nazis. When this was challenged by Wedgwood, Strauss and Rhys Davies,† Eden promised to check his facts again; he was obviously answering from a faulty brief. A Foreign Office official commented: 'Eden had a rough passage in the House. If I were Secretary of State I should be rather angry with certain people in the War Office.' To which another official added a marginal comment: 'Mismanagement of this kind is bound to shake public confidence in the efficacy of the Security Services.'[10]

Although it was claimed on several occasions that class 'B' and 'C' prisoners had been aboard, the Government spokesmen were in fact correct in stating that all the Germans had been class 'A'. The confusion had arisen through the erroneous assumption that all the 'A' internees were Nazis or Nazi sympathizers. The list of those drowned includes names like: G. Lewy, F. Marcus, L. Baruch, A. Blumenthal, F. Schlamowitz, J. Kohn, H. Krebs and H. Mankiewicz – none of them very likely to be a Nazi sympathizer.‡ Equally, not all of the Italians were fascists; none of them had been through any tribunal and amongst them were a number of ex-trade union officials and refugees from Mussolini's régime.

The trouble was that no government department really knew the correct story. Journalists and anxious relatives were referred from the Home Office to the War Office and from there to the Ministry of Information; nobody could give them a satisfactory answer. The various refugee aid organizations were equally in the dark as to who had been drowned and who saved.

---

* In view of the fact that the prisoners spent only one day aboard the ship, the story is an unlikely one. Perhaps the incident was meant to refer to the earlier *Duchess of York*. The information about a swastika having been nailed up in the wardroom which resulted in riots and in two hundred Nazis being battened down in the ship when she was struck, came from H. N. Brailsford in *Reynolds News* of 14 July. He was also the first to state, correctly, that there had been at least two hundred refugees aboard.

† MP for West Houghton (Lab).

‡ FO 371/25210. Protests made at the time, such as for instance in the *Manchester Guardian* of 5 July, that young 'C' class refugees who had been living in the Cambridge area had been interned in May when the Eastern counties became protected areas, and had been transported on the *Arandora Star*, have not been substantiated. They may well have been on some of the other Canada-bound ships.

Only the Foreign Office assessed the situation correctly. In a memorandum from the Refugee Section, addressed to the POW Section, R. E. Latham mentions that amongst the Italians lost on the *Arandora Star*, was the well-known anti-fascist Vice-Consul of the Republic of San Marino. Umberto Limentani, a former Italian trade union official had been listed by the War Office as drowned, yet the Foreign Office knew that he had been saved and was now on his way to Australia. Amongst the Germans was an ex-BBC man. The story related in the memorandum confirms that there had been no boat drill on board, nor any instructions as to how to behave in an emergency.

In the end everything had to be improvised. This man claims that an Army Captain insisted that only his escort soldiers should be allowed into the few lifeboats, but that he was overruled by a senior ship's officer. Latham mentions another Jewish refugee as drowned; yet the Home Office had authorized his release from internment on 7 July. The memorandum also contains the interesting observation that 'the instructions to the tribunals issued by the Home Office permitted them to order internment on grounds other than hostile sentiments' and that this was the reason why so many people were classified as 'A' and interned immediately because they had 'left sympathies'. Many of them were now at the bottom of the sea.

A committee of interned Italians sent a letter to the Foreign Office through the Brazilian Embassy, asking them to thank the officers and the crew of the Canadian destroyer *St Laurent* for all they had done in the rescue. One Foreign Office official suggested that this should be publicized, but another commented: 'I think the rarer the occasions on which the horrid words *Arandora Star* appear in the press the sooner the discreditable incident will be forgotten.'

However, the incident remained in the public eye for a while, and on 12 August the Cabinet bowed to parliamentary pressure and asked Lord Snell to undertake an enquiry into the *Arandora Star* affair, as well as into the conditions at Huyton Camp which had also caused a lot of disquiet.[11] Lord Snell submitted his report to the Cabinet on 24 October.[12] He confirmed that the internees aboard had by no means all been dangerous characters, in particular not the Italians. It had been thought advisable at the time to remove as many people as possible because of the emergency, and in their own best interests. The report was discussed in Cabinet on 7 November.[13] It was decided that although Parliament had been told originally that the enquiry would be held, no undertaking had been given to publish the findings. As public interest in the matter seemed to have died down, it would be a pity to revive it. The report was therefore never published.★

The sinking of the *Arandora Star* became headline news throughout the Western World. The American press in particular gave it ample coverage. The *New York Times* reported on 7 July that the German Government had accused Britain of being in flagrant breach of the law by deporting prisoners, and without prior notification to the other side. In actual fact, the German Government did have prior notice of the operation, even if they were probably not advised of the exact details.[14] The Swiss Consul in Liverpool, visiting the camp at Huyton, told the German internees that their government had been advised through the Swiss that the British authorities intended to send internees to Canada for their own safety. The internees told him that they would resist any forcible transportation.

At their daily press conference at the Ministry of Propaganda, the German press was instructed not to make any mention of the sinking of the *Arandora Star* until the government had received details of those drowned and of those saved so as to prevent any unnecessary disquiet.[15] Once they had been given details through the Swiss, the German Foreign Office advised the next of kin of those drowned in the following terms:[16]

> During an attempt to remove German civilian prisoners by force to Canada Mr .... has sacrificed his life for the glory of Greater Germany. The ship was sunk as a result of the war at sea.

No mention anywhere that the life had been sacrificed as the result of a German torpedo.

★　　★　　★

The next ship to sail for Canada, the ss *Ettrick*, again aroused a fair amount of disquiet and public attention. Because there were now only a few 'dangerous characters' that is, class 'A' aliens, left in UK internment camps, the boat was loaded with 1,307 'B' and 'C' German

---

★ On 8 August the Minister of Shipping told the House that the total number of persons aboard the *Arandora Star* had been 1,569, including, presumably, the ship's company. Lifeboats had been provided for 750 of them and rafts for a further 1,088. Also available had been 2,000 lifejackets. He denied that anybody had been locked up during the torpedoing. This is also not mentioned in any of the reports in the German Foreign Office archives, presumably it did not occur.

internees in addition to 1,348 German prisoners-of-war and 407 Italians. The 'B' and 'C' internees had been taken from the Isle of Man. They had been told to pack up at short notice and according to one witness, William Powell, now Head of the Modern Language Department at a London Polytechnic, had been given no choice, nor were they told their destination. When they saw the size of the ship waiting for them in Liverpool they realized that they were overseas bound.

The *Ettrick* set sail on 3 July at a time when the internees had not yet heard about the sinking of the *Arandora Star*. They were therefore less apprehensive than subsequent transports. The authorities heard about the disaster when the *Ettrick* was just a few hours out of Liverpool. They immediately recalled her. The *Ettrick*, just as the *Arandora Star* had been, was flying a Swastika pennant just below the Red Ensign, to indicate that she was carrying POWs. It had been hoped that this would stop U-boats from attacking her. It obviously had not worked for the *Arandora Star*. The *Ettrick* therefore sailed again in a convoy with a destroyer escort – this time not flying the enemy flag.

The 'B' and 'C' internees were shut up in the hold of the ship. They very much resented that German Army and Air Force personnel had been given the passenger cabins. They were convinced that this had been done because prisoners-of-war were under the protection of the Red Cross and the Geneva Convention, whilst nobody cared how internees were being treated. Walter Wallich, later a senior BBC producer, and his friends spent the whole journey in a locker-room marked: 'Sergeants Luggage'. Amongst the civilians was Prince Frederick of Prussia. Victor Ross, a Cambridge undergraduate in his final year, now Managing Director of a leading publishing house, first met the Hohenzollern Prince in an empty Walls sausage factory, used as a first staging post for newly rounded-up internees. Prince Frederick or Count Lingen as he was known throughout his internment, always identified himself with the refugees and refused to have any truck with the Nazis. True to the concept of *noblesse oblige*, he always offered to help no matter how menial the task was. After a stormy passage, it was the Prince who organized the mopping-up of the bile by a squad of volunteers, naked but for their gumboots. They did not wish to soil the only set of clothes which they owned. None of the refugees, in contrast to the Nazis, was allowed on deck throughout the voyage. Their first breath of fresh air and glimpse of the outside world came as the ship began to sail up the St Lawrence River. One internee felt like Floristan coming up from the dungeons.

According to the Intelligence Officer on board, Captain Milne, the ship was overcrowded and the conditions sordid.[17] The journey was on the whole uneventful; their trouble only started after the ship had docked in Quebec. The POWs as well as the internees were paraded on deck, and were kept standing there for about twelve hours without being given any food or liquid refreshment.[18] They were then taken ashore where they stood around the quayside for a further six hours, still without any food, by which time most of them were in a state of complete mental and physical exhaustion. It was then that Canadian soldiers, belonging to a French Canadian regiment, conducted a bodily search of every prisoner as well as a rough rifling through their luggage. Victor Ross recalled somewhat wryly:

> These soldiers did not know who we were nor why they were in the war, nor did they care. On the night of our arrival they robbed us of everything except our virtue. Their searches were conducted in two shifts; during the first all our valuables were taken away and receipts issued; during the second search they just took the receipts.[19]

The incident, particularly the wholesale pilferage, caused quite a stir in Canada, with echoes in the British press and at Westminster. As late as 23 March 1941, Captain Margesson, Secretary of State for War,* refused to convene a Court Martial because, according to him, an investigation had shown that the complaints only concerned over-crowding and discomforts on the journey. But only a few days later, Osbert Peake† had to admit that there had been a loss of goods and money, amounting to at least £1,200.

The two government departments concerned obviously did not see eye to eye on this issue. The War Office had issued an internal state-ment claiming that the fact that no complaint had been received from the internees throughout the entire length of the search, should be sufficient to absolve British personnel from any further responsibility. In the light of the state of exhaustion in which the internees were at the time of the search, a senior Home Office official was shocked by that statement.[20] He suggested that the Home Secretary 'should rub the nose of the Secretary of State for War well into the true facts'. In the end the Canadian Defence Department admitted liability. Total compensation of $1,296.50 was eventually paid to the internees, equally shared between the British and Canadian Governments.[21]

---

* In reply to a question by Geoffrey Mander.
† In reply to a question by George Strauss, 1 April 1941.

Just as later on in Australia, the Canadians had been inadequately briefed on what sort of people they were getting.* They were under the impression that all of them were dangerous Nazis or blackshirts, who had been seized as security risks and were somewhat surprised when some of them asked for kosher food after arrival at their first camp. Amongst those who were disembarked from the *Ettrick* was a group of priests dressed in their cassocks. Insults were hurled at them as they passed through the dockyard. The Canadians believed that they were some of those ss troops who had been dropped on Rotterdam in disguise and who had not yet had a chance to change their dress.

Geoffrey Shakespeare, Undersecretary of State, Dominions Office, claimed in the House on 10 July that the Dominion Governments had been informed that the 'B' class internees were neither criminals nor hostile to this country, but were victims of Nazi oppression and should be kept separate from POWs and hostile aliens. If any such message had at this stage really been transmitted to Ottawa or Canberra, it certainly had not filtered through to the lower echelons in either Dominion. In fact, it must be questioned whether either government was properly put into the picture until complaints began to be voiced in Britain. After all, the Canadian High Commissioner had told his government just over a month before, that all the civilians which the British Government wanted to send them were 'potentially dangerous persons'. He must have received that briefing from somebody high up in government.

The last internment ship to sail for Canada was the Polish liner *Sobieski*. Apart from 450 POWs and 405 Italians it contained one thousand Germans and Austrians, of whom for the first time the largest proportion were class 'C' refugees from Nazi oppression. Our eye witness here is an engineer, at the time a young Jewish bricklayer, now a leading Canadian dam designer. Like many other children he had been brought out of Germany just before the outbreak of war (his parents later perished in a gas chamber), and had been taken to Richborough Camp where all these youngsters were given vocational training. On 12 May, the whole camp was suddenly surrounded by a

---

* It is true that the Canadian High Commissioner wired Ottawa on 4 July and 6 July that some of the internees on the *Ettrick* and the *Sobieski* were category 'B' and 'C', but it seems clear that the Canadian authorities had no real understanding as to just what that meant. They had originally offered to take 'dangerous characters' and that is what they were expecting.

barbed wire fence and the inmates declared interned. After a stay on the Isle of Man many were taken to Glasgow to board the *Sobieski*. This refugee remembers:

> Our group was assembled on the upper deck of the Isle of Man steamer. A wild rush towards the lower deck started where the transfer from one boat to the other was to take place. But somebody changed his mind and instead of arranging the transfer at the lower level as we had been told, the gangway was opened on the upper deck. We thus became the first to board the liner which was to bring us to our new and still unknown destination. The ship was already half filled with German prisoners-of-war and thus could not accommodate the entire Isle of Man group. Many of us had to be left behind. We only found out many years later that they were shipped to Australia. If the ship's officers had stuck to their original plan and made the transfer on the lower deck I would now be an Australian and not a Canadian.

His journey was uneventful; the German prisoners-of-war on the whole behaved properly towards them. When once they chanted their favourite '*und wir fahren gegen Engeland*' he pointed out to them politely that they were obviously sailing in the wrong direction. The only unpleasant incident which he remembers occurred when a group of young orthodox Jews were performing their religious rituals and some German POWs who were billeted side by side with them, mocked and caricatured them.

It took all these refugees a considerable time to convince the Canadian authorities as to who they really were, but when they finally succeeded, their treatment changed quite dramatically, particularly after the Home Office had sent out its emissary to liaise with the Canadian authorities and sort out the various internees, with a view to possible repatriation and release. On the whole the Canadian story had a good ending.

8 'That Fatal and Perfidious Bark'

NOTHING ELSE which occurred during the internment period remotely touches the stark, almost unreal horror of the journey of His Majesty's troopship *Dunera* from Liverpool to Freemantle, Melbourne and Sydney, with intermediate stops at Freetown, Takoradi and Capetown. The passage lasted from 10 July to 7 September 1940, when the ship reached its final destination. The *Dunera* was an old, converted troop transport built to take a maximum complement of two thousand people. There were, in fact, 2,873 people aboard, of which 2,732 were internees made up as follows:*

Category 'B' and 'C' Refugees:
from Huyton Camp	1,150
Central Camp, Isle of Man	230
Onchan Camp, Isle of Man	350
Ramsey Camp, Isle of Man	250
Lingfield Camp	308

Survivors 'Arandora Star'†
Italians	200
Category 'A' Germans and seamen	244

The remainder were the ship's company and the escort troops. The military complement was made up from British companies in the

---

* Captain Margesson, Secretary of State for War, Commons reply 21 January 1941. These figures do not entirely tally with those given in chapter seven. They are culled from a report written in 1941 by the spokesman for Camp Eight. They leave a balance of only 140 officers and men for the escort which seems too low. One or the other of these two sets of figures must be incorrect. This is most likely the number given by the Secretary of State. Statistics on every aspect of the internment story, given from time to time in Parliament by spokesmen of the various Ministries, differ so often that one cannot but wonder about their accuracy.
† All the *Arandora Star* survivors were redeported to Australia almost immediately, except for those who had been injured during the sinking and were too ill to be moved again.

Pioneer Corps, as well as from various regiments of the line, such as the Royal Norfolks, Suffolk and Queen's Own.* One internee says that there were many ex-jail birds amongst the soldiery who had been granted a Royal Pardon upon joining the Army. They had been considered unfit for normal combat or garrison duties, but entirely suitable as guards. The soldiers were under the overall command of Major William Patrick Scott, AMPC, who for the journey had been given the rank of Acting Lieutenant-Colonel, OC Troops.

The internees had arrived at the quayside in Liverpool from different locations after very different adventures and mishaps. 'A' category Germans and Italians were all survivors from the *Arandora Star*. The 'B' class internees had been arrested in May and had already spent several weeks behind barbed wire, having been shunted from camp to camp and ending up on the Isle of Man. But the largest contingent, those coming direct from the two mainland camps at Huyton and Lingfield and totalling over 1,450 men, were all category 'C' refugees from Nazi oppression, who had only been interned for a week or two. None of them had any premonition or had been given any hint that they were about to be transported over ten thousand miles across the world. When they saw the gaunt troopship's silhouette looming up in the grey mist beyond the dockside tracks, they felt confident that they were about to be taken on a short and choppy trip across the Irish Sea to the Isle of Man. Only a few of them wondered about the size of the ship. Most of them were therefore in an expectant and unworried mood.

Peter Stadlen, the pianist and music critic, had arrived in a transport from Huyton Camp. 'We were picked by the Sergeant Major at random' he told me, 'without any regard to our age, fitness or professional qualifications. It was pure chance that my brother and I stood in the same file and were therefore shipped together.' In Stadlen's case the Home Office had already decided to release him again, but by the time the order reached the camp office he was already on the high seas. He did not come home again until two years later. Siegmund Nissel, now one of the Amadeus Quartet, then at Huyton, had been told to get ready to move; he went into hiding until the transport had left. He was never punished.

The *Arandora Star* complement were under no illusions. They had

---

* The recollections of several internees about the regiments vary. The information may therefore not be entirely accurate, or comprehensive.

just survived a testing ordeal. When they saw the size of the ship they realized immediately that it was much too big for the Isle of Man; they expected another attempt would be made to ship them across to Canada, perhaps with equally disastrous results.

The 'B' class internees who had only arrived that morning from the Isle of Man, realized that they were about to be transported somewhere far away. Through the camp bush telegraph most had heard about the *Arandora Star* disaster; they thought they were bound for the same destination and were apprehensive. Only a few guessed their correct destination. They were the married ones who had been given to understand that if they volunteered for transportation to Australia, their wives and children would either accompany them on the same boat or follow on the next one. But only very few on the *Dunera* had actually volunteered; the overwhelming number were in total ignorance of their fate.*

When all this was subsequently discussed in Parliament, it became evident that neither the Home Office nor the War Office had any clear idea who was on board, how they had been selected, and what promises had been made to the married ones and never kept. In none of the debates did the true facts of the journey ever properly surface.

To whatever category they belonged and whatever their previous experiences in internment had been, the internees are agreed on one thing. From the moment they were handed over to their guards and set foot on the gangway leading up to the ship, they were subjected to treatment such as they had never experienced before in their lives, except for those who had previously been in German concentration camps, where it had been much worse, but where they had been prepared for it. The guards' behaviour was totally out of character with the kindness and consideration which had been shown to them before their internment, and with the normal behaviour of British officers and other ranks. The mistreatment did not cease – despite all their protests – until their arrival, when they were handed over to Australian escorts.

The internees were disgorged from several special trains, and slowly shuffled their way across the quayside. They were carrying their gas-masks and what had remained of their possessions. In the case of the *Arandora Star* survivors it was practically nothing; with the others

---

* Yet as late as 13 August, Osbert Peake assured Sydney Silverman that everybody who had been sent to Australia had volunteered to go. Silverman did not believe him. How right he was!

there were battered suitcases – often shoddy *ersatz*-type rucksacks, or canvas holdalls. They were told to dump their gas-masks on the quay and board the ship. The soldiers were shouting and swearing at them to get a move on, jostling them, poking them up the gangway with their bayonets. A German sailor alleges that when they were not moving fast enough a British officer yelled at them '*Macht keinen Quatsch, sonst werdet Ihr erschossen*'.*

The moment each one of them set foot on the ship, his case was roughly torn away from him and thrown helter-skelter on to an ever-increasing heap. Few cases were able to withstand such treatment. Many burst open, others were ripped open by the soldiers' bayonets and the contents spilled over the deck. Officers and NCOs stood by and said nothing to stop the vandalism. Each internee was then searched and whatever could be found on him was taken away, money, fountain pens, watches, lighters, pipes, religious objects, even false teeth, and, what was much more important for most of them, their previous personal identity papers and correspondence, such as confirmation that they had a registration number for an eventual US visa, or relating to an application for release.† When someone protested he was told cynically by an officer: 'Where you are going to, you won't need these papers any more.' Only a refugee himself can probably appreciate the fear and feeling of hopeless nakedness if one is deprived of one's identity papers.

The young Italian who had lost everything on the *Arandora Star* had been issued, at a transit camp in Greenock, with a set of army clothing, including a battledress jacket and a pair of boots. Both these were now taken away from him and for the rest of the journey he had to walk about barefoot. He too lost his only remaining possession, a fountain pen; other Italians were deprived of their watches and wallets.

As soon as these first searches had been completed, the prisoners were urged down to the bottom of the ship, where they were shut up in the holds which at one time had served to take troops to far-flung parts of the Empire. But this time these long, dark and cavernous holds were bare of everything except for a few benches and some trestle

---

'Don't be daft, otherwise we'll shoot you.' Letter in the *Auswaertige Amt* IV II ZV 58.
† The confiscation of the dentures is mentioned in an article in the Australian edition of *Reader's Digest* of December 1973, headed: 'BY DUNERA, a Cargo of Talent'. Cyril Page, the author, calls the *Dunera* a 'floating concentration camp'.

tables. Eventually they were supplied with some hammocks, but there were only enough of them for the elderly and for the invalids; the great majority throughout the eight weeks journey slept either on the tables and benches or on straw palliasses on the floor. When later on in the tropics the heat down below became unbearable, some tried to sneak upstairs on deck; those who were caught were punished.

During the voyage the *Arandora Star* survivors fared relatively better than the rest of the internees. They had, of course, been inured for a longer time to hardships; some were, no doubt, of a tougher mettle, but there is also evidence here, as there is throughout the internment story, that certain officers sympathized more with, and accorded better treatment to, genuine Germans than to the mainly Jewish refugees.

The ship had been wired off into several compounds; the Italians were put into a large cabin, perhaps previously a messdeck, with tables and chairs in the centre and hammocks slung at the side. Everybody was issued with one blanket which in the intense heat and stench which soon developed was more than enough. The German sailors accommodation was superior to everybody else's; every one of them had a proper hammock. The Italian says that the refugees had the worst quarters on board, the washing and toilet facilities were quite inadequate. For 980 'B' and 'C' refugees in the fore part of the ship there were sixteen toilets of which never less than three at a time were out of use, and thirty-two washbasins, which had to be used for personal hygiene, the washing of dishes, cutlery and of clothes.

Soap was rarely available; water mostly came from the sea and as the internees had been deprived of their belongings they only had the shirt, the socks, the underwear in which they stood. They had lost their shaving kits, their toothbrushes, their combs; in fact they had nothing. Just a few had managed to conceal their safety razors and after a few days were imprudent enough to shave off their sprouting beards. Their razors were immediately confiscated. The remaining refugees on the aft deck were even worse off. They had no washing facilities and no toilets and had to cross a small gangway on the deck and then a narrow passageway so as to take their place in the never-ending queues.

Hans Wetzler, later to become chairman of a firm of export merchants, kept a log of his journey to Australia and of his sojourn there. He records that he shared his quarters with a rabbi, six inmates of an Orthodox old age home, a blind man and two cripples. They were all allowed to sleep in the hammocks.

At 11 pm on their first day the prisoners were given their first meal, fish served incongruously on china plates. Few people ate much; the majority were in a state of nervous exhaustion or collapse; their only hope was that before the next day was out they would arrive on the Isle of Man and their Kafkaesque nightmare would then be over.

The ship sailed at daybreak the next morning, and almost immediately ran into bad weather. The *Dunera* was tossing about badly, the air in the holds was stale and foul. A chain reaction of seasickness soon developed which few escaped. There were no paper bags; it was impossible for most to get anywhere near the toilets and it needs little imagination to visualize the scene, the filth, the smell in those holds.

In order to reach the washroom some of the prisoners had to mount two decks and then walk along a narrow gangway which had been wired off and which day and night was only lit by a dim blue lamp. The gangway saw a perpetual motion of people in both directions, bumping into each other; some of them were sick, others were carrying slop pails which constantly spilt all over the place.

A similar storm wrought havoc whilst they were crossing the Bay of Biscay, when the latrines overflowed and flooded into the sleeping quarters. Some of the German seamen, who were much better inured to these rough sea conditions, were then allowed into the refugees' quarters and with rubber 'squeegees' mopped up the floor. One refugee says that he can never forget the smell in those dungeons, a mixture of vomit, kippers and tropical heat. Until this day he cannot stand to smell, let alone eat, a kipper.

Whilst the boat was storm-tossed in the Bay of Biscay at around 9.00 pm on the second day out, there was suddenly a dull thud, followed shortly afterwards by an explosion. The prisoners were first told by an officer that this was an anti-submarine exercise, but later learned that a German submarine had launched two torpedoes; the first had just missed the *Dunera*, the second had glanced off the stern. The German radio in fact later announced that the *Dunera* had been sunk. No lifevests or rings had been issued, no boat drill had taken place, nobody except the *Arandora Star* people knew how to behave in such an emergency. On this occasion the refugees were better off than the others. In their open hold they had access to the top deck, but they were of course forbidden to go up and find out what was happening. The Italians and the category 'A' Germans and seamen had been locked in their cabins. When they heard the explosion they hammered at their doors, but the soldiers on guard had disappeared. If the ship had been hit, they would have drowned like rats. Later the guards returned and when they heard the Italians still hammering and shouting behind locked doors they fired a few rounds into the air to calm them down. The refugees heard the shots and that frightened them even more.

Only on the third day were the bulk of the prisoners allowed on deck. A few had been detailed on the first day at sea to help the soldiers with the mountain of piled-up baggage. The Italian was one of them. He was told to break open every piece of luggage, remove from it every piece of wearing apparel and stack the shoes, the socks, the shirts and trousers in separate heaps. He was then told to toss overboard the suitcases with whatever remained in them. They went down, one by one, with books, family photographs, stamp collections, letters from wives and children, manuscripts, including a novel, the fruit of many years work, whatever personal possessions an internee had considered important enough to carry with him on his long road through the camps. A violin was deliberately broken to pieces by a soldier and then tossed into the deep. There were two Italian doctors on board; they lost all their medical equipment that way. Apparently, however, not everything was quite vandalized because a few internees at the end of the journey were handed back a few of their possessions, which they had long since written off as permanently lost.

By now it had become clear to everybody that they were heading well beyond the Isle of Man. The convoy was travelling in a zig-zag fashion in a generally westerly direction and so most people now speculated that they were bound for Canada. It was only after many days at sea that by observing the sky at night through the portholes, that some internees were able to speculate on the ship's likely destination. Even then many thought they would be landed somewhere in Africa.

Hans Wetzler was working as a potato sack carrier in the Quartermaster's store – one of the few privileged to do some work (others had volunteered to join a deck scrubbing squad or worked in the kitchen or the bakehouse). He was one of the first to hear one day that their destination was Australia. Others did not know it until they were within a few days of the Australian continent; their guess was at first that they were heading for the Gold Coast, then for South Africa and finally for New Zealand. It was a guessing game which provided a never-ending topic of conversation.

From the third day onwards the prisoners were allowed on deck for a brief airing and for exercises which now became a regular and welcome feature of their daily routine. The deck was lined with soldiers at six yards intervals, with fixed bayonets; whilst at each end a machine gun was mounted behind sandbags, ready to open fire. The prisoners were shouted at to get a move on whilst they trotted round the deck at the double, but they did not mind; it was a welcome relief from the stench below and from the monotony. One incident of these daily PT exercises, confirmed by several eye witnesses, is that an NCO in a bad temper deliberately smashed a milk bottle into the path of the internees, who had to run over the well scattered pieces of jagged glass.

But, as in internment camps on dry land, the spirit of man proved indomitable and irrepressible. On the very first Friday evening, amidst the filth and the smell, a rabbi held his first Sabbath service. The chronicler of this, not himself a very religious man, says this was the most moving and unforgettable service which he ever attended in his life. A young Cantor chanted all the traditional Hebrew songs and the rabbi, Dr David, preached a sermon full of hope. From then on Jewish services were held regularly below decks. The Roman Catholics held theirs in the open and a number of Jewish prisoners attended these Sunday services also, not so much because they were veering towards catholicism, but because it gave them additional opportunity to get some fresh air.

The tragicomic, self-mocking Jewish humour also soon asserted itself. On the day after the first religious service the first cabaret was arranged below deck. It consisted of various comic turns, sing-songs and jokes of the 'gallows-humour' type. The inmates sat around on the floor in semi-darkness, dirty and unkempt; the air was foetid; it reminded one internee of the picture of an old slave ship which he had seen in a museum. Another remembered a scene in the German film classic 'M', when shadowy characters of the Berlin underworld cluster together in an old warehouse to sit in judgement on a child murderer. One of the regular contributors to these cabaret performances later became a very well-known band leader in Britain. Another contributor was one of the ship's seaman cooks, one of the few who showed kindness to the prisoners.

Learned lectures and seminars on a variety of subjects also soon began, anything to transport the mind away from the sordid surroundings into a more congenial atmosphere. As the *Dunera* was sailing down the West Coast of Africa, for instance, an internee, Professor Beckermann, held a seminar on 'Africa, its lands and its People'. A young mathematician, now holding a chair at Melbourne University, lectured on mathematical problems; Peter Stadlen, then a concert pianist, now even better known as the music critic of a national newspaper, talked about Schoenberg and Weber, his teachers in Vienna. On the birthday of the bard, a professor of the German language talked on 'Goethe's Importance in the German Literature'.

Dr Franz Borkenau, a well-known anti-fascist author, lectured on contemporary politics; Dr Buchdahl held philosophy classes. A 'Dunera Mass' was composed and performed by a scratch choir. Language classes and first aid courses, held by qualified linguists and medical doctors, were arranged. The youngsters on board were given every opportunity to further their education but the ambiance and the total absence of any teaching material, of even pencils and paper, made this a somewhat thankless task for the teachers. Chess tournaments were organized on improvised boards cut from wooden planks and with make-do chessmen made out of stale bread. Their own pocket chess sets were all lying at the bottom of the deep. Without any books, without any paper and with hardly a pen amongst them, out of their inextinguishable store of memories, they recreated a world of the spirit, exactly in the same way as it was being done, but under conditions less harsh, in every internment camp at home.

The convoy had been sailing in a generally southerly direction, the rest of the ships now veered westwards as they were bound for America, whilst the *Dunera* continued on a southerly course. Ploughing now through calmer waters, the passengers no longer suffered from seasickness and for a while the sanitary conditions improved, but not for long. On 23 July an epidemic of diarrhoea spread through the ship and soon the lavatory situation grew worse than before. People had to queue up for twenty to thirty minutes before they could reach the sanctuary of a toilet, and often could not make it. A memorandum of complaints submitted afterwards by the prisoners cites the case of a Mr Fliess who tried *in extremis* to reach a lavatory by a forbidden gangway, and was stabbed by a guard with his bayonet through the barbed wire. Bleeding profusely he was taken to the ship's hospital, but was fortunately found not to be seriously injured.

The diarrhoea had probably been caused by the poor quality of the food which consisted mainly of frozen meat and tinned preserves. Each prisoner also received one apple per week. The bread was soggy and insufficiently baked. Diarrhoea was not the only disease rampant. Due to the lack of washing facilities and the poor standard of hygiene, many people began to suffer from skin diseases such as impetigo and furunculosis. The small hospital on board was quite inadequate and although the medical officer tried his best assisted by a number of internee doctors, it proved impossible to render assistance to all those who needed it.

The searches and thefts of personal valuables continued throughout the journey. Some prisoners had been able to hide a few of their precious possessions. One internee reports that a few of his peers preserved their wrist watches by tying them round their penises. Another internee was successful in hiding a compass which, in conjunction with their observations of the stars in the night sky, enabled them to get a rough idea of the ship's course. But the searches continued throughout the journey; on several occasions when the prisoners had been herded on deck to do their exercises, soldiers rifled through what was left of their belongings; sometimes there were bodily searches.

On the twelfth day of the journey, Leo Roth, a refugee, was asleep on a bench when around two am a patrol of two soldiers spotted a golden signet ring on his outstretched hand. They shook him awake and told him to hand over the ring. His finger was swollen and it proved impossible to remove the ring. He was then bodily dragged into the washroom where, with the help of soap and water, the ring was wrenched free. But force had to be used to such an extent that the finger had to be bandaged in hospital the next day. The man complained but he was told to shut up; the ring was never recovered.

The different classes of prisoners had elected spokesmen who time and again tried to lodge complaints about their treatment with the officer commanding the escort troops, but it was to no avail. When the elected leader of the category 'A' prisoners protested against the constant thefts, the co suggested that they should put their remaining valuables into little black bags, which he provided, and hand them to him for safe keeping. Nothing was ever returned to any refugee. According to one account the spokesman, the Calor Gas director, Dr Eichenberg, eventually demanded the return of their possessions, whereupon the officer denied all knowledge and when the spokesman persisted, he was put under close arrest.

A class 'C' internee who belonged to the deck-scrubbing squad, remembers that he watched the Commanding Officer help himself to trifles from the bayoneted suitcases lying on deck. One of the German sailors says that one day two soldiers came to their cabins and offered the Nazis the chance to help themselves to some of the things which they had looted from the Jews' luggage. The sailor claims that they all declined. There is not one passenger on the ship who has a single good word to say about the Colonel commanding the troops. One internee was present when a rabbi complained about the abominable treatment which they were receiving from his soldiers. His answer was: 'If you don't shut up, I will have you strung up by your beard from the masthead.'

On 24 July the *Dunera* rode into Freetown harbour, in Sierra Leone. Throughout their stay in this, as in all the other ports, the prisoners were not allowed on deck and as their portholes were blacked out and kept closed, they could see nothing. The only windows which had to be kept open were in the WCs. Thus whenever the *Dunera* touched port queues formed outside the lavatories so that people could mount the lavatory seats and catch a glimpse of the outside world. Each internee was allowed two minutes.

After Freetown there was a brief stop at Takoradi on the Gold Coast and then a somewhat lengthier stay at the Cape. Here the competition to stand on the lavatory seats was particularly intense. One internee remembers in particular his emotional reaction to the sight of Capetown with the beautiful backdrop of Table Mountain, a vista of majesty and perfection he had forgotten had ever existed.

One particular unpleasant junior officer, a Lieutenant O'Neill, is mentioned in every single account. One internee recalls that on their last day in Capetown this officer returned to the ship in an advanced state of inebriation. He began to beat up a couple of refugee boys in hospital and when they protested threatened to put them into the bunker, which was regularly used as a punishment cell. A number of beatings by this officer, or by NCOs in his presence, have been authenticated, usually ending up with the prisoner in the 'glory-hole'. Another man – one of those mislabelled refugees in the class 'A' contingent – remembers that one of his deckmates was put into chains for insubordination. When he came back to them he had a broad white streak in his coal-black hair.

After the *Dunera* had rounded the Cape and entered the Indian Ocean, the sudden heavy swell caused another bout of seasickness, but by now many internees had become hardened to the vicissitudes of the voyage; their lectures, cabarets, chess playing and interminable arguments on esoteric as well as very mundane subjects, went on as usual. One man remembers a Friday evening Sabbath service with the congregation swaying backwards and forwards, not because of any devotional intensity but because of the rolling of the ship, with several worshippers actually being thrown against the side of the ship.

On 21 August many internees were on the boat deck for their daily exercises, guarded as usual by machine guns and soldiers. Suddenly one of the refugees broke ranks and ran towards the ship's railing. Before a guard could stop him, he had jumped overboard. For a while the ship hove to, a rubber ring was thrown into the shark-infested waters, but the man was never recovered from the deep. He was an Austrian named Weiss, on his way to the Argentine, whom the war had stopped in Britain. On the day of his suicide, his Argentinian entry permit had finally expired.

On the same day, the vice-chairman of the Austro–Jewish ex-servicemen's organization died in the ship's hospital from natural causes. There was a brief religious ceremony on deck, then his body was lowered into the sea. It was the last communal act on board ship.

The end of the journey was now in sight; the internees' spirits rose. They began to admire the lovely sunsets and watched the dolphins leaping from the sea. The artists on board memorized the scenery in rough pencil sketches which later on in camps they turned into water colours and oil paintings.

As the *Dunera* neared the Australian continent their treatment showed some marginal improvement. They now received regular news bulletins and, as the news about the progress of the war was becoming more hopeful, so their spirits rose. Soap became more freely available, fresh water had been taken aboard at Capetown, it was again possible to wash one's clothes. A few Italians were detailed to cut the hair of the hirsute refugees, razors were suddenly issued and the prisoners ordered to shave. The few suitcases which had escaped being thrown into the sea were now restored to the lucky owners; the approaching end of the journey lifted everyone's spirits.

Physical assaults had now virtually ceased, though not entirely: one of the class 'C' prisoners was suffering from severe mental depression and was being kept in the ship's hospital. When the *Dunera* docked at Melbourne, he went into an officer's cabin, put on his uniform, started to shave off half his beard, then climbed through a porthole and tried to slide down the side of the ship. He was spotted and was allegedly so severely beaten by the senior Provost Sergeant that he suffered a fracture of his nasal bone as well as the loss of teeth.

The language of the NCOs and of many of the private soldiers continued to be rough and unfriendly – all quite unlike the relationship which most of the internees had managed to establish with their guards in the camps in Britain. The tone on board had been set at the top;* some of the officers showed a friendlier attitude and a measure of compassion – the testimony of at least one senior officer at the Court Martial showed that – but the rest, and, in particular, the Commanding Officer, treated the two thousand refugees as if they were the scum of the earth. All the accounts agree that the bullying and the mental anguish which that caused was much worse and much more debilitating than the occasional physical violence.

Throughout the journey the ship had been a hothouse bed of the wildest rumours about where they were going, what would happen to them once they got there, and what was happening in the wide world outside. Nothing was too fanciful or too far-fetched not to be believed by somebody. Amongst the category 'A' Germans and the seamen, the Nazis were taunting the mislabelled Jewish refugees that they had heard on first class authority that Germany had begun to invade Britain and how soon their wives and children would all be strung up. Amongst the refugees a rumour suddenly sprung up that a boat containing their wives and children had overtaken them and that their families would be waiting for them at the dockside in Australia.

On 27 August the *Dunera* docked in Freemantle. The refugees quartered midships and those aft had been kept apart, each with their own elected spokesman. After the ship had tied up the two sections were paraded separately, ready for an Australian inspection. A party of officers came on board. The senior officer asked the first group whether there was anybody amongst them who could speak and understand English. The elected spokesman of the refugees, a Mr Eppenstein, came forward and reported to him. Eppenstein had been educated at a public school and had gone to Cambridge; his accent was impeccable and he can be forgiven if for the occasion he accentuated it deliberately. There exist two different reports on the Australian officer's reaction. One recalls that the Australian said in a surprised voice: 'Why, this is an Englishman; I thought we were getting a boatload of Germans.

---

* A German seaman says that one day two junior officers apologized to them for the atrocious behaviour of some of the troops. They said they were unable to stop it because it 'came from the top'. *Auswaertige Amt* archive, file op. cit.

The other remembers him saying: 'England seems to have given you a very good education; why are you then fighting against her?'

The second inspection was less humorous. The elected spokesman of the other group, a Dr Wiener, who during the voyage had been involved in a number of clashes with officers, had prepared an address and began to explain to the Australians who they were and how they had been treated. He was interrupted by Lieutenant O'Neill, who barked at him: 'Shut up or I'll shoot you.' Undauntedly Wiener went on with his catalogue of grievances; the Australian officer listened without comment. But that night he came back with his staff and after inspecting their hold was heard to mutter 'Horrible, simply horrible'.

Despite all the superficial improvements which had been carried out on the boat during the last few days, the Australians were clearly shocked by the conditions on the ship. A medical inspection was arranged but the MOs seem to have been chiefly interested in the palms of the internees' hands. They were worried that there might be some blacks among the prisoners.

The *Dunera*'s next port of call was Melbourne, where the Italians, the German sailors and the category 'A' aliens were disembarked. They were handed over to Australian escorts and marched to the railway station. Their reception was significant. A German refugee remembers that the guards had been told they were getting all German submarine crews; the Italian reports that his guards thought they were all parachutists and fifth columnists who had been caught in civilian disguise. However, it did not take the Italian internees long to break down the barrier. By the time they had reached the station the officers, paying for it with their own money, had cleared out the station buffet, buying for them whatever comestibles were available.

The 'B' and 'C' class refugees were carried on to Sydney, where the ship finally docked on 7 September. Just before handing his wards over to the Australians, Lieutenant-Colonel Scott assembled them on the promenade deck and told them: 'Once you are in the hands of the tough Aussies you will look back on the marvellous treatment which you have been given here.' He was apparently not joking. He also promised them that he would tell his Australian fellow officers just what sort of people they were.

The refugees listened in silence. All they cared for was that their Odyssey had at long last come to an end; anything that might be in store for them was bound to be better than their health cruise. They marched off the ship to a friendly reception from their new warders;

127

and were loaded aboard a special train and taken up country to their new home, 450 miles away.

The *Dunera* carried the only load of internees ever sent to Australia, but it had been intended to send more. On 7 July, Neville Chamberlain reported to the Cabinet that in accordance with a prime-ministerial directive to send abroad as many internees as possible, a vessel, capable of carrying three thousand of them would sail for Australia on that day and that two further vessels, capable of taking another 6,500 internees would sail on 16 July.[1] If the latter transports were not needed they could be used to evacuate children.

Chamberlain emphasized to his ministerial colleagues that no internees would be sent abroad who were married with wives and children, and where a separation would cause special hardship; neither would they deport those who were required for the war effort nor those who had been interned by mistake. The Home Secretary was most anxious that the greatest care should be taken in the selection of the internees for shipment. A Foreign Office comment on this is 'Selected by whom and on what principles?'[2]

'Jews would never be mixed with Nazis and Fascists,' the Lord President said, in good faith, no doubt. 'But,' he added, 'if we must adhere to a strict sailing timetable, then it might well be unavoidable that categories of internees will be included which the Home Secretary desires to be excluded.'

The Lord President recalled the warning given by Joe Kennedy to Lord Halifax and added his own concern about possible reprisals against British prisoners-of-war and civilians in enemy hands. He suggested that they should for the moment go ahead with the planned sailings for Canada and Newfoundland,* but that the Australian sailings might be delayed in order to carry out a more careful selection. In the end the *Dunera* sailed three days after the originally planned departure date of 7 July, but the selection process had been anything but 'careful'.

The first of the great Commons debates on the whole internment question took place on 10 July, on a motion to adjourn the House. That was the very day on which the *Dunera* set sail; the deportation to Australia therefore only played a minor role in the debate. The questions raised and the criticisms voiced, as well as the ministerial

---

* Newfoundland and New Zealand had also been envisaged as deportation destinations, but in fact no internee was sent to either country.

statements, were primarily concerned with the basic policy and all its anomalies, as well as with the conditions in the British camps. Unfortunately, no member of either House had been at the dockside in Liverpool when the *Dunera* was loaded.

In so far as the debate touched overseas shipments at all, it was mostly concerned with Canada and with the *Arandora Star* tragedy, of which more and more particulars were gradually coming to light. Eleanor Rathbone made an impassioned speech in which she urged that nobody should be deported on whom no real suspicion rested, and that a deportee should be allowed to take his wife and children with him. Britain should not wash its hands of all responsibilities once she had got rid of these aliens, but should make sure that they were treated well in whatever Dominion they eventually landed. She articulated the refugees' sentiments thus: 'We want to serve the common cause here. Let us serve in the fighting forces, in industry, in any occupation to which we belong. But if you have no use for us, do not send us abroad as prisoners-of-war but find us room in some colony or dominion or in the USA to enable us to start a new life in freedom again.' Miss Rathbone added that this was a question which affected the nation's prestige. 'We don't want it to become known that this is a land of oppression and not of the free.'

Osbert Peake answered that wherever possible only the most dangerous internees were being sent overseas and that Australia had agreed to take whole families, who would, however, remain interned there, but perhaps in a greater measure of liberty. Not a single one of these statements proved to be correct, but most probably no blame attaches to the responsible Minister. The Government was possibly being misled as much as Parliament.

On the following day, Richard Law, Financial Secretary to the War Office, repeated that they were hoping to arrange for wives and children to accompany deportees, or to follow them to Australia. When the Home Office was later criticized in Parliament for having broken their promise and having made internees volunteer for Australia under false pretences, great play was made of the fact that this had not been a promise but only a hope. The internees remembered otherwise.

A publication cyclostated in Onchan Camp* tells of four hundred

---

* 'Royal Avenue', a stencilled broadsheet, published in the Onchan internment camp on the Isle of Man.

category 'B' men who had been separated from their families since they were arrested in May, though the families were interned on the island not very far away. The men were told that a meeting had been arranged with their families for the purpose of discussing with them the prospect of going together to Australia. They had bought chocolate in the canteen for the children, picked bunches of flowers for their wives; they had been taken by train to Port St Mary, where at the Ballaqueenie Hotel there was an emotional reunion. One ten-year-old girl, hugging her father, shouted: 'Now you are going to stay with us for ever, aren't you, Daddy?' A senior officer addressed them and told them that whilst there was no guarantee that all the families could actually travel together on the same ship, they would before long be reunited in Australia. They had two days to make up their minds; if there were not enough volunteers for the first transport, it would then be a question of 'you and you and you'. After that there was great excitement; many who had sunk roots in their new home country, who had jobs or businesses, were unwilling to go; others were unsure, weighing up the advantages of going to a country, free of bombs and invasion scares, against the risk of torpedoes *en route*. In the end, of those who had met their wives, only sixty volunteered.

These 'B' class women and their children in the end never left the camp until they were finally released towards the end of the following year. 152 category 'C' women, who had never been interned and who had also been given the chance to join their husbands for the trip to Australia, agreed. They gave up their jobs, sold up their homes, took their children out of school and, if they had lived in the country, journeyed to London, awaiting a final movement order. It never came. The Home Secretary later implied that the Australian authorities had backed out of their promise at the last moment.

Major Layton, the official later sent out to Australia by the Home Office, recalls that the Australian authorities were loth to allow the setting up of married camps for fear of encouraging the breeding of Australian-born children.

Many questions remain unanswered, as at every other stage of the internment story. If the Home Office had been in serious negotiations about this particular problem with the Australian authorities, surely the latter should have been familiar with the background and status of the internees who were being sent to them. Yet when they eventually arrived not a single Australian official, whether in uniform or in mufti, seemed to know that he was not dealing with dyed-in-the-wool

Nazis. It was always the same story, at first in the British camps and now in Canada and Australia: at what stage of the lines of communications was the message not passed on, and was it just inefficiency or deliberate intent?

The enforced deportation of refugees continued to be a topic of interest, both in Parliament and in the press, but it was mainly the tragedy of the *Arandora Star* and the other transports to Canada which attracted continued attention. As it took many weeks before the first letters and reports filtered through from Australia, it was not until the beginning of 1941 that news about the journey of the *Dunera* began to attract attention in Parliament.*

On 21 January, the opening shot was fired by Colonel Josiah Wedgwood, seconded by Edmund Harvey, who asked the Secretary of State for War a number of awkward questions. What was the maximum number of people which the *Dunera* was equipped to take? How many had actually been transported? What had the sanitary arrangements been and had any complaints been received and been investigated? Was it true that the luggage had been ripped open as the internees came on board and had they been deprived of their money, their valuables, and of much of their clothing? Would the Secretary of State enquire into the alleged suicide of one internee?

Captain Margesson, who had only recently succeeded Anthony Eden at the War Office, replied that they were shortly expecting the return of the first party of the escorting officers and men. They would then set up an enquiry into the various allegations. His information was that there had been 2,873 internees aboard and that the accommodation and sanitary facilities had been adequate. A report from the Australian Society of Friends as well as evidence from internees would be carefully considered by a Court of Enquiry.

In view of the public disquiet, Colonel Wedgwood pressed the Secretary for War on 12 February, to hold the *Dunera* enquiry in public, but the Financial Secretary, Law, replied that this was not normally done. However, although not all the officers and men concerned had returned, enquiries had already been set afoot. Six days later the last of the escort troops had returned, and, according to Captain Margesson, evidence was now being collected from them, but the Secretary of State refused to be drawn by a suggestion of Colonel Wedgwood's that a Court of Enquiry should not only be concerned

---

* Apart from a letter in the *Manchester Guardian* of 15 November 1940, which mentioned a few of the hardships which the *Dunera* prisoners had suffered.

with the punishment of the guilty, but also with reparations to the victims. The Colonel was not satisfied with the replies and on 25 February forced through a debate on the adjournment of the House to deal with the whole subject of aliens aboard maritime transports.

Replying to Wedgwood's pungent accusations, Law told the House that preliminary enquiries about the *Dunera* had shown a *prima facie* case for a Court of Enquiry, and that some internees had suffered losses. However, the Advocate General had advised that it might take months to assemble all the essential witnesses and that court martial proceedings could be instituted more quickly. Meanwhile, the Government had decided to compensate the internees for their material losses, and were now investigating how this could be done most quickly. They would not wait until all the evidence had been collected, even if this might prove somewhat expensive to the Exchequer.

For a while public interest in the topic faded again, but on 13 May 1941, in reply to a question by Colonel Wedgwood, Captain Margesson announced that as the result of the enquiries which had been made, orders had now been issued for court martial proceedings against the officer commanding the escort troops, his regimental sergeant major, and one sergeant.

Three courts martial were held between 20 and 25 May. The accused were: Acting RSM Charles Albert Bowles who faced twenty-one charges; Senior Provost Sergeant Arthur Halliwell facing four charges, and Major (former Acting Lieutenant-Colonel) William Patrick Scott, charged on two accounts. Halliwell was found not guilty on all charges except one, for which he was severely reprimanded. Major Scott was also found guilty on one charge. He too was severely reprimanded, but with no loss of his seniority. The Regimental Sergeant Major was acquitted on nineteen charges but found guilty on two concerned with the theft of money. He was sentenced to be dismissed from the service and to serve twelve months' imprisonment.

The verdicts did not create much of a stir in the British press, probably nobody had any inkling of what had really happened on that journey. No internee was present for interrogation; if sworn statements had been taken from them they were not read out in court. But the proceedings did not escape the attention of the German press. The official Nazi organ – the *Voelkische Beobachter* – headed its report, full of *Schadenfreude*, with the caption: *Raeuber bestehlen Gauner.**

---

* Robbers thieve from criminals.

Only Colonel Wedgwood would not let go. On 31 July Captain Margesson, in reply to a question, gave the House the final results of the three courts martial. Wedgwood's only comment was: 'Instead of a proper enquiry all we had was a hushed-up court martial.'

Claim forms had been issued to the internees in Australia in respect of their losses. They were quite exhaustive and it was not easy for the internees to supply all the details required, such as where, when and for how much the various purloined articles had been purchased. A number of internees would not or could not submit completed claims. On 20 January 1942 Sir Edward Grigg, for the War Office, told Mr Harvey that a total of £5,900 had been paid out to 519 claimants who had since returned to the UK (or something like £12.00 per internee). A further 1,300 claims made by internees still in Australia would be settled out there. The total value of the property recovered from searching the kitbags of the returned escort was £100.[3]

Later, in an Australian camp, an ex-public schoolboy who had been waiting to go up to Cambridge when he found himself interned and shipped on the *Dunera*, set down some quotations from Milton and Coleridge, which seemed to sum up the refugees' feelings about the unhappy ship: 'It was that fatal and perfidious bark, built in th'eclipse and rigg'd with curses dark'; and, 'There passed a weary time. Each throat was parched . . . a weary time, a weary time.'

The internees had arrived in Sydney, in the words of one of them: 'physically and mentally exhausted. Beaten and sworn-at we left the ship. The chapter of the *Dunera* had come to an end.' The chapter of their internment in Australia was about to open.

9   *The Road to the Isle*

> Companions quarrel about trifles and get the least possible pleasure from
> each other's society. You feel a constant humiliation in being fenced in by
> railings and wires, watched by armed men and webbed about with a tangle
> of regulations and restrictions.

THIS IS HOW AN INTERNEE of an earlier period described the
claustrophobic tensions inside a barbed wire encampment. The quota-
tion is actually from Winston Churchill's *My Early Life* and relates to
his imprisonment during the Boer War. But it could have just as well
been a description of the state of mind prevalent amongst many of the
latter day internees; a state of mind which has been labelled 'internitis',
a somewhat contagious disease to which many of the refugees, old and
young, male and female, succumbed at some stage or other of their
internment. But the psychological impact of imprisonment, of enforced
isolation, was by no means uniform. Some, particularly amongst the
younger ones, treated the situation with a sense of adventure or looked
upon it as a beguiling challenge. Once the novelty had paled, it gave
way in some to anti-climactic despondency; others again were sustained by it until their release. But most of the older ones, in particular
those who but recently had been inmates of Buchenwald and Dachau,
were from the outset either broodingly depressed or openly angry;
either way they were apprehensive Jeremiahs transmitting their gloom
and panic to their fellow internees.

Because the interlude was so wholly out of character with either
past or future, the experience left indelible recollections upon the
alumni of these camps. It probably did not change the basic chemistry
of anybody's character, but it undoubtedly developed or accentuated
whatever overt or latent characteristics there were.

In some, internment awakened a social conscience, an awareness that
man is not an island; in others it showed up their selfishness, their
asocial nature. Internment camps were forcing houses of innate
characteristics. Its effects were most marked and lasting on the younger
internees. To some it provided proof of how they could rise to an
unusually challenging occasion; for others it provided a taste of

authority and gave rein to their organizational talents. Some of these camp officials later became prominent politicians, businessmen and civil administrators. Part of their apprenticeship in accepting responsibilities and learning man management was spent in these camps.

For many it was a unique opportunity to mix at close quarters with famous men, artists, scholars, journalists and scientists. Since 1933 the education of these young refugees had been sketchy, often hardly existent. Now they had a chance to broaden their knowledge in the camp schools and universities, to be introduced to an appreciation of music and of the visual arts; by sheer force of circumstances to subordinate their own interests to the common weal. What in the outside world the army taught its conscripts and the seats of learning their students, was available here, without the traumas of essays and examinations and without the coarseness of barrack life.

For the majority of the male refugees, that is to say, for all the 'C' ones, internment came during the last week of June or during the first two weeks of July 1940, when all over the country some additional 23,000 refugees were rounded up. To those who lived in parts of the country sparsely populated by refugees it came quite unexpectedly during the first forty-eight hours. Those who lived in the refugee belt of North-West London mostly had advance warning. Some of them were able to take evasive and sometimes successful action. It soon became known that the police never called between 5.00 pm and 7.00 am. People would therefore leave their homes or boarding houses at cock's crow and sit around Lyon's teashops or Corner Houses; some spent all night there, playing cards, wandered about in the Royal Parks, or hidden in the recesses of the Hampstead or other public libraries until the witching hour of five o'clock had passed. If a police officer found that his quarry had gone out he would sometimes, but not always, announce that he would call again the next day. Some refugees would then stay put for the next morning's call, either because, for them, a police officer's message was a command, or because they were convinced that ultimately everybody would be caught anyhow. But others were more enterprising; they escaped internment altogether.

Some of the people rounded up and taken to the nearest police station had to be released again because they were engaged in vital war work and were holders of special permits exempting them from any possible internment. But even some of those, despite all their protests, were shunted into internment camps whence it sometimes took weeks for them to return. A few unlucky ones were even taken overseas before the muddle or deliberate obstruction was discovered. In their case it was many months before they came back, a misfortune not only for them, but perhaps also for the essential war job they had been performing. A refugee NCO in the Pioneer Corps, who had been evacuated from Boulogne, was home on special leave. He too was arrested because the police officer would not believe that a German national could possibly be serving in HM forces. He was eventually allowed to go home again after producing at the station his AB64* and his special leave pass.

Occasionally a refugee was even able to convince the police officers that he should not really be interned. Professor Hans Eysenck recollects: 'The police came twice to arrest me. I managed to talk them out of it each time, which certainly would not have been possible in Nazi Germany.'

Had the Home Office simply requested the refugee organizations to notify their wards or made a public announcement that, for example, every 'C' class enemy alien between sixteen and sixty years of age, whose surnames started with the letters A, B, or C, had to report on 26 June, between eight and nine am, at his local police station with a small suitcase, only a few refugees would have tried to evade the summons. The early morning knocks, the black Marias, the hit and miss way in which internment was carried out had been quite unnecessary. If there really were some genuine suspects amongst these 'C' aliens, they were given every opportunity to go underground anyhow.

The actual internment procedure, the various Stations of the Cross on the way to the Isle of Man, or to more distant shores, differed from case to case. But there was a common pattern in most of them. I was one of those rounded up; this is my story which I shall now briefly tell. It is quite typical of how many of the interned refugees fared.

I had grown up in Berlin, of solid, old-established, *petit bourgeois* German–Jewish stock, and had just started to read Law at Bonn University when the advent of the Nazis put an end to any future academic career. I had come to Britain in 1934 and was working in an office in London's West End. In 1936 I had got married to my boyhood sweetheart.

At the outbreak of war, my wife, a daughter of one year of age, and I were living in a small house in the Eastcote–Pinner district of

---

* A British soldier's pass book.

Middlesex. Immediately after war was declared I volunteered to join
HM Forces, heard nothing for several weeks, passed my tribunal as a
'refugee from Nazi oppression' and was eventually told that I could
join one of the newly-formed, unarmed alien companies of the
Auxiliary Military Pioneer Corps. I declined, I was ready and anxious
to fight with a weapon in my hand, but was not prepared to serve as a
second-class soldier. I joined the Air Raid Precaution Service (ARP)
and was given crash courses in lorry driving and in first aid. For the
next few months of the phoney war period we whiled away our time
by playing cards or driving our ambulances through the darkened,
deserted streets of West Middlesex.

One Sunday in June we were listening to the wireless in the next
door neighbour's house (as enemy aliens we had been deprived of our
own some time before) and heard that by an Order-in-Council our
area had been declared a protected one, which all aliens had to leave
within forty-eight hours. Our good neighbour obviously would not
believe that this expulsion could possibly apply to either my wife, our
baby daughter or to myself, the ambulance driver. But alas, it did. The
inspector at the local police station, where because of my ARP activities
I was quite well known, advised me not to set up house elsewhere, as
one never knew what part of London might next be affected, but to
seek temporary shelter with friends in a more remote area. We had to
vacate our house within forty-eight hours and I was advised by my
police friend to store our furniture. Only my wife was allowed to
return a few days later to supervise the removal of our worldly goods.
Fritz Hallgarten, the wine shipper and author of several books on
wines, and his wife, who had evacuated themselves some time before
to a small village in Hertfordshire, immediately offered us a roof.

Around six am on day one of the general internment, two police
officers roused us by their knocks and requested a search of the house
for forbidden or dangerous objects. Their manner was pleasant; we
were allowed to dress and have breakfast. There was not a word about
any possible internment. By eight am they had confiscated a box
camera, an atlas, and bus and underground maps published by London
Passenger Transport. They then asked my friend to accompany them
to the local station in case the inspector wished to ask him a few
questions. By way of a mere afterthought they told me that I might as
well accompany my friend. They denied that they had any instructions
to arrest either of us but, at the insistence of our wives, allowed us each
to pack a small valise. 'It is really quite unnecessary; you will be home

before the morning is out.' They agreed to our request to park the car at the end of the road and allow us to walk to it unaccompanied to fox the neighbours. They also willingly complied with our request to stop the car at the village shop so that we could buy some chocolate, soap and razor blades, all of immense benefit later on.

As we pulled up in front of the Hemel Hempstead Police Station, so did a number of other cars and black Marias. We were led into the entrance hall of the station. There we sat on our suitcases or on the floor, or walked aimlessly around. No inspector ever interrogated any of us; nobody would answer our questions. The air was thick with rumours, gloom and foreboding. I remember an old man, certainly in his seventies, who had only the year before come out of Dachau. He showed me his weals and scars; he was totally disorientated, convinced that he was about to suffer the tortures of another concentration camp. We tried our best to cheer up all these miserable people, but on the whole our forced humour fell flat.

Once the local haul had been completed we were driven to the central catchment centre, a territorial drill hall in Watford. Here we encountered our first strands of barbed wire, hastily thrown across windows and exits. More and more refugee files were led in, some looking bewildered, others panting under the weight of their suitcases. Late in the afternoon a convoy of RASC trucks drove up and we were handed over by the police to the army. We were loaded aboard and driven off. We had become wards of the War Office. So far nobody had told us anything. At this most critical moment of the war, when everything seemed to be collapsing around us, we had suddenly been wrenched from our families, our jobs, our friends, our responsibilities; many of us, educated, articulate, concerned members of society, had suddenly been thrown into total isolation, guarded first by police officers and now by soldiers who were totally uncommunicative.

This was the time when all the signposts had been removed from Britain's roads so as to confuse possible parachutists. I was standing at the tailgate of our truck and tried hard to spot identifiable landmarks. I told my fellow travellers that we were being driven in a generally southerly direction, which immediately convinced them that Southampton was our destination where we would be loaded aboard a ship and transported to Canada. We had, of course, no idea that Southampton was no longer used for the transatlantic route and that Liverpool or Glasgow would have been our goal had we been destined for immediate onward shipment.

By the time dusk was falling I had spotted Windsor Castle in the distance, and guessed that we were somewhere in Berkshire. Suddenly the convoy halted. In front of us we saw a barbed wire fence; we seemed to have arrived at our destination. We had in fact reached the winter quarters of Bertram Mills' Circus near Ascot. Early in the war the stables which used to shelter lions and elephants from the cold had been turned into a prisoner-of-war camp for captured German seamen. The camp had been standing idle for a while, the last inmates had been the ship's company from the ss *Mecklenburg*.* It was totally unprepared to receive civilian internees. A ludicrous situation now developed. We had halted outside the barred gates and there our trucks stood for what seemed to us several weary hours. We later learned that the camp Commandant had received no prior notice that he was getting fresh guests and had refused to admit us until the War Office confirmed that all was in order. It took some time to locate the responsible Staff Officer and night had fallen before the gates finally swung open.

Naturally no preparations had been made for our reception; we had eaten nothing since our dawn breakfast. There were many elderly persons amongst us, people who suffered from diabetes (a favourite ailment of the Jewish bourgeoisie) or gastric complaints. It had been a very long day; everybody felt mentally and physically spent. The small army skeleton staff tried their best to help. Volunteers were called to get the kitchen going. I realized at the outset that what would keep me sane was hard physical work, as much as possible. I joined the small group for kitchen fatigues. The enormous coal-fired range had not been used for some time, the chimney had not been swept; it was hard to light it with the smoke pouring backwards. But by midnight we had a mug of tea and a 'doorstep' of bread and margarine ready for everyone. Afterwards we were led to bales of straw and told to fill our palliasses. We helped the old and the invalids to bed down some-where in the stables and it was well into the next day when we finally fell asleep.

Memories of the next few weeks have faded; only occasional shafts of light illuminate a particular tableau; the grimy, smoke-filled cavern of a kitchen, where we toiled for much of the day; the aimless wandering back and forth along the barbed wire strands; the keyed-up gatherings at the gate whenever a new batch of internees arrived. They

---

* *Auswaertige Amt* RX II ZV 57. The camp was designated as POW No. 7.

were the only harbingers of news from the wide world outside; just like the heralds on the ramparts in Greek dramas who told the audience how the war was going. I also remember one other link with the outside; the milkman, who everyday brought us world news, as digested by him, which was then passed on from mouth to mouth, often distorted in the process.

Of all the hardships which we had perforce to bear, the total isolation at this most critical moment in the war was the hardest. Most of us had wives outside; many of them had to look after young children. They had no money; they were strangers, alone with no family to whom they could turn, with no roots and few friends; it was weeks before they heard from us or we from them. France had fallen. Britain was fighting alone; that much we knew and little else. The soldiers were under orders not to tell us anything, but we knew that an invasion attempt was a distinct possibility. Just before internment we had read how, a few weeks before the débâcle, the French had interned refugees at a stadium outside Paris and how, as part of the armistice arrangements, they had handed the camp over to the Nazis lock, stock and barrel, with every refugee still inside. I well remember how, as soon as I woke up every morning, I peered outside, half expecting that our soldiers had been replaced by jackbooted ss troops; how relieved I was when I saw the familiar figures in khaki battledress, stomping up and down outside.

I can also still see us assembled one evening on roll-call parade, waiting for an address by the camp commandant. Our camp elders had told him how the lack of reliable news was depressing us all and was creating a potentially troublesome situation. The frozen aloofness of his usual facial expression had somehow thawed when he told us that we need not worry any longer. 'Things are looking up for England', he said to the assembled internees, 'the Navy has sailed into Oran and has sunk a good many French warships. The tide is turning.' At this such a spontaneous burst of cheering, clapping and stamping of feet broke out that the old chap was visibly moved.

From that moment onwards things began to change. The privates and NCOs talked to us; every day a news bulletin was posted underneath the daily orders; letters from our families were beginning to trickle in. Deep down, none of us had ever really come to terms with the thought that Britain could be successfully invaded and beaten. But from that moment on I became convinced, quite irrationally, that Britain was to be ultimately victorious even if I had no idea how and when that might come to pass.* Such certainty made temporary internment much more bearable. Many of us now accepted that however innocent we were, however unfair the internment of thousands of refugees was, if that was the price to be paid in order to put acts of espionage and of sabotage beyond the pale of any possibility, then it was a small contribution to be made with the best grace possible. I stopped worrying about myself, but nothing could assuage concern about my family until my eventual release.

We were also helped at this time to see our internment in a more balanced manner, with much less of a sense of personal hurt and grievance, by news of the way the British public was responding to our internment and of the increasing feeling in Parliament and in the press that an injustice had been done which should be put right as quickly as possible. In this most critical phase of the war, when everything was at stake, the House of Commons had found time, on 10 July, to debate for hours the fate of a few thousand German refugees. We heard about it through newcomers, the tail-end of those interned. It helped our morale no end and restored a lot of tattered faith.

As a kitchen hand on permanent fatigue, I was considered an essential cog in the running of the camp. I thus stayed on until, some time in mid-July, the last batch of internees were loaded aboard a train. After a night's stay under the Tote at Kempton Park racecourse, our special train took us to Liverpool, and thence to the Isle of Man. As we were speeding towards Hemel Hempstead, quite near to our house, Fritz and I dropped a message to our wives, asking the kind finder to deliver it to them. Alas, it never reached them. I will reappear again in this story at Hutchinson Camp.

* * *

The sudden, precipitate decision to extend internment to 'C' class aliens meant that the accommodation available in the existing internment camps was quite inadequate. Overseas deportations were easing the problem to some extent, but far more people were being rounded up every day than could be transported to the Dominions. New camps, mainly on the Isle of Man, were being hastily improvised. There had

---

* It is interesting to compare at what point of time one began to believe that Hitler would ultimately lose the war. Sir Herman Bondi told me that he became convinced already earlier on, when he heard that after Dunkirk Hitler had turned his thrust towards Paris instead of pressing home his attack on Britain.

also been a steady intake of Germans interned in the British colonies and brought to England. Amongst them were some of the most rabid and anti-semitic Nazis.

By the time general internment commenced, the two holiday camps in Devon had been closed, but Lingfield was still open and so was Kempton Park, which became the main reception centre for Southern England.

Other places hastily converted into internment camps in the North included a disused cotton mill near Bury, a housing estate near Liverpool and a tented encampment on a Shropshire heath. Some internees stayed only a short time in these mainland camps before they were ferried across the Irish Sea or overseas. Others were shunted through several camps before they reached their final destination on the Isle of Man, in Canada or in Australia. The two southern racecourses, particularly Lingfield, had been used as camps for some time; conditions were therefore bearable there. Warth Mill, Huyton and Press Heath were put together at short notice; conditions there were at first unpleasant, and at Warth Mill downright scandalous.

At Kempton Park, as at Ascot and at almost every other camp, no preparations had been made for these sudden influxes, nor could they have been made because it was all the result of such a hasty panic decision. No briefing was given to the troops about the background of their prisoners; nor could it have been given, because the officers had also not been properly briefed. At Kempton Park the sentries were Grenadier Guards, used to the rough language of the drill square and quite out of sympathy with the sometimes cowed, sometimes complaining, always neurotic foreigners. Their commanding officer was much more easy going and understanding, so easy going in fact that after a further spell as Commandant of Warth Mill he was relieved of his post and court martialled for retaining, illegally, articles belonging to internees. He was sentenced to eighteen months imprisonment and cashiered.

But he was also quite a shrewd psychologist. From the moment that the gates of an internment camp had swung shut behind an internee, his overriding preoccupation was how he could set about getting released again. No word in the English language was bandied about as much, was so much on everybody's lips as that magic word: release. Even those who spoke little or no English never used its German equivalent in their 'emigranto' vocabulary. The Commandant realized that nothing would occupy his charges better and make them less restive than the hope of an early release. At that time no government policy had as yet been formed, no White Paper had been published about the grounds on which the Home Office might consider release; no application forms had been issued, no tribunals appointed to examine these applications. But no matter; applications were invited from all who were interested. They could be written on any available paper, even toilet rolls. A deadline was set; suitably qualified internees were asked to help others in making up their applications. These were collected and taken to the Commandant's office . . . where they were all promptly destroyed.

Food, as everything else, was at first inadequate. A black market soon developed. One day one of the sergeants pushed a barrow laden with apples into the camp, which were snapped up immediately by those nearest to the gate. The apples then made the rounds of the camp, being sold and resold again and again, every time fetching a higher price.

It was in these early days, sometimes within hours of first internment, that small groups formed themselves. Often they crystallized around a younger, more incisive type of man, usually somebody who had lived in England for some time, spoke the language better than the others and knew his way about. Whenever possible these groups stuck together on their journey from camp to camp and formed friendships which have lasted until today.

Confinement in camps was conducive to, and intensified religious activity, particularly amongst the Jews. Even those who had not been inside a synagogue for many years, or who had only attended divine service on the high holidays, weddings, Barmitzvahs and funerals – and that was the great majority – suddenly felt the need for spiritual reassurance through communal prayer. At Kempton Park an altar had been rigged up behind the tote, where daily prayer meetings were held. An Austrian journalist recalled the scene in the *News Chronicle*: instead of the punters, tipsters and tic tac men, there were now Jews of all ages, some with prayer shawls and skull-caps, some with only a handkerchief draped over their head, some swaying backwards and forwards, others just praying silently, whilst in the background he saw some Nazi youths, wearing long, brown jackboots, jeering the congregation.

The camps contained a considerable number of clerics of various denominations: rabbis of all religious hues, from strictest orthodoxy to liberal reform; Lutheran pastors of the German Confessional Church, Jesuit priests, even a few ministers of the Anglican Church. They often did wonderful work amongst their captive flock and rekindled faith in them. Sometimes they also engaged in theological disputations; sometimes they had their amusing or off-putting personal tiffs. The progressive rabbis, for instance, were usually on better terms with their Christian colleagues than with their orthodox brethren, who looked down on them as heretics. For many 'non-aryans', that is to say half-Jews, baptized Jews or Jews brought up without religion in a totally assimilated household, this was an imposed first experience of observing Jewish rites, of witnessing a Jewish conscience at work. For some it became the first step of an eventual return, the pace of which was only accelerated after the war, when the full horror of the holocaust was revealed; others were repelled by the intolerance and unco-operativeness sometimes displayed by the more orthodox Jews, who braved famine, in the early weeks often near-starvation, in the observance of their dietary laws, yet who occasionally treated their fellow Jews with disdain or scorn.

The racecourse at Lingfield, emptied of its Nazi seamen and class 'A' internees, now also became a temporary home for the 'C' refugees. Amongst them was Claus Moser, then a lad of seventeen, whom Huyton later introduced to statistics and who in the passage of time became a distinguished civil servant. He had been taken at his parents' home together with his father, and his slightly older brother. He did not stay at Lingfield for very long but his experiences there have left an indelible memory.

The Moser family guessed that they would not tarry at Lingfield for very long; the air was thick with rumours and speculations. They were a closely-knit family; the father, a frail gentleman, went to the Commandant and obtained his promise that whatever happened the three could stay together. The very next day the whole camp was called on parade, names were read out of all those who were to move on immediately to Huyton. The father's name was on the movement order but not those of his two sons. The father stepped forward and in front of the whole parade addressed the Commandant: 'But, Sir, you promised me last night that my sons would not be separated from me.' The officer shouted at him to shut up and step back; the father left and the boys stayed behind. Soon after the father got to Huyton he was admitted to hospital with a collapsed lung. He stayed there for several months until he was finally released. The incident at Lingfield had been a terrible shock for him, nobody had ever shouted at him like that and he could not understand how a British officer could break his promise.

In due course the elder of the two sons, but not his brother, was told to get ready for a move which, it was rumoured, would end up in Canada. He stuck to his ground; he would not obey unless his brother was included in the party. That was impossible because the lad was too young, and in the face of the elder boy's quiet determination, the Commandant gave in. His name was taken off the list; a few days later both boys left together and by good chance rejoined their father at Huyton. But many families were not so fortunate; in some cases a father went to the Isle of Man, one brother to Canada and another to Australia. Some of these instances were brought to public notice; no plea that there was a panic on can really excuse the carelessness or callousness with which families who had travelled together a long and often tough road were separated.

By the end of June, the stables, the tote and the grandstands of Lingfield were almost empty again, most of the resident internees had been sent to the Liverpool docks for onward embarkation or to Huyton. Only a few people who worked as clerks in the commandantura had been left behind. The camp stayed almost unoccupied until early in August 1940, when the Home Office began to shift transmigrants from the Isle of Man to a place somewhat closer to London. An internee, a young lawyer who had been on the staff of Bloomsbury House, was moved from Onchan to Lingfield in order to help would-be immigrants to the USA to learn how to fill in their forms and fulfill the various conditions stipulated by the stringent US immigration laws. The two governments concerned had now solved the problem which had baffled the Canadian and Australian authorities and which had prevented the direct movement of any internee from the Dominions to the United States. As R. A. Butler, Undersecretary of State at the Foreign Office, explained in a letter to Dr Leslie Burgin,[1] internees were now being released a few days before their expected date of embarkation so that they could come to the US embassy and collect their visas as free men. The Bloomsbury House staff member recalls that at one time there were as many as seven hundred internees at Lingfield waiting for the completion of their US formalities. Only a proportion of them eventually reached America; berths became harder and harder to obtain and after Pearl Harbor transatlantic civilian passages virtually ceased to exist.

Chaim Raphael, then a young Jewish scholar, seconded from Oxford, was working at the time as an Intelligence Officer at Lingfield, processing the visa documentation.[2] He has described the feverish anxiety of all these would-be immigrants, each one of whom was considering himself a special case and was constantly pestering the camp officials about his papers and his problems. The Commandant told him that to look after his first charges, proud, healthy and independent Nazis, had been a pleasure compared with these middle-aged wrecks, whining about their fate. But another 10, who was responsible at that particular time for camp welfare, says that all the officers were sympathetic towards the predicament of their charges and that their relations with them were friendly and understanding.

One day Raphael stepped away from the turmoil and the fuss into a quiet darkened room where a small group of orthodox Jews were grouped around a rabbi, who was explaining to them the *Midrash* of the Book of Lamentations. It was the Ninth Day of the month of *Ab*, the day on which in the year AD 70 the temple in Jerusalem had been destroyed; a day on which devout Jews traditionally fast and pray, with ashes in their hair. For this small group of internees the Lamentations had a special relevance. The scene deeply moved Raphael.

Of three internment camps in the North-West, Huyton, near Liverpool received the lion's share of public concern, though it was by no means the worst case. Eleanor Rathbone was the first to complain about the conditions at Huyton (during the adjournment debate on 10 July 1940). On 24 July she and Graham White visited the camp on behalf of the Parliamentary Committee for Refugees. They came to the conclusion that conditions there were utterly unsuitable for the basic needs of the several thousand interned people. Some of them were so delicate in health or so old that they should not have been interned at all. Others had been engaged on vital war work, were students about to take finals, or refugees on the point of emigration – all victims of mistakes made by the police under hastily drafted and imperfectly understood regulations. The internees' most bitter complaint concerned the delays in postal deliveries; followed by the inactivity and boredom forced on people most of whom had been used to a studious and active life. The postal delays were in fact the single most important factor in sapping camp morale as it took sometimes several weeks for letters to travel from London to Liverpool or to the Isle of Man. All incoming mail had to be passed through one central censoring office in Liverpool, which was hopelessly understaffed; all outgoing letters were censored by the individual camp 10s. It took a considerable number of parliamentary questions, letters to the editor, and visits to camps by parliamentary and ecclesiastical delegations before the situation really improved. But as to Miss Rathbone's other complaint about boredom, for most of the refugees that did not last long. Its remedy did not depend on outside assistance; it lay in the refugees' own hands. They lost no time in solving the problem.

On 4 August, *Reynolds News* complained that amongst the refugees at Huyton there were many cripples and even blind people, and that one house was full of advanced TB cases. The *Daily Telegraph* of 23 August reported that cooking had to be carried out in the open air, even when it was raining and that the food was nearly always cold. There was no hot water supply and only very inadequate hospital arrangements. Despite all the assurances in Parliament, Nazis and anti-Nazis had not been separated.

An article in *The Times* on 23 August contained a comment from a solicitor who had visited Huyton for consultations. He too admitted that the conditions were bad in the camp, but added:

> It must be admitted that the majority of these people are Austrian nationals one of whose inherent characteristics is a lack of initiative and improvisation. If British nationals were interned under the same conditions they would have been able to make themselves more comfortable.

The charge that the internees lacked initiative and improvisation is a travesty. Of course not all the internees were sufficiently skilled and practical to be able to improve conditions by their own resources – some academics were 'all thumbs' – but it was a constant marvel to see how with practically no tools and precious few raw materials the amenities were improved, and how much initiative and improvisation flowered in the camps.

Under increasing pressure, the Cabinet asked Lord Snell, leader of the Labour peers, to conduct an enquiry both into the *Arandora Star* affair and into the conditions at Huyton.[3] The Home Secretary was also asked to set up a separate departmental enquiry into the Huyton situation, prior to the transfer of responsibilities for internment camps from the War to the Home Office. Lord Snell submitted his findings in November, but the Cabinet decided that as public interest in Huyton had meanwhile died down, it would be a pity to revive it. The report was therefore never published.[4]

The report is a succinct and, on the whole, damning document, highlighting the problems and shortcomings of the camps better than any individual eye-witness account. Most of its observations have equal relevance to other camps; it therefore merits examination here in some detail.

Camps had been set aside at the outbreak of war, Lord Snell reported, to provide for the possible internment of twenty thousand enemy aliens. By January 1940, fourteen of those had remained unused and were therefore handed over to the civilian authorities to be used for other purposes. In May 1940 it was suddenly decided to intern all 'B' class aliens and all those who lived in the coastal areas; in June this order was extended to all enemy aliens regardless of classifications and location. New camps therefore had to be improvised at very short notice, one of which was Huyton. It had to be readied in less than a week to receive its first intake. The camp consisted of an empty housing estate, completed just before the war, to which were added adjoining rooms or tents. The houses consisted of three to four rooms and accommodated twelve persons each; they were bare of any furniture but had running water in the bathrooms. The tents housed four internees each, who were given groundsheets. In wet weather the tents became sodden and muddy because they were not well water-proofed. The sanitary arrangements were unsatisfactory and the tented accommodation unsuitable for the type of people who were put into it. The tents were dismantled in the latter part of July.*

Messing took place first in marquees, later in hutments, and was carried out in relays. The only furniture at first available were 340 beds for four thousand internees; the rest were given straw palliasses and three blankets each. Due to a general shortage at Western Command it took a long time before enough tables, benches and other simple pieces of furniture could be provided. There was a shortage of cleaning materials and of toilet paper; no towels could be provided but each internee was issued with two ounces of soap each week. Due to a shortage of coal only one bath per month was permitted. All other ablutions had to be performed with cold water.

Despite clear instructions issued to the Chief Constables, they had arrested many people suffering from diabetes, cardiac diseases, gastric afflictions, paralysis and blindness; even some cripples and mental cases.

---

* The Swiss Consul in Liverpool in a report to his government (G3XVI 1940/ HWH/AS/60) in file RX II ZV 57 at the *Auswaertige Amt*, says that the houses on the Woodfall Estate in Huyton had not all been completed. The rooms were un-papered; there were no electric lights, no black-out provisions and no common rooms.

Lord Snell estimated that over forty per cent of the Huyton internees were over fifty years old; a good many were over sixty. At least one third were unfit in one way or another. Only three houses had been set aside for the invalids, which was quite insufficient. A number of bedridden internees were forced to sleep on mattresses on the floor in overcrowded rooms, left to the attention of their fellow internees. There was only one medical officer for four thousand people; however, he was later assisted by medically trained internees. There had been a serious shortage of medical supplies, particularly of insulin. An outside dentist visited the camp once a week, but he was never able to attend to all the urgent cases.

The standard of food was adequate but unsuitable for the infirm. There had been occasional shortages and the quality of the cooking was not good. At the request of the Chief Rabbi, Lord Snell added, arrangements had now been made for the supply of kosher food. People were allowed to write two letters per week of twenty-four lines each. At first these could only be written on official forms normally supplied to prisoners-of-war, of which there had been a great shortage. The report does not explain the reason for the shortage, but an internee recalls that the special paper used for these forms contained a concealed layer of chalk which made the use of invisible ink impossible. The reason why there was such a shortage of this special paper was that the owner of the company manufacturing it, as well as his chief engineer, were interned. The factory had come to a temporary standstill.*

Lord Snell mentions that the internees had at first been allowed neither radios nor newspapers. This total isolation coupled with the postal delays had a very bad effect on morale; it had been unwise and unnecessary. The restrictions had now been lifted. The Commandant and his staff had tried their best to alleviate the conditions but the constant arrivals and departures and the lack of sufficient camp staff, had put records into a state of great confusion until finally the offer by internees to help in the clerical work had been accepted.

Lord Snell realized that the internment of enemy aliens coincided with the evacuation of the BEF from the continent, which had put a great strain on the resources of the Western Command, but the War Office should have foreseen that a large number of the internees were not like healthy young soldiers but elderly and frail, and should have

---

* Recorded by Kurt Steinberg whilst he was at Camp Hay in Australia.

provided better amenities for them. Even when this was eventually realized, the authorities were unable to take much remedial action however sympathetic the Commandant (there had been three of them in quick succession) and his staff had been. Most of the internees were friendly to this country. They had been taken at short notice from their homes and families; for a considerable time they had received no letters nor any news about the progress of the war. When later lists were posted of those to be shipped abroad, distress became acute and widespread.

* * *

At Huyton, as at almost every other camp, cultural and educational activities started from almost the first day. They followed the election of an internal camp administration with its own little hierarchy of leadership. Huyton was in most respects not very much different from all the other camps. The early atmosphere inside is perhaps best illuminated by what Alfred Lomnitz describes as the Huyton camp song – *the Moorsoldaten*,* a haunting stoic tune, first sung in the German concentration camp *Boergermont* in the moorland country near the Dutch–German border, which one of the ex-prisoners of that camp who had now been interned at Huyton, had taught his fellow internees.[5] Its words and music express the frustration, the despair leavened with hope, which incarceration creates.

But Huyton did not spell despair for everybody. As conditions improved so did the spirit of the inmates. The truly catholic variety of talent and knowledge could not be suppressed; for the majority it soon triumphed over many of the material hardships, if not always over mental anguish. On the whole the young people met challenges better than the old ones. For some of them their spell inside an internment camp had a formative, even decisive, influence on their future life.

The future Sir Claus Moser was about to go up to the London School of Economics, when he was interned. Whilst at Huyton he was asked by a somewhat bored mathematics don, not much older than he was, whether he would like to help him to compile a census of the inmates. It gave him his first taste of accumulating and evaluating such data. He became so interested that when he was released a few weeks after, he decided to read mathematics and statistics. Much later he

---

* The soldiers of the swamp.

became head of Britain's statistical services and of the Bureau of Census. He remembers that when he told the Director of the LSE where he had been, Carr Saunders mentioned that the freehold of the housing estate which had been requisitioned for Huyton Camp belonged to his wife. The young man is now the distinguished chairman of the Covent Garden Opera House.

He was not the only young man whose future career was positively influenced by the internment experience. Siegmund Nissel, a seventeen-year-old refugee from Vienna, had come to Britain with a children's transport. The only precious possession which he had been able to take with him was his violin. He was a promising musician but much too poor to afford lessons in London. In due course he was interned together with his violin, and passed through the usual stations, Kempton Park, Huyton and the Isle of Man. In camp his talent was noted and he was able to be taught. He joined in trios, quartets, and small chamber ensembles and took part in camp concerts. He got close to another equally gifted boy. Wellwishers in the camp, impressed by their talent, arranged that once free they could have lessons with Max Rostal, but for the moment there was no way in which they could be released. Eventually they applied under paragraph twenty of the last White Paper, which covered 'persons of eminent distinction who have made outstanding contributions to Art'. The advisory panel who had to judge whether a musician qualified as such a person, was chaired by Ralph Vaughan Williams. The two boys of sixteen and seventeen, not even yet at the threshold of a career, got such glowing testimonials from music lovers in the camp that Dr Vaughan Williams recommended their release to the Home Secretary. In due course they were joined by another young man, fresh out of Press Heath Camp, and later by a fourth one, a young Englishman, all pupils of Rostal. After the war they formed the Amadeus String Quartet. For one young Viennese the year in internment had been decisive in shaping his career. The ability to practise all day without having to worry about his daily bread, the stimulation and encouragement provided by so many other people interested in music, gave him an opportunity which he might possibly have missed under different, more 'normal' conditions.

Press Heath was a hastily erected tented camp, situated four miles from Whitchurch, which under adverse weather conditions would have been quite uninhabitable, even for seasoned young soldiers. There were no duckboards; people slept on groundsheets and straw palliasses. After sunset utter darkness reigned, except for the brightly illuminated perimeter fence and the occasional pale fluorescence of the moon. Fortunately, the summer of 1940 was an exceptionally hot and dry one. For the young and fit ones conditions were therefore bearable, even enjoyable to some extent, but difficult for the rest. A report by the Secretary of the Federation of Synagogues states that the camp housed 1,200 people under canvas and that there had been an insufficiency of food.[6] The Board of Deputies took up the complaints and on 24 September the Home Office replied that they were hoping to close the camp completely by the end of the month.[7] But on 8 October Herbert Morrison admitted in the House that the camp was still open. He was expecting it to be run down by the end of October.

One of the internees, the Goethe scholar Professor Friedenthal, in his *roman à clé*, mentions that the meals at Press Heath consisted mainly of herrings.[8] Barrels of salt herrings in fact provided the staple diet in all the camps. Army cooks, and at first also the amateur chefs amongst the refugees, could do little to make that monotonous diet more palatable but with experience the internee *chefs de cuisine* managed to produce marvels from that rather unprepossessing raw material and there are reports from at least two camps that eventually these herrings tasted just as delicious as river trout. In his fictionalized account Friedenthal also highlights comments by the camp commandant which are typical of the general ignorance of these officers due to a lack of proper briefing. The commandant could not understand why the internees were all so concerned about the security of their papers and documents which had been taken from them. After all they did not need them any longer in the camp. On another occasion the Colonel told the assembled row leaders: 'I see from your papers that so many of you are Jews. How is it then possible that you have sided with Adolf Hitler?' When it was explained to him who they really were, he replied that if that was true, then it went beyond his comprehension that they should have been interned. We come across such ignorance time and again amongst the camp officers in Britain and abroad, including even the Intelligence Officers. They had either not been briefed at all or had been given entirely incorrect information. Was this sheer oversight or ignorance of the people concerned in the War Office, or was there a more sinister purpose behind it?

*   *   *

The camp which stands out amongst the rest and which can be likened to *Dunera* in dry dock, was the disused Warth Mill.* Most people stayed there only for a few days, but whether it was just one night or several weeks, the impressions of that satanic Mill have remained indelibly impregnated in the memories of all who passed through it. It had not been used for years and was in an advanced state of decay. Its floors were pitted, filthy, tesselated with puddles of machine oil and grease. The building was infested with rats, mice and other vermin, which during the night could be heard scurrying about; many an inmate, lying on his palliasse, received nocturnal visits from one or the other of these creatures. On an average two thousand internees were imprisoned here. There was no furniture of any description, neither tables or benches; people had to eat their meals standing up or squatting on the greasy floor. There was no electric light. What light there was during the daylight hours filtered through a glass roof. Many of its panes were broken. Whenever it rained, which fortunately was not often, puddles of water accumulated everywhere. The washing facilities consisted of eighteen cold water taps. Later additional basins and lavatories were built, but they were some distance away up a hill.

The sentries belonged to the Lancashire Regiment. After the usual initial hostility they soon relented and a brisk trade developed with them covering such forbidden essentials as newspapers, cigarettes and unrationed food, in that order of priority.

Several internees remember a group of German and Austrian Jesuit priests who were particularly cheerful and helped greatly in boosting camp morale. It is altogether interesting to compare the comments of various internees on camp morale because they often tell more about the character of the internee himself, than about any general atmosphere. One inmate's most vivid memory of Warth Mill is that it brought out the worst in people. Because of the lack of tolerable accommodation and the shortage of food, everybody was fighting to get as much as possible for himself. It was *chacun pour soi* all along the line. Yet another internee says that whilst some inmates became withdrawn and despondent, many others were helpful and were able to ignore the appalling conditions. The same internee remembers an inflammatory speech, full of complaints, made by a

---

* See pamphlet issued in May 1941 by the National Council for Civil Liberties 'Internment and Treatment of Enemy Aliens'. Also Judex: *Anderson's Prisoners* op. cit. The composite picture also draws on the accounts of several inmates.

former member of the Austrian Upper House, which, he says, the camp authorities with typical British tolerance simply ignored.

Just as on the *Dunera* the miserable surroundings only encouraged the desire to escape from reality, albeit only for an hour or two. An internee remembers how within three or four days of their arrival their first open air concert was held and how deeply he was moved by a rendering of Schubert's *An die Musik* cycle, sung evocatively by a Jewish Cantor.

✶　　✶　　✶

Conditions in the other camps did not greatly differ from those on the racecourses. In Scotland the principal internment camp was at Donaldson's Academy near Edinburgh. An inmate there shared his accommodation with a lion tamer whose primary worry was how his lions would survive without him. The great majority of internees were educated, middle-class refugees, but it must not be overlooked that there was a considerable leaven of people of working-class origin, people who had found themselves in Britain at the outbreak of war for reasons other than racial or political persecution. Some of these were quite strange characters; we will meet them again when we come to the island camps.

It was rare in these early days for internees to be allowed to receive visitors, but it happened occasionally, particularly in the case of owners of factories and other businesses whose decisions or signatures were needed so that their firms could carry on in the interest of their employees – and often in the interest of the country, for many were engaged on work of national importance. A Scottish solicitor was able to interview a few of such clients at Strachur Camp and later wrote a memorandum to the Home Office on his visit.[9] He bitterly complained that although his clients were desperately anxious to hear news from him about their families, he was not allowed to discuss anything else with them but the particular business at hand. The Camp Commandant was rude to him and made as many difficulties as possible. He also warned the solicitor not to discuss the camp conditions with anybody outside nor to contact any of the wives of any of the internees who were not already his clients. Eleanor Rathbone, the parliamentary paladin of the refugees, visited the camp on 15 August and thereafter conditions improved.

During July and August 1940 the various camps in England and

Scotland were gradually emptied and most of them closed altogether; the inmates had by then been transferred to the Isle of Man, shipped overseas or released. Only Lingfield remained open as a transit camp prior to release for internees returned from overseas, for people who were in the penultimate stage of emigration to the United States or for the occasional refugee who had managed to reach Britain from occupied Europe, and who had to be interned pending verification of his credentials.

From late 1940 onwards the blessed isle in the Irish Sea had, with few exceptions, become the repository of all the interned enemy aliens who had not been deported.

10 *Hutchinsons Camp*

A Short Guide to Internment

To exercise discernment, in the matter of internment
is a gift possessed by few.
One needs a mind eclectic and a turn for dialectic
With a ticklish job to do.

One must always be suspicious of talents meritricious
That foreigners display.
If they are intellectual blighters, scientific chaps or writers,
One condemns them right away.
Yes, that is our simple plan,
Intern them if you can.

And if criticism is vocal in Parliament or Press,
Just make bold to say:
To frown on cerebration, as a menace to the nation,
Is our good old British way.

Anti-Nazi propaganda is one to understand a
Thing we may or mayn't desire.
Libertarian fanatics should be taken to their attics
And kept behind barbed wire.
Where the hatred of oppression has the force of an obsession
The danger may be small.
But with those who have been da capo in the hands of the Gestapo
One should take no risk at all.

So that is our simple plan:
Intern them if you can.

(*Dogberry*, published in the *News Chronicle* on 20 August 1940)

★   ★   ★

I woke at seven o'clock in the morning. The sun had risen a couple
of hours ago over the distant sea. It was a lovely fresh morning,
the promise of another hot, cloudless day. Nothing had so far stirred,
but then a bugle sounded reveille. Very slowly Hutchinsons Camp

came to life. Men of all ages, dressed in all manner of raiments, pyjamas, bathrobes, vests and underpants, tumbled out of the requisitioned stuccoed boarding houses on to the greensward for their daily PT exercises. Half an hour later they congregated outside their various houses for the daily roll-call ritual. The Regimental Sergeant Major, impeccably dressed, his cane smartly swaggering in step with his feet, appeared. With him were a few junior NCOs and occasionally a Lieutenant. The RSM liked his wards to be fully dressed, shaved and smartly turned out for the parade, but he was fighting against overwhelming odds. The internees shuffled around in their bathrobes and dressing gowns, bleary-eyed, with no pretence of falling in 'smartly in three ranks'. There was another roll-call at 'tattoo' time when the flag was hauled down, but it was not much better. In fact, those roll-calls were hilarious spectacles. The number of prisoners were counted and often recounted; each time the result was different. When they were finally reported 'all present and correct' the final figure often did not tally with the official camp records. For a regular soldier roll-calls of such an undisciplined 'shower' were a nightmare!

*　　*　　*

'Under escort in the Isle of Man'

At the peak of internment the Isle of Man, a favourite holiday resort for the North of England, whose first known invaders had been the Vikings, contained two camps for women – Port St Mary and Port Erin, situated on the Rushen peninsula – two camps for Italians, known as Palace and Metropole; one camp for British subjects interned under

18b; and six camps for Germans and Austrians: Hutchinsons, Central Promenade, Onchan, Peveril (Peel), Mooragh (Ramsey) and, later on, Sefton. Some of these were in due course vacated again and their remaining inmates transferred to others; one of the women's camps was turned in 1941 into a mixed one; only a few remained in business until the end of the war. Hutchinsons was one of the largest and best known of them. It was there that I found myself for a while and it is the one camp which will be described here in detail.* Most of its features and human interest stories were replicated in the other camps, but it stood out in one respect: whether by chance or design it had a large contingent of practitioners of the visual arts, painters, sculptors, illustrators and etchers, who gave the camp an atmosphere all of its own.

*   *   *

The contingency plans worked out before the outbreak of war did not provide for the siting of any internment camps on the Isle of Man, although the island had been used for that purpose during the First World War. The decision to use it again must have been taken sometime during the early spring of 1940.

The word 'camp' usually conjures up an image of a cluster of huts or a row of field grey tents in some isolated spot, windswept, at the end of a single approach road, fenced in by a stockade and guarded from the outside world by watch-towers and searchlights sweeping the night sky. All that the camps on the island had in common with such a vision were the fences and the sentries.

Hutchinsons was scenically in the most attractive position. It was situated high up on the slope of a hill. It consisted of a number of houses grouped around three sides of a square, one further row of houses abutting one of those built-up sides, whilst on the fourth, unbuilt-up, side there was a lovely open vista towards Douglas and the Irish Sea beyond. Just as in the previous war, the government had requisitioned a number of terraced boarding houses and surrounded them with a palisade of barbed wire fencing. The landladies, who in halcyon pre-war days had made their living by catering for the summer tourists, had been told to clear out (except in the women's

---

* The picture of Hutchinsons Camp is drawn from various sources. Apart from my own memories I have profited in particular from those of Dr Hinrichsen Professor Weissenborn, Fred Uhlman and Fritz Hallgarten.

camps where they stayed behind), and had taken with them every-thing that was valuable or precious or had locked it away in their attics. All that was left were the bare essentials of furniture, such as beds, tables, chairs and occasionally wardrobes. Some of the houses also boasted a few broken upright pianos which had not been tuned for years. Nevertheless they provided the basic instruments for the musical activity which soon mushroomed.

No blackout curtains had been provided and the army, in their wisdom, had simply painted all the window-panes midnight-blue and all the electric light bulbs red, including an occasional lamp hanging on an outside porch, so that at night Hutchinsons looked like the red light district of some sleazy harbour town. Obviously, these arrange-ments were quite unsatisfactory as they plunged the inside of the houses into total gloom and even during the day made reading, chess playing or any other kind of activity needing vision, impossible. One of the first tasks, therefore, to which the internees set their hands, was to beg, borrow or steal – often by breaking open the landladies' locked attics – bits of material and to fashion them into curtains. The next step was to obtain a fresh supply of pearl coloured bulbs and lastly to scrape clean the windows. This last task gave rise to a new form of graphic art. Professor Helmut Weissenborn, formerly of Leipzig, a well-known teacher of graphic arts and an artist of some repute, armed himself with razor blades and, not content with merely scraping off the blue colour, engraved the panes with his own designs. Some had a classical or mythological subject, some were floral fantasies, lit up by the sun coming up across the sea; one was a copy of part of the Sistine Chapel ceiling, some were humorous and others slightly erotic. One window depicted Adam and Eve, with the apple engraved: $1\frac{1}{2}$d. This apparently offended some of the orthodox Jews, but the non-Jew Weissenborn atoned for it by engraving the windows of the Kosher House with biblical designs. In exchange their cook baked the breakfast rolls for his house. Weissenborn was by all accounts as accomplished a chef for his house-mates as he was an artist.

Each boarding house catered for itself, with one of the resident internees volunteering to act as *chef de cuisine* and daily fatigue details performing the unskilled kitchen chores. The Isle of Man Government in due course published a booklet, 'Three Hundred Recipes, Based on the Dietary for the Isle of Man Internment Camps'. It was a suggested feeding routine instituted at Hutchinsons by the commandant, Captain

H. O. Daniel, and was based on the weekly rations, varying every day over a three-week period, and contained recipes for soups, main courses as well as desserts, including such delicacies as Lancashire Hot Pot, braised Windsor Steak, Bechamel Potatoes, Rice Croquettes and Jam Turnovers. Some of the amateur chefs no doubt drew inspiration from these recipes, few of which had ever figured on a continental's menu; others, with the help of spices and herbs, procured through the canteen, and their own artistic imagination, occasionally produced culinary masterpieces. When they were eventually released, their wives had some pleasant surprises. Many a judge who had never before held a drying-up towel in his hand, could now throw his weight about in the kitchen.

Hardly anybody was ever taken straight from arrest to the island. There was usually at least one, often several, intermediate transit camps between apprehension and final destination. Several hundred internees at a time were usually transported in special trains to Liverpool then ferried across the Irish Sea in the ships which in normal times took the Lancastrians for their 'Wakes' holidays. The trains and the ships were guarded by escort troops. The diplomatic relations between the soldiers and the internees had by then become much less distant and much more informal. One internee remembers how a young soldier in his railway coach had taken his rifle to pieces in order to clean it and was then unable to put it together again until some of the prisoners took it from him and assembled it again correctly.

Initially idle crowds of Manx men and women were always watching the arrival of these ships, but the novelty soon wore off. From Douglas the internees were marched up the hill – this again soon ceased to attract much attention – and welcomed at the camp gate by a small reception party consisting of the Regimental Sergeant Major and some of his NCOs. The RSM at Hutchinsons was reputed to have been the head porter at a West End block of flats. He personified authority for the internees in a much more immediate sense than any of his superior officers, and although quite friendly and approachable, was treated with almost as much awe by the internees as by his troops.

The officer in charge of the transport handed his charges over to the RSM who divided them into batches of thirty and then had each batch taken to one of the empty houses, allowing friends to stay together.

The arrival of new intakes was an important event in the camp calendar and a welcome break in the monotony of the early days. The old hands stood around the camp gates trying to spot familiar faces. If

'Inspection',
Prees Heath Camp

'The Fifth Columnist'

'Food Carrier'

'Gala', Prees Heath
Camp

'Friendly Aliens
Avenue'

'Waiting for the
Happy End'

Waiting for the Happy End

W.JONDORF

Internees on the Isle of Man

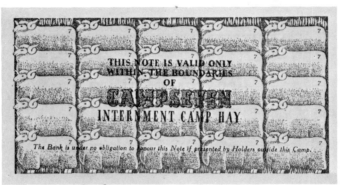

Camp Currency from Australia

one did find a friend and there was room in one's house one could usually arrange for him to join the house community.

A week or so after my own arrival I was watching a batch of new arrivals marching up the hill slowly, under the weight of their valises, when I spotted my own father amongst them. He had escaped from Germany after the *Kristallnacht* under somewhat dangerous circumstances and had been living in London since then. I had not seen him for several weeks and had not even known that he too had been interned. It was a fortuitous and emotional reunion.

The requisitioned boarding houses normally had a lounge/dining-room on the ground floor and a number of bedrooms on the first and second floors, each equipped with two double beds. These beds posed problems. Continentals were used to twin beds and had rarely shared an all night connubial couch with their partners, marital or otherwise, let alone strangers. Initially this problem was the cause of a lot of friction and disputes until somebody suggested that the top mattress was put on the floor so that each of the unwilling bed partners could have his own exclusive sleeping berth, even if it restricted perambulation in the bedrooms. These revolutionary arrangements applied more to the older men; the youngsters had no such hang-ups and the double beds may have contributed to some extent to the incidence of homosexuality and of lesbianism which developed in both the men's and women's camps. It worried the internal camp administration at Hutchinsons to such an extent that they confidentially requested the commandant to arrange for a mixture of Bromide in some of the basic foods. Later, when this leaked out, it became an endless topic of conversation which part of the daily diet contained the bromide; the general consensus favoured the porridge.

A typical day in the camp began with the morning roll-call. Such daily counting of the sheep was really quite superfluous. Nobody ever managed, or as far as is known, even wanted to escape. There was really nowhere to go. There is in fact a story of what occurred, somewhat later on, when internees under escort were occasionally taken to a local cinema. Whilst in the picture house an internee fell asleep and missed the bus back to camp. Nobody noticed his absence but he became alarmed when he woke up alone in a darkened cinema. He managed to engage a taxi cab to take him 'home', but when he arrived at the gate the sentry refused him admittance until his credentials could be proven. The name of the film is not known, but the episode could hardly have occurred on the very first cinema visit by the

Hutchinsons internees. On that occasion they saw Chaplin's *Great Dictator*, then in its first year. The film made a very deep impression on people for whom Chaplin's tragicomic carricature of Hitler had especial poignance.

After roll-call there was time to finish one's ablutions, and tidy up one's bed before the breakfast gong sounded. Thereafter people were free to do whatever they liked – there was not too much choice – except for those who were on domestic fatigues. Each house drew its rations from the Quartermaster's Store and made its own culinary arrangements. A strict roster of duties was kept in every house and except for the invalids, nobody, not even the camp officials, was excluded from the performance of domestic chores. An internee who was one of the house fathers and who was also in charge of camp welfare arrangements almost lost his jobs because he had paid somebody else to do the washing-up and sweeping for him. Luncheon was served at 1.00 pm, supper at 7.30 pm; by 10.30 pm all lights had to be out. It was a healthy, sensible routine.

From the beginning the internees were encouraged to establish their own camp administration with the army keeping as much as possible outside the barbed wire fences. One internee has likened this to the strategy underlying the success of the British Empire, that is to say, to allow the local Rajahs or chiefs authority over their native subjects, but to keep security and external relations strictly under British control. Each house elected a house father; each row of houses a street father, and at the apex of the pyramid sat the camp father, the native ruler who was the principal link to the District Commissioner, or in this case the Camp Commandant. At first the army wanted to call these camp officials house captain and camp captain, but the internees preferred the less military appellation father. Alongside this fatherhood a miniature camp civil service evolved; internees were chosen to be in charge of welfare, of educational facilities such as the university and the technical college; of the camp newsheet; of concerts and art exhibitions; of other leisure activities and of the canteen.

For a while I was in charge of the canteen, a position of not inconsiderable 'patronage'. One of my 'perks' was a twice weekly visit under escort to the Woolworth store in nearby Douglas, in order to buy whatever unrationed food and other small comforts were available. I thought at the time that I had discharged my duties tolerably well but when researching for this book I came across the first issue of the weekly camp newsheet, and found the following tribute to my work:

Dear Press Chief: I would like to say something about your canteen but I do not know enough language in English to express exactly what I mean. If you are independent you should take a thick broom and work like a charwoman. There is much rubbish in the corners. Chin-up, Yours I.C.

The managers of the various camp activities each had their staff of helpers and assistants, but the personnel constantly changed, particularly once releases started in earnest. It was therefore not easy to establish a pattern of continuity.

The first camp father, a non-Jew, had been a private secretary to Thomas Mann and was himself an authority on both Goethe and Mann. The problems which he and his staff faced were considerable. In the first place they had to convince the Commandant that the great majority of the internees were decent, loyal people, smarting under a sense of grievance and that it was in the Commandant's own interest to provide as much material help and to bend the rules as much as possible to enable the camp staff to keep the internees usefully occupied and mentally stretched. Captain Daniel, the Commandant at Hutchinsons, was a fair, quiet, open-minded regular officer, perhaps more familiar with musical comedies and convivial stage parties than with classical concerts, more with cricket and football than with chess and debating societies, with ordinary people than with 'cloud-cuckoo-land' professors and dadaist or expressionist painters. He probably could never quite understand the behaviour and demands o some of his more weird charges, but he tried to help wherever he could within the limits of the army's resources. Fortunately for the internees, the Intelligence Officer, Captain Jorgensen, who in peacetime had been a broker on the Baltic Exchange, spoke first-class German, was familiar with the background of the majority of the internees and able to help where the Commandant or the RSM were often baffled.

In quite a short time the Commandant became proud of 'his' internees and of his camp. He liked to think that the camp was better cared for and that he had a happier ship than the other commandants; one of his ambitions was that Hutchinsons should beat Peel on the football pitch.*

He encouraged the planting of shrubs and flowers and the gardens

---

* Two Swiss officials visited the camp on 8 November and interviewed the Commanding Officer, Captain Daniel. Their comment: *'Ein Musterlager'* (an excellent camp). *Auswaertige Amt* Archive RX II ZV 189.

were put in the charge of a former Berlin banker who once upon a time employed a squad of gardeners in the grounds of his Tiergarten villa. Through the camp technical school the commandant organized the installation of a loudspeaker system so that every day he was able to speak to the internees whilst they were having lunch in their dining-rooms. His addresses were a mixture of war news, camp information, strictures and pep talks. When the idea of starting a chamber orchestra was first mooted by some internees, he thought what they wanted was a brass band, but he fell in with their idea and helped to get them the necessary instruments.

The Commandant took great personal pride in the one well-known musician who was interned in his camp. Marian Rawicz, an Austrian, had before the war, together with his compatriot Landauer, become very popular as an interpreter on the piano of light classical, particularly Viennese, music. The story went that they had been brought to England by the Prince of Wales and that they were both interned as they returned home from performing before Queen Mary. They had been sent to different camps but Captain Daniel soon succeeded in having Landauer transferred to his charge. The broken-down pianos would not do for two virtuosi, so he managed to obtain the loan of two baby grands. I can still picture a lovely summer's afternoon on the crowded square, the internees crouching on the lawn, the officers and their ladies sitting on chairs in front of them and the sentimental strains of Strauss, father and son, beautifully coaxed from the second-rate grand pianos by these two maestros, wafting across the distant sea. It was one of the highlights of the camp sojourn.

On the whole, therefore, relations with the army were good; the problem which the internal camp administration faced with their fellow internees, was much more daunting. It was no easy task to mould into a bearable community such a heterogenous lot of people, under such unusual and taxing conditions. René Elvin, an interned journalist, called it a '*Zwangsgemeinschaft*', a community based on imposed togetherness, which, he says, could not be moulded into a lay monastery or into a modern utopia because of its lack of freedom.[1] The barbed wire, the very symbol of all that we were fighting against, became an obsession, an *idée fixe*, which made it impossible for a lot of irremediably individualistic people to submit to the common weal. No doubt that was the reaction of many internees, particularly the older ones, but it was by no means universal.

There were the high spirited, often bored, schoolboys, liable to play

CONCERT

By invitation
of the Commander of Hutchinson Camp, Douglas,
Captain H.O.Daniel

Thursday, 7th November, 1940
8.00 p.m.

VIOLIN: Dr. C. Sluzewski
PIANO: Prof.R.Glas and H.G.Furth

--

PROGRAM

I) F.HANDEL: Sonata for Violin and Piano F major
Adagio - Allegro - Largo - Allegro

Violin: C. Sluzewski
Piano: Prof.R.Glas

II) J.S.BACH: Concerto for Violin and Orchestra
E major. Second movement: Adagio

Violin: C. Sluzewski
Piano: Prof.R. Glas

III) L.v.BEETHOVEN: Concerto for Piano and Orchestra
E flat major (Emperor - Concerto)
Allegro - Adagio un poco moto -
Allegro (Rondo)

Solo part: Prof. R. Glas
Orchestra part: H.G. Furth

Concert programme from Hutchinsons Camp

irreverent pranks and jar the nerves of some fastidious or cranky elders, who insisted on being called '*Herr Geheimrat*' and '*Herr Oberregierungsrat*' and who, like the Aristos, had learned nothing and forgotten nothing. There were the physically sick or handicapped, the mentally disturbed, the religiously devout or intolerant, and those who mocked them. Some were able to ignore the barbed wire fence and, in

the words of one internee, could say with Tolstoy's Pierre Besukov:
'My immortal soul can never be imprisoned'; others suffered from a
permanent depression. There were those who were cheerfully willing
to help and those who had no trace of any community spirit; those
who bore whatever discomforts initially arose without much complaint, and those who were only interested in their own creature
comforts and who always reported sick whenever there was work to
do. There were those who were keen to widen their horizon by
attending lectures and those who complained or played cards all day
long. There were some who had vowed not to speak a word of
German again until Nazidom had been wiped from the face of the
earth and those who either knew no English or refused to speak it
because they were cross with Britain. The *lingua franca* of the camp
however was English, spoken in all its variations and nuances, from the
accent-free literate, to the crude 'emigranto'. An example of this
peculiar lingo is the text which a pastor chose for one of his Sunday
morning services. Translating from the German '*Der Geist is willig
aber das Fleisch ist schwach*' he announced his sermon as 'The ghost is
willing but the meat is weak'.

The majority of the inmates were assimilated, middle-class German
and Austrian Jews, of a similar background and education, though of
all shades of temperament and behaviour; on the whole they were
much more 'German' than 'Jewish'. But there were also other groups,
each adding spice as well as problems. The most unusual group were a
number of long-term resident Jews, who had no connection whatso-
ever with the so-called 'German *Kulturkreis*'. They had been born in a
part of Poland, Galicia, which before the First World War, when
Poland had not existed as a sovereign state, had belonged to the
Austro-Hungarian Empire. They had come to Britain around the turn
of the century, as a result of religious persecution or of economic
pressure and had mostly settled in the East End of London or in the
predominantly Jewish parts of Manchester and Leeds. They had been
either too poor or too ignorant to apply for naturalization; as far as the
authorities were concerned they had remained Austrians until the
Anschluss when they had automatically become citizens of the Greater
German Reich. Had they only been born after 1919, they would now
have been welcomed as Polish allies. They had been left alone during
the First World War, many of them had British wives and sons or
grandsons fighting in the armed forces; they had all been rounded up
in June. They were decent, god-fearing elderly people who since their

arrival in the ghettos of this country had never been outside Britain or been separated for one day from their families. They spoke either Yiddish or their own brand of English. They were bewildered, unable to comprehend what was happening to them and often lacked the inner resources to overcome the indignities of their present environment. The attitude of a few – not many – toffee-nosed 'Herren Doktoren' also did not help them.* They could be seen every day wandering aimlessly along the perimeter fence. No group in the camp was less likely to contain Nazi sympathizers or potential fifth columnists than these unfortunate people.

Their case was soon taken up in the press and in parliamentary questions. Fortunately they had a champion who vigorously spoke up on their behalf. That was Nathan Laski, a prominent Manchester Jew, father of Neville KC and Professor Harold; a patriarch, greatly revered in his community. He complained to a great personal friend, Winston Churchill; he complained to another friend Clement Attlee; he told the Board of Jewish Deputies in forthright language that they were not doing enough, but he made little progress.† The first White Paper containing specific categories under which internees could apply for release, made no provision for these long-term residents. Churchill's private secretary told Laski in fact that such long-term residence was in fact no proof *per se* that the aliens concerned were loyal to the allied cause. However, under constant pressure, a clause covering these cases was later added to the White Paper and by the middle of 1941 they were all back again with their families.

There were also smaller identifiable groups: German and Austrian trade union officials and other members of social-democratic and left-wing organizations, including a few members of the pre-Nazi German and Austrian parliaments; there were journalists, writers, musicians and visual artists; members of the Left who had fought in the International Brigades; members of the old aristocracy or of the conservative opposition to Hitler; Catholic and Protestant clergymen and a few people who did not belong to any of these groups.

Amongst these untypical people was an elderly man from Bremen who had been employed in the circus all his life. He had fought for

---

* The strained and unusual circumstances by no means eliminated social snobbery. On the contrary, they sometimes accentuated it.
† Letter to Churchill, dated 9 August 1940; to Attlee dated 28 August; and to Brotman, Secretary to the Board of Deputies, dated 9 August; all at Bloomsbury House.

Britain in the First World War and had been awarded various decorations; he had been discharged as a Company Sergeant Major and had lived in England most of his life without ever having been naturalized. He bore his fate with fortitude; every morning he silently paraded up and down outside the Commandant's office, sporting all his medals and campaign ribbons. The Commandant took up his case personally; he was one of the first to be released.

There was another man, the son of a German father and an English mother, born in Germany but brought to England as a baby when his parents split up. He never saw his father again, spoke no German and had had no idea that he was German until the police came to pick him up. In camp he refused to wash or to shave or to attend any of the parades. He was repeatedly put into detention but refused to co-operate until he was released.

Perhaps the oddest duo were twin brothers, coal miners who spoke with such a broad Scottish accent that even the guards had difficulty in understanding them. Their parents had stayed briefly in Germany where the twins had been born and where the father had worked in a Ruhr pit. The family had returned to Scotland when the boys were infants, but their nationality had never been regularized. They kept a chart in their room on which, day by day, they recorded how much coal had been lost to the war effort because of their imprisonment. The Intelligence Officer took a particular interest in their case, as in the long-term residents and in the boys interned from boarding schools, and the twins were among the first to be released.

For anybody who was prepared to make the best out of a bad situation, a situation which he had neither sought nor could control, internment could be turned into a positive experience, enlarging horizons, deepening knowledge, furthering latent abilities. One internee later compared it to Mann's 'Magic Mountain' where Hans Castrop gathered a wealth of knowledge and experience. But, of course, for understandable reasons, many internees reacted very differently and suffered scars of mental anguish which took a long time to heal.

In the early weeks of their incarceration many internees were tormented by fear of invasion. One of the options open to the Nazis, which was often discussed amongst the *cognoscenti* in the camp, was an occupation of Ireland as a basis for an invasion across the Irish Sea. People were convinced that in such an eventuality, the government would abandon the Isle of Man, just as they had evacuated their garrison from the Channel Islands once the German troops had reached the French coast. Death of all refugees at the hands of the Nazis appeared a distinct possibility. Some people suggested that as soon as this appeared imminent, the internees should break out of the camp, steal whatever pleasure boats and fishing smacks could be found and sail them to England. Others advocated a desperate last stand such as the Spartans at Thermopilae. Fortunately as the evenings lengthened, invasion of Britain or of Ireland or of anywhere else seemed to become less and less likely and people could again concentrate on their two principal preoccupations: release and making life in the camp as interesting and bearable as possible.

Perhaps the people least affected by rumours or boredom were the artists who, with few of their customary tools and materials to hand, in next to no time became amazingly creative. Sixteen painters and sculptors, all interned at Hutchinsons, had written a letter to the *New Statesman* which the journal published on 24 August.* 'Art cannot live behind barbed wire, whatever attractive picture is painted by some newspapers. We came to England because we saw in her the last bulwark, the last hope for democracy in Europe. We are asking our British colleagues and friends and all who are interested in art to help us obtain our freedom again.' Unbeknown to them, their friends had already taken action. Eight days earlier *The Spectator* and other journals had published an open letter urging the release of all interned refugee artists. That letter had been signed by Augustus John, Jan Gordon, Vanessa Bell, her companion Duncan Grant, James Bateman and Muirhead Bone. The *cri de coeur* of the imprisoned artists is borne out by the testimony of one of them, Helmut Weissenborn. He says that this was the worst period of his life. Treatment was fair and humane, but the very fact of imprisonment is, for an artist, beyond endurance. Yet despite all the mental anguish, of feeling caged in, these artists were amazingly creative and interacted extremely well with the other internees with whom in outside life they had little contact, and who knew even less about them.

The artists themselves were quite a heterogenous lot. Amongst them was Fred Uhlman, who happened to be the son-in-law of the Under-secretary of State for War, a peer of the realm. Until his emigration to Paris he had been a lawyer, but then developed into a talented painter.

---

* Such letters to the press were permissible provided they had been properly censored.

Two of his drawings from that period are included in this book. He wrote an amusing account of his life which includes many vignettes of his internment.[2] He thinks that in one way captivity was much harder to bear for internees than for ordinary criminals. A criminal, once convicted, can settle down and make the best of it because he knows the maximum stretch he has to serve. But for him it could have been a day, a week, a year, many years; he just did not know. He says that Professor Weissenborn was not the only artist who decorated the boarding house windows. Others followed his example; one of them was a big game hunter who had for years observed African wildlife with the eyes of a bushman. His window full of zebras, giraffes and monkeys was equal to those done by the professional artists.

Other artists were Fritz Salomonski, a Max Liebermann pupil, who because of his resonant voice also doubled up as a Jewish Cantor; Erich Kahn, a Kokoschka pupil, who painted scary nightmares anticipating a bleak future for mankind; the sculptor Siegfried Charoux, one of whose statues now stands in front of London's Festival Hall. There was Eric Stern,* one of pre-Nazi Berlin's best known stage designers, the sculptors Gerhard Ehrlich and Mueller-Blensdorf, and the painter H. Fechenbach.

But above all, there was Kurt Schwitters, co-founder of Dadaism, a giant, a polymath of a man, who not only painted and sculpted, but was also a prodigious poet. Sometimes he gave recitals of his own poems; one which sticks out in memory was written to be read by stammerers. Schwitters and his son had come out of Norway after the German invasion. His work had been neglected for years; he was desperately poor and would become so again after his release. But in the camp he had a captive audience, he was in his element and could give full rein to his ebullience and *joie de vivre*. He was not only full of talents, but also full of quirks. His socks were so full of holes that they hardly existed. For reasons unknown he preferred to sleep on the floor in a makeshift dog basket into which he crawled at night; he always barked before he went to sleep. One night there was an answering bark at the foot of the boarding house stairs. There lived in the camp

---

* I remember with pleasure a performance of *Pagliacci* which Stern produced about a year later at a theatre in Chester when both of us had advanced to privates in the Auxiliary Pioneers Corps. Our Alien Company provided most of the orchestra and the male singers; the ATS the sopranos and Western Command the audience. His scenery and costumes, made out of bits and pieces of war surplus stores, were breathtaking.

another internee whose life-long yen it had been to bark like a dog, but inhibition had always prevented him from giving voice to his craving. Now at last he could engage in a nightly duet with Schwitters, much to the discomfiture of some Manx cats. Fred Uhlman remembers that Schwitters sounded like a Dachshund; the elderly Viennese businessman more like a mastiff.

Schwitters earned pocket money to pay for canteen comforts by painting portraits of some of the more affluent fellow internees. They were traditional pictures and are perhaps not amongst his best work.

Canvas was hard to come by and Schwitters painted or assembled collages on and with whatever material he chanced to find or to 'liberate', such as cigarette packets, seaweed, shells, pieces of cork, string, nails, broken glass, deliberately broken-up tables and chairs, lino ripped from the floor or just walls. The story goes that after he eventually became famous, connoisseurs journeyed to the Isle of Man to see whether the returning landladies had left any of his murals intact, but to no avail.

His *pieces de résistance*, beyond doubt, were sculptures fashioned out of stale remnants of porridge, which he assiduously collected from breakfast tables. They had the colour of Danish blue cheese and exuded a faintly sickly smell. Alas, they did not survive long; the mice soon got at them. Uhlman's epitaph on Schwitters is: 'The Till Eugenspiegel of painters; he played the fool but he knew exactly what he was doing.'

Schwitters was undoubtedly the leading spirit amongst the camp artists and helped in establishing in one of the houses an 'artists' café', a poor man's *La Coupole*, where the painters and sculptors met every afternoon and where several exhibitions of their work were mounted.

Whenever functions were held in the camp, such as concerts or poetry readings, programmes were duplicated in the camp office for which the artists provided the illustrations. Professor Weissenborn recollects that he designed and then printed his illustrations from lino cuts. The material usually came from bits of linoleum found in the attics or occasionally, but not often, torn off the floor.

After a visit to the camp on 1 October, the General Secretary of the YMCA commented that: 'the ingenuity of the internees in improvising materials is astounding. Murals have been made with jam, porridge, ink, herring skins and olive oil. What a pity if that work were lost.'*

---

* Report by Mr Barwick in the *Auswaertige Amt* Archive RX ZV 189. One wonders how the report found its way to wartime Berlin.

House of Lords,
6, Stanley View,

Hutchinson, Douglas,
I.O.M.

25 decembre 1940

MENU
—

Escargots de Release
ou
Soupe de Patates Bonne Femme

Oie Rôtie à la Commandeur

Gigot d'Agneau
Riz à la Pékinoise
Orge perleé à la Szafir
Salade de légumes

Gâteau de Noël
Compote de Fruits

—

Moka

Deux Call Rolls

H. E. B.

Hutchinsons Camp menu, Christmas 1940

Hutchinsons was full of once and future Very Important Persons. In its early days it housed over thirty university professors of international repute, who had come to England at the invitation of either Oxford or Cambridge, as well as prominent journalists, musicians, writers, prominent businessmen, a plethora of talents. Here is a random list of a few names:

Professor Fehr:	Berlin oculist; pioneered operation on detached retina.
Heinrich Fraenkel:	Journalist with several anti-Nazi books to his credit. Chess editor *New Statesman and Nation*.
Richard Friedenthal:	Professor of German Literature. Wrote standard work on Goethe. Friend of Stefan Zweig, later his literary executor.
Professor Glass:	Musicologist.
Max Gruenhut:	Criminologist. Professor of Law at Bonn, later Oxford, where he created a new school.
Professor Hass-Heyer:	Textile designer, started School of Textiles in camp.
Professor Heinemann:	Philosopher.
Professor Koenigsberg:	Historian.
William Kohn:	Art Historian, specialist in Far Eastern Art.
Rudolf Olden:	Political editor '*Berliner Tagesblatt*'. After release drowned on way to America.
Alfred Unger:	Writer and graphologist. Whilst at Hutchinsons submitted to the War Office detailed plans on how to defeat Germany.
Egon Wellecz:	Composer and expert in early Byzantine music.

Another internee was Karl Leder, who had been the head of the School of Dancing at Dartington Hall, and had been co-choreographer of an anti-fascist ballet, called *Chronica*, with which the Ballet Joos was then touring South America under British Council sponsorship. Kurt Joos, the other creator of the ballet, head of this dance company, and pioneer of contemporary ballet in post First World War Europe, had been interned at Huyton, whilst the designer of the ballet, Heinz Heckroth had been shipped to Australia.

Charles Martin, director of Dartington Hall, bitterly complained to the Foreign Office that these internments were making a poor impression in South America, where the ballet was trying to promote Britain's image.

Not all the academic luminaries agreed to participate in the curriculum for the camp university. Some refused because they did not want to teach purely from memory, without their notes or books, others because they were too disturbed and did not want to contribute to any activities which could make incarceration more tolerable and thus give the authorities an excuse for prolonging it, but most of them willingly put their knowledge at the disposal of their fellow internees. It was not easy to plan a timetable or a course of several lectures because neither teacher nor pupil knew just for how long he would be around. This constraint applied in particular to the well-known academics who were amongst the first to be released again. In the light of these handicaps the organization of the camp university was a doubly creditable achievement.

The first lectures took place within three days of the opening of the camp, and eventually covered most of the subjects normally taught at a university. The whole enterprise was organized by an architect and town planner, Bruno Ahrends, who was ably assisted by a young art historian, Klaus Hinrichsen. Initially they had no books or teaching aids, nor any classrooms. The first classes were in fact informal get-togethers or tutorials on the lawn. But with great persistence and the help of the Commandant, they eventually got most of what they wanted. To show the catholicity of the subjects covered, and also their occasionally arcane nature, here is a typical timetable for the weekending 27 October 1940.

Sunday	11.45	Dr Reich: Agricultural Seminar: Bacteria in the economy of nature.
	4.00	Dr Wiener: Vignettes of History: From Prince Metternich's secret files.
	7.45	Professor Isaak: History of Therapeutics (continued).
	8.00	Mr Stadler: History of Mediaeval Culture (continued).
Monday	12.00	B. L. Frank: Physical Chemistry: Nutrition (Hormones; enzymes and vitamins).
	2.45	Mr Rosenberg: The Rise of English Democracy.
	4.00	Dr Wartenberg: From the Childhood of Aviation.

	4.30	Dr Unger: Greek Philosophy: Plato (continued).
	8.00	Recital: German Poets (Hoffmannstahl, Rilke and Altenberg).
	8.00	Dr Bratu: Circle Francais: Quelques aspects de la pensée francaise actuelle.
Tuesday	11.45	Chemical Colloquium.
	4.00	Mr Sheppard:* India the Jewel of the British Empire.
	8.00	Great Historians: Gibbon, Macaulay, and Trevelyan.
	8.00	Youth Group (see special programme).
Wednesday	4.00	Dr Lachmann: Law and Lawyers in England and in Germany.
	8.00	Technical School (see special programme).
	8.00	Reverend von Deutschhausen: Evangelical Bible Lesson.
Thursday	2.30	Concert: J. S. Bach.
	4.00	Dr Preuss:† Vignettes of History: Portraits from the Third Reich (Meissner, Schacht and Feder).
	8.00	Dr Krapalik: The Jewish Exodus from Vienna 1938/1939.
	8.00	Mr Zuntz: How the Bible came down to our Times.
Friday	12.00	B. L. Frank: Physical Chemistry.
	2.45	The Banishment of the Jews. Mr Loewenberg.
	4.30	Dr Unger: Greek Philosophy: Plato (continued).
	4.00	Debating Society Meeting.
	8.00	Study Group on Photography.
	8.00	Bruno Ahrends: Why Town and Country Planning is Indispensable.
Saturday	4.00	H. Bardt: The Economic Structure of South America and the Problems of Emigration.
	8.00	F. Burschell: Recital from Faust (continued).
	8.00	Professor Marx: Study Group on Goethe.

---

* He was not an internee but a Manx vicar who like several others went beyond the call of his pastoral care and helped the internees greatly. The attitude of the cloth was in contrast to that of most of the Manx officials.

† Preuss himself had been a senior civil servant in Berlin. Meissner was Hitler's State Secretary, the same post which he had held under his Weimar predecessors. Schacht was the economic wizard who had conquered inflation. Feder was the 'economic expert' of the Nazi Party.

Alongside the 'University of Liberal Arts', there existed also a technical school, which had been started by an electrical engineer, Dr Warschauer, who remained an enigma until the end. He bore a name which usually denoted Jewish origin but he denied all connection with Judaism. From the first day of his internment he claimed that it had all been a ghastly mistake and that he would be released within a few days as he was engaged on very secret and important war work; yet he remained inside until the end of the war. From time to time mysterious people would arrive from London and be closeted with him at the Commandantura. Nobody knew who they were and why they had come, but it was rumoured that they were from Scientific Intelligence, come to pick his brains. He was supposed to have invented a pioneering system of electronic eavesdropping, nobody in the camp then knew what that really meant, which he had then sold to the Gestapo in exchange for permission to leave Germany, but nobody knew anything for certain. He was not popular with his fellows but he was an able and efficient organizer of his technical school. He was also one of the very few who was able to put his inmates to some useful war work: the cleaving of sheets of mica.

An entertainment which puzzled many inmates, particularly the older ones and those who had not been long at liberty in Britain before they were arrested, were the meetings of the Debating Society, modelled on Oxford Union lines, even though there was a distinct shortage of dinner jackets and *pukkah* Oxford accents. Motions were discussed, such as: 'It is better to have loved and lost than not to have loved at all' or 'That this house considers that the pen is mightier than the sword'. Motions such as: 'This house will not fight for King and Country' were, of course, quite out of the question. It went beyond the comprehension of some of those curious enough to attend these debates, that people should want to argue for the sake of arguing irrespective of their own convictions. But for those taking part, it was all good fun to hone the edges of their debating prowess, even if the accent was peculiar and the syntax sometimes slipping. It may have sounded weird for those brought up in the German school system, or on a German *alma mater*, but it was a useful introductory lesson into the mysterious ways in which British democracy works.

A Hutchinson Camp March
(Song of the Internees)

TEMPO DI MARCIA

Words and Music by
EDW. E. VERDIERS

Hut-chin-son, Hut-chin-son, Hut-chin-son! 1. Pi - o - neers of Free-dom, fight for hu-man right, ral-ly round the stan-dard free, force was ne-ver right. Car-ry on the sa-cred cause where e-ver you may be, close up the ranks of free-dom, don't be a re-fu-gee!

Great Bri-tain is our Al-ly in the cause of Li-ber-ty, let's fight the force of E-vil to-ge-ther to be free! Free-dom will ne-ver die, our plight is not in vain, there'll be a day of Vic-to-ry, and we shall be free a-gain, for — Free-dom will ne-ver die, our plight is not in vain there'll be a day of Vic-to-ry, and we shall be free a-gain.

1. Pioneers of Freedom
fight for human right,
rally round the standard free,
force was never right.
Carry on the sacred cause
where ever you may be,
close up the ranks of Freedom,
don't be a refugee!

2. Swing the torch of Freedom,
hold it without fear,
never let's surrender
that which to us is dear.
Faith and Hope are pillars firm
firm as strong as our belief,
God will not fail grant us
His blessing in our grief!

'A Hutchinson Camp March'

One problem which could not be solved at Hutchinsons, nor at any other camp, was to turn idle and often able hands to some useful work. Constant suggestions were made in Parliament; the Home Secretary and his spokesmen always promised sympathetic consideration, but no internal workshops were ever established (except for the pilot mica project), and because of local and TUC opposition, no way was found to send working parties into outside factories. Many internees continued to be condemned to relative idleness. Only a few of them were able to help the farmers in their fields outside.

Physical activity was also restricted. In the morning PT classes were held on the square; some internees jogged around the perimeter fence rather like people on cruise liners running around the promenade deck. There were regular organized walks under escort (with an internee occasionally carrying the rifle of a tired soldier) and an occasional game of football. Only much later were the Hutchinson internees allowed to go for an escorted swim off the beach.

When, late in August 1940, recruitment began for the alien companies of the Auxiliary Military Pioneer Corps, the volunteers, awaiting their call to arms (or rather to unarmed service) were taken out of camp under escort and urged by the stentorian voice of the Sergeant Major, received their first squad-drill, a kind of pre-recruit indoctrination, which, bearing in mind that at the end of the exercise the recruits again reverted to the status of His Majesty's prisoners, was really bizarre.

Overshadowing everything else was the question of release. There were a few people who had no special desire to leave the camp, either because they were too scared to return to blitzed London, or because they had nowhere else to go nor nobody else to go to, and had found in the camp the security and companionship which they knew was lacking outside or because they were cross with Britain for interning them. They had not asked to be interned and saw no reason why they should now beg to be released. But whatever positive virtues people had managed to extract from internment, the overwhelming majority of internees had only one desire, to get out as fast as possible to get back to their families and their lives, to do their best bit in the common effort, to obtain redress for injustice which they had suffered and to wipe out the stigma with which they had been branded. Typical of the sentiments of many is the signature which a socialist ex-Mayor of Vienna, an internee at Hutchinsons, appended to a letter which he wrote to the new Home Secretary Herbert Morrison, whom he knew from the pre-war Socialist International. He signed himself: 'Maurer, internee of Schuschnigg's, then of Hitler's and now of Attlee's concentration camps.'

This was the time when Ghandi, the Mahatma, was very much in the news; he too had been interned during the war. The favourite catch phrase at Hutchinsons became 'Ma-hat-ma released' an Austrian variant of the 'proper' German, 'Man hat mich released', often an expression of wishful thinking.

When the government eventually published its first White Paper specifying what categories of people were eligible for release, there was deep disappointment at how very few people the eighteen categories included.[3] We will comment on these White Papers later, but it must be stressed that from the moment the first White Paper was issued, people became so preoccupied with trying to fathom out how they could fit or wriggle into any of the available categories, that camp activities necessarily suffered. Once the first trickle of releases came through, the thought uppermost in many people's minds was: Could I possibly be amongst the next batch? Influential friends and lawyers outside were mobilized; the very fortunate or well-connected managed to get their cases raised in a parliamentary question. Every morning, when the names of those about to be released were to be posted, one felt like one was attending a draw for the Irish Sweepstake. Departing friends were loaded with messages and requests; those remaining drew tighter together. Life went on but thoughts were becoming progressively concentrated on the morrow outside.

I I 'I do like to be beside the seaside'

HUTCHINSONS HAD KURT SCHWITTERS; Onchan Camp had another one of these larger-than-life characters, tall and rotund Jack Bilbo. An adventurer by nature, an artist by talent, a fibber by inclination, he was something of a modern Baron Munchausen. His parents, called Baruch, had been theatrical costumiers in Berlin. He had run away from home at the age of seventeen, joined a circus, roamed the world, and spent some years in the USA. He had run a café in Spain and had come to Britain in the wake of the Spanish Civil War. He was a painter and sculptor of no mean talent; he was also an author, who had written a book entitled *I Was Al Capone's Bodyguard*, relating his adventures in the gangster-ridden Chicago of the nineteen twenties.

In the camp he regaled his gullible fellow inmates with tales of hair-raising adventures. One day he announced that he would be giving a lecture 'Why I have been silent until now', hinting that in reality he was a Very Famous Person, but refusing to be drawn any further. To a capacity audience he later revealed that he, Jack Bilbo, was also Ben Traven, the author of *The Treasure of the Sierra Madre*, *The Totenschiff*, and of many other novels with a South American background; the man who had mystified journalists and critics for years, whom nobody had ever seen and who was supposed to be living in total seclusion somewhere in the Mexican hinterland. He told his audience that he was only now disclosing his secret because he wanted to help them. The President of Mexico had been his attorney in days past; he had sent him a wire asking him to take him away from his imprisonment and not only him, but all the others who were equally victims of an unjust persecution. He was sure his great friend would not let him down. Not everybody believed him, but there were quite a few who thereafter scanned the horizon every day to see whether they could spot the promised ship from Mexico. An internee, working in the Orderly Office, actually saw the cable; Bilbo must have talked the censoring officer into letting him send it.

Like everybody else, Bilbo tried his hardest to get out. When one morning on sick parade the Medical Officer asked him why he was reporting sick, he replied: 'I want a woman, I want to be released.' The White Paper had no special category covering sexual frustration as grounds for release, so Bilbo was forced to apply to join the alien companies of the Pioneer Corps. He did not stay long there and was soon discharged as being unsuitable for hard work. He then opened an art gallery, first in London and then in Weybridge. In 1948 he published his autobiography, an elaborately printed, exquisitely illustrated book.[1] In this he admitted that he was indeed not Ben Traven nor had he ever been anywhere near Al Capone and that the pictures in his book showing the two gentlemen together had been faked. Eventually he went back to the town of his birth and opened up a curio shop in West Berlin. To people who visited him there he is supposed to have retracted his retractions. He is dead now.

He gave Onchan a special ambience, but otherwise the camp was not very different from Hutchinsons. Its approximately 1,500 inmates belonged to both categories 'B' and 'C'; it had been opened for business a few weeks before Hutchinsons and, unlike Hutchinsons, had been a last staging post for many who were shipped overseas.

The camp consisted of a number of the usual boarding houses, strung along the seafront and isolated by barbed wire fences. Its basic organization – internal self-government to the extent to which it was compatible with good order, discipline and security – was similar to all the other camps. The 'camp father' was called here 'camp supervisor'. In addition to the normal duties of his position he had been given another, most unenviable task, namely to select internees for overseas deportation. This had not been the procedure in any of the mainland camps, but in Onchan the army neatly passed the buck, and the inevitable odium, of selection to the internees themselves.

Early in July the supervisor was told that three hundred internees had to be readied for overseas shipment within forty-eight hours, no destination being mentioned. How the quota was to be filled was up to the supervisor and his staff. If he could not get enough volunteers it would be up to him to pick the rest by whatever criteria he considered fairest. This caused an uproar in the camp and for the next two days was the sole topic of excited discussion. Only a few volunteered; some of them were adventurous youngsters without any particular ties in England. Others were transmigrants waiting for US quota visas. They had been told that it would be easier to enter the States from Canada or Australia. It turned out that the very opposite was the case.

The supervisor then decided to put on his list all unmarried internees, including the formidable Jack Bilbo. Bilbo threatened that he would have to be carried out of the camp struggling and was eventually again taken off the list. The quota was still not filled; the supervisor refused to force any married men and the Commandant agreed that it would be cruel to send family men overseas. He advised the War Office that he had been unable to fill his quota, which then most likely was made up from mainland internees, none of whom were given any advice or choice, nor even told that their destination was an overseas Dominion. This particular human cargo was sent to Canada. A few days later the married internees, whose wives were also interned on the island, were given a chance to meet their spouses for the first time so that they could decide whether they wanted to go to Australia together, but again only a few volunteered.*

The cultural and educational activities blossomed at Onchan and at most of the other camps as richly as at Hutchinsons. There were art exhibitions – the camp housed Ludwig Meidner, a painter of considerable talent; one of the few people who had no desire to be released and was happy with his paintbrush and his peaceful surroundings. There were regular chamber music concerts and solo recitals with instruments provided by charitable organizations; there was a cabaret and even a 'Café Corner House'. The camp university had a regular lecture programme containing a variety of literary, philosophical, technical and scientific subjects. There was no lack of teaching talent. The inmates published a cyclostyled weekly newspaper, the *Onchan Pioneer*, which cost two pence and of which altogether forty-seven editions were issued. The last one was published on 20 July 1941† 'in great haste because the camp is in the process of being closed down.' The swan-song issue contained an appreciation of the Reverend Duffield: 'Never forget the Vicar of Onchan who has been our greatest friend.' Just as at Hutchinsons, the local Church of England vicar had, as a matter of course, included the internees in his pastoral care, regardless of their religion. He had lectured them on 'The English Point of View'; he had been one of their lifelines to the outside world; he had told the authorities: 'Restore the freedom to the refugee to

---

* Their meeting has already been described in Chapter Eight.
† The last four issues are available in the Wiener Library.

whom you have granted hospitality. Let them work with you in the common struggle against Nazism.'[2]

The tensions, the emotional and psychological problems endemic in any situation where humans are under abnormal conditions, confined and condemned to live in close proximity, posed the same challenge at Onchan as elsewhere. As in other camps there was a certain amount of homosexuality, but most of the men had practised it before internment. There was even a couple who had emigrated together from Germany; one of them was an 'Aryan', the other a Jew; in Nazi eyes, a felony compounded by racial pollution. At Onchan they were given an attic room all by themselves and lived in harmony with all the other residents of their boarding house.

At Hutchinsons and at Onchan, the general mood of the internees was on the whole reasonably buoyant, with people trying to wring the best out of an unpleasant, inescapable situation. There was a lot more despair and despondency at another camp, the Central Promenade Camp, right in the centre of Douglas. Its two thousand inmates were quartered in the usual terraced boarding houses strung along the seafront. The barbed wire fence had been staked right along the centre of the promenade; therefore there was much less space available for the internees than at Hutchinsons; on the other hand, they had direct access to the beach. The inmates were nearly all 'B' and 'C' cases who had been interned in May when the coastal counties had been declared protected areas; 1,700 of them were Jews.* Amongst them were several rabbis who had been well known in Germany. One of them had, until his internment, been looking after a Brighton and Hove congregation. Another was a lecturer at Edinburgh University. When the threat of deportations was very much in the air, they together addressed a *cri de coeur* to the Agudas Israel, a Jewish Welfare Organization, stating that the prospect of being packed away like cattle, sent to another continent, completely separated from one's family, was unbearable. 'Have we to abandon all hope?' they asked.

A Central Promenade Camp alumnus, newly released, complained in a letter to the *New Statesman* that 'many of the internees there are elderly men, suffering from a variety of diseases, unable to participate in the daily walks on which they are accompanied by guards carrying fixed bayonets.' He also said that the recreational facilities were pitifully inadequate.[3]

---

* According to a report by Rabbi Schonfeldt who visited the camps on behalf of the Chief Rabbi – at Bloomsbury House.

Dr Bell, the Bishop of Chichester, paid a visit to the camp. On 6 August in the House of Lords he criticized the 'unforgettable depressing picture, seeing men of high quality wandering aimlessly about behind high pallisades of barbed wire.' According to the Lord Bishop, one hundred and fifty of the internees had previously been incarcerated in German concentration camps. Amongst the internees was Sebastian Haffner (real name Raimund Pretz), the author of *Germany–Jekyll and Hyde*, perhaps at that time the best known anti-Hitler publicist in Britain, and after the war a distinguished *Observer* correspondent. His original tribunal had put him in category 'B'; he was therefore interned rather early on, but again released for a while in order to proof-read his book. By the time it was published he was back again behind barbed wire.* Another newspaper man in the camp was Walter Nissen, London correspondent of the *Basler Nationalzeitung*, who in his dispatches had always taken a pro-British line. The cartoonist Willy Wolpe who had lampooned Hitler for years, was also in Central Promenade Camp.

Mary Hills' impressions of this camp were similar to the Bishop's.[4] She thought conditions there were worse than at Wandsworth Jail. There was not a bit of green grass anywhere, no central recreation area, no meeting hall; all that people could do was to wander about aimlessly. Her verdict: 'Doubtless historians will in future argue whether National Socialism's racial mysticism and appeal to base instincts have been more or less cruel than the British who after offering asylum then imprisoned those who accepted it.' This is no doubt an emotive and quite unfair comparison, but it is indicative of the depth of feeling which visits to the camps aroused in some well-wishers.

But although conditions and morale at Central Promenade Camp seem to have been much worse than in other camps, intellectual activity prospered just as much. They had their little university conducting lectures and seminars on a variety of subjects, and according to another released internee, whose letter the *Spectator* published on 29 November 1940, many internees did accept the situation and tried to make life as bearable as possible.

---

* Haffner was not the only author with the distinction of being rewarded by internment for anti-Hitler publicity. Franz Borkenau's: *The Totalitarian Enemy* was published shortly before he found himself on the *Dunera* en route to Australia. Heinrich Fraenkel was another well-known journalist interned despite his many anti-Nazi articles.

'I do like to be beside the seaside'

In the three other and smaller camps on the Isle of Man housing German and Austrian refugees, Mooragh near Ramsey on the East coast, Peveril near Peel on the West coast, and Sefton outside Douglas, life was organized on very similar lines as elsewhere. The inmates were plagued by the same frustrations, the same human failings; they were encouraged by the same challenges and achievements; they had their artistic and educational activities, their café-house gossipers and card-players, their irritable old and irreverent young, their bickerers and pacifiers, their mopers and their cheerers. As everywhere else, internment brought out the best in some, the worst in others; it scarred and it improved, often all at the same time.

12 *The Women's Camps*

What is the barbed wire doing,
Set up everywhere I see?
Is it meant to keep the world out
Or protect the world from me?
            Livia Laurent[1]

LESS THAN FOUR THOUSAND German and Austrian women were
interned during the war. Their mix was different from the men; their
camps were organized on different lines; they were under the
exclusive suzerainty of the Home Office with no confused responsibilities between two Departments of State as was the case with the
male internees. But their physical and emotional problems – fear and
anger, despondency and hope, rejection and acceptance – were not
very different.

None of them were sent overseas. But whilst only a very few men
passed through any of HM prisons, and then only for a night or two, the
majority of the women were incarcerated for several weeks, alongside
common criminals. Some were in provincial jails, but most of them
were put into Holloway Prison in North London. Not all of them
were fastidious, middle-class wives and daughters, brought up in
cultured, sheltered, aseptic homes, but even for those who came from
a tougher background or whom life of late had treated roughly, the
trauma of being clapped into a common jail was worse than the men's
first impressions of their improvised camps. There might be some aura
of adventure about a race track, a circus quarters, a bivouac of tents,
even a rat-infested cotton mill; there was none about a notorious
jail.

Because no ordinary category 'C' women were ever interned, the
ratio between refugee and non-refugee women differed from the
men's. At outbreak of war a number of German domestic servants had
been employed in mostly upper-class British households. Some of
these were interned immediately; a larger number availed themselves
of repatriation to the fatherland. The rest had been examined by the
tribunals and put into a category 'B'. They were mostly apolitical but

with a few exceptions their loyalty was clear-cut; they were Germans and they wanted Germany to win the war.

But a considerable number of these domestics were not professional servants at all, but refugees, educated middle-class girls whose only chance of being admitted to England and of earning a living, had been to go into domestic service. Some married couples, perhaps a lawyer with his teacher wife, had been working as a team of butler and cook; some single girls were parlourmaids or 'tweenies'. At first it had been a bit strange for them to dine in the scullery and to be addressed as 'Rosenthal' or 'Kohn' without any prefix. As soon as they were allowed to do so, most of them moved on to do war work in the factories; they much preferred it.

In addition there were also at Holloway a number of non-refugee women in a higher social bracket: some were wives of German businessmen and engineers, others British-born women who had become German by marriage or women who had been arrested in distant parts of the Empire and been brought to England for intern-ment. All the others were female refugees who through bad luck or the whim of a tribunal had been put into category 'B'.

The round-up of the 'B' women began on 26 May. The police arrived in the early hours of the morning and often had to wait for the women to get dressed before taking them away. Some of those who wanted to were allowed to take their children with them. Amongst the first 1,200 arrested were a good sprinkling of infants. Several of the older women were in tears but some of the younger ones joked with the policemen.[2]

A typical case is a young Jewish journalist, Margot Pottlitzer, whose only chance to earn a living had been to work as governess to a family in Gloucestershire. The chairman of her tribunal in Cheltenham, quite a well-meaning gentleman, had created a classification all of its own, a kind of 'upper C', declaring her and all others before him to be genuine victims of Nazi oppression, but imposing upon them all the same, all the restrictions reserved for 'B' cases of doubtful loyalty. Hence they were all interned in due course. The young lady was by then looking after some children in Norfolk, where, on 4 June, a Chief Inspector of Police in charge of the district personally came to arrest her. He told her where she was going and advised her to take warm underwear along as it might be quite cold in Holloway, and also on the Isle of Man. Most courteously he gave her ample time to pack her things and after driving her to King's Lynn station, both he and his wife accompanied the girl in a locked first-class compartment and then a taxi, right up to the grim gates of Holloway Prison, where they shook hands with her and wished her well.

The big reception area there had been subdivided into two parts; one was reserved for the ordinary prisoners who had been returned from sentencing and were awaiting transfer; the other for the refugees who were constantly being brought in in small squads from various parts of the country. The refugee women hung around this area for varying lengths of time, some of them for as long as three days, sleeping on the floor, getting on the first day only a cup of tea and two biscuits; otherwise being left entirely to their own devices.

Eventually they were called up, one after the other. Their money and cigarette lighters were taken away; their personal details recorded and their identity papers retained. Despite their protests a wardress examined their hair for lice. Thereafter they were locked into a bathroom for their ablutions with the water being turned on and off from the outside by a wardress. The tub was so filthy that many disdained to immerse themselves in it. They regretted it afterwards because they did not get another chance for a proper ablution for several weeks. Next they were issued with bedsheets and then taken to an upper floor where they could pick their own favourite single cell in a wing which had been specially cleared for the internees. From then on they had few contacts with the ordinary prisoners except for Sunday religious services, to which many went regardless of their own denomination, sometimes to more than one, just in order to escape their cell isolation and to meet other women. No Jewish services were held, the usually very small intake of ordinary prisoners of Jewish persuasion would not have warranted it, but they did have full support from various Jewish welfare organizations. The Hon. Lily Montagu, sister of Lord Swaythling and *Grande Dame* of Liberal Judaism, visited them and was appalled by what she saw: 'There are Jewish women there between sixty and seventy years of age, all victims of Nazi persecution, all in miserable solitary confinement.'[3]

British women interned under Defence Regulation 18b were housed next to the refugees. On the whole they were better off because they had relatives and friends who could visit them regularly and bring with them extra food and comforts. The refugees had fewer and poorer friends and relatives and as inadequate censorship arrangements were holding up their letters for days, it was difficult for them to get in touch with people outside.

The wife of the Hamburg shipowner, who has been mentioned earlier, also found herself in Holloway. She had been arrested in Bristol a few days after her husband, but had been allowed to take her five-month-old daughter with her. Because there were no facilities to look after a baby in an ordinary cell, she was put into a ward in the prison hospital, but when her bed was needed for an urgent operation case, she was told that she had to get rid of the child. With the kind and quite illegal assistance of a prison officer, she managed to contact her mother-in-law who came to collect the baby, whilst she joined the other prisoners in their exclusive wing.

On the whole the interned women at Holloway were treated like prisoners on remand. They could wear their own clothes and, if they had money, which few of them had to any extent, could buy extra food and comforts. Once a day they were allowed to exercise in the yard for one hour. However, many escaped the claustrophobic loneliness of their solitary cells by volunteering for various chores such as fetching food from the kitchens, dishing out mugs of tea and breakfast porridge from big zinc buckets, sweeping and washing the corridor floors, or working in the garden, the linen store, or – most coveted of all – in the prison library.

Despite the barriers to intercommunication and the ban on socializing from one cell to another, the prisoners soon established a frail but viable community life. They lent each other what few books they had brought along; they shared with each other what fruit, cakes or chocolate a prisoner had obtained from a parcel or a visitor. They tried to lift up each other's spirits and for many of the older refugees this was much more needed than physical sustenance. Although some of the servant girls were secretly sewing swastika flags to greet the conquering heroes of a successful invasion, relations between them and the Jewish refugee women were on the whole not bad, certainly better than in the men's camps. This may be due to the fact that the more rabid Nazi maidens who had been interned during the first few weeks of the war, had by then been repatriated. A total of sixty such women had been sent home via Holland. Of these, forty had been domestic servants, all members of the Nazi Labour Front organization, who, according to a report by the official in the German Foreign Office responsible for looking after Germans interned abroad, had been arrested at the outbreak of war. The total number of women interned up to the end of 1939 was 180. Sixty of them were repatriated, twenty-five were Jewish and the rest did not want to come home because they did not want to leave behind their interned husbands.[4]

One of these repatriated Nazi ladies complained to the German Foreign Office that in Holloway they had been kept in single, unheated cells with stone floors.[5] They had to sleep in their underwear which they could only change once a week; their bedlinen was changed every six weeks; they each had one towel to dry their bodies and their crockery. Food was so poor, she says, that they all suffered from recurring stomach upsets; they had no books or newspapers. This woman had been imprisoned for the first few days in Manchester Jail, where, she claimed, she shared her cell with a convicted murderess under sentence of death. By the time the 'B' women refugees reached Holloway in May and June 1940 some of these alleged shortcomings no longer existed and conditions had been progressively improved in so far as this was possible.

Most of the 'B' women stayed at Holloway for between four and six weeks. As accommodation became available on the Isle of Man, they were shifted in batches. The journalist-governess was told at midnight one night to pack up her things and, together with others, was then moved to another wing of the prison, so recently vacated by an earlier batch of transferees that the sheets had remained unchanged. They remained locked in their new cells for three days without any exercise or outside contact, then were taken in coaches to Euston Station, thence railed in locked compartments to Liverpool where they stayed the night at a seamen's hostel. The Bishop of Liverpool visited them there and tried to comfort them. Next morning they crossed the sea to the blessed isle.

A Jewish seamstress from Vienna, who had worked in England as a parlourmaid, was arrested in May and not allowed to take any suitcase with her. 'You will be away only for a couple of days' she was told. For the next eight weeks she only had the clothes she stood in. She and a number of others, including sniffling children and crying babes-in-arms, were taken straight to Liverpool and lodged in prison there.

Two days later the women were marched along some main streets to the dockside with women bystanders spitting at them and shouting anti-Nazi obscenities. Some of the marching women remembered Vienna, just two years before, when they or their menfolk on their way to concentration camps, had to suffer similar indignities. Only then the obscenities had been anti-Jewish.

The seamstress remembers that the ship carrying them across was so overcrowded that she and many others, including children, had to stand up throughout the whole storm-tossed journey. But she soon recovered her spirits when the storm abated, the skies cleared and she saw the lovely island coming closer with the sun setting behind it.

* * *

Cast your eye for a moment on the Isle of Man; a delectable spot with plenty of good food; a spot where many of us would like to spend a short holiday. Well, there are some people who are spending a very long holiday there at the British taxpayer's expense but they are not British. They are interned aliens, all avowed or suspected enemies of this country. The manner in which they are being coddled is driving many people on the island pretty well crazy. Our treatment of these people carries humanitarianism to the verge of insanity. A correspondent writes: 'the whole island is furious because mixed camps are to be allowed. We ask ourselves why British soldiers exiled from their wives and sweethearts should be compelled to assist in the spectacle of men and women living happily together making love, breeding more Nazis? The women are the worst of the lot. They openly boast that their children are being brought up to revere Hitler as a god.' 'Resent' seems a mild word under these circumstances.[6]

This was written by Beverley Nichols, whom Lafitte described at that time in his book, just published, as an 'ex-pacifist, ex-Buchmanite, ex-Mosley supporter, ex-pro-Nazi',[7] just a year after these men and women had been interned and when at last married couples had been promised permission to share their internment. Many of them were middle-aged Jewish couples who might have had some genetic difficulties in 'breeding more Nazis'. An internee's comment, in the *New Statesman*, on Beverley Nichols' calumny, was that: 'We learnt to "revere" Hitler in Dachau and Buchenwald.'[8]

The *Daily Telegraph*, almost a year earlier, wrote of a holiday atmosphere at one of the women's camps, 'the women sunbathing in their beach-wear and having unlimited tennis and bathing and the shopkeepers doing a good business.'[9] It all sounds too delightful and desirable. ('Anyone for tennis?') What was the reality?

On 30 May 1940, Sir John Anderson had announced in the House that 3,200 women between the ages of sixteen and sixty had been interned. In November he told the Cabinet that the number had risen to nearly four thousand.[10] Out of those three hundred were expectant mothers.[11] This was approximately ten per cent of the total number of

German and Austrian women in the UK.* By the end of the following year 1,198 were still interned of whom 430 belonged to category 'A'; 604 to 'B' and 171 to 'C'.†

The women were housed in two camps on the Rushen peninsula, one in Port St Mary and the other in Port Erin. The peninsula faces Erin Bay with its rocky coast, interspersed by beaches, and with green hills as a backdrop. This is the most attractive part of the isle and if lovely landscape were all that is needed to make people happy, the women certainly had it.

Unlike in the men's camps the women were not totally segregated from the indigenous population, nor were these really fenced-in, self-contained camps in any sense of the word. Major parts of the two villages had been taken over; boarding houses and small hotels had been requisitioned but the landladies and hotel staff had not been evacuated. Amidst the sequestered houses were others in which the local inhabitants continued to live. The various shops in the villages served both the natives and the internees. There was a single wire fence all along the extended perimeter of the villages beyond which the interned women were not allowed to stray and through which only such locals were allowed to pass as had legitimate business within. The relationship between the shopkeepers and those natives who were left inside on the one hand, and the interned women on the other, were correct but impersonal; fraternization was frowned upon. In one of the houses the landlady's husband was a local CID officer; he barely exchanged the time of day with his wife's houseguests.

The landladies were the key people to morale in the two camps. They were responsible for housing and feeding their guests for which they were paid £3 per week per person. No doubt they would have preferred to continue catering for their regular holiday sojourners. Many resented the imposition. The accommodation varied; some houses could only cater for six women; others for as many as fifty.

---

* An undated memo by the Home Secretary to the War Cabinet (FO 371/25244) gives the exact figure as 41,400 whilst the other memo (WP(G) (40) 309) mentions a figure of 38,500.

† Herbert Morrison replying to Edmund Harvey on 11 November 1941.
During a meeting of the Council for Aliens on 12 December Eleanor Rathbone asked how class 'C' women could possibly be on the Isle when they had been told by Osbert Peake that none had ever been interned. The Home Office representative replied that one hundred of them had been interned on personal grounds; the remainder had been re-classified as 'A' by Regional Advisory Committees. But what about such 'C' plus cases as the journalist/governess?

The largest establishment was the Ballequinie Hotel which took several hundred internees and which had retained its own staff. In all other places the interned women were expected to perform all the usual household chores, except for the cooking, which was done by the lady of the house.

As in the men's camps, the standard sleeping accommodation was double beds. The same initial embarrassments arose, but instead of one bed partner pitching her mattress on the floor, the women rolled up a blanket and laid it in the middle as a demarcation line. Lord Farringdon complained in the House of Lords on 6 August about a terrified sixteen-year-old Jewish girl who had to share her bed with a bullying Nazi maiden, but such unholy bed-fellowships seem to have been rare.

Many of the girls and women had been together for some time, usually in Holloway Jail; they had formed groups of the like-minded, and struck up friendships, they stuck together when on arrival they were allocated to various houses. Children were invariably put together with their mothers. Some mothers had at first left their children behind in the care of somebody else, but once they had settled down the children joined them.

Relationships with the landladies varied, depending on the extent to which the social background and interests between landlady and inmate jelled. One woman, who said that the internees in her house were all 'intellectuals', did not get on at all with her fierce Scottish landlady, who was simply not on the same wavelength as they were. Another, less sophisticated, girl got on so well with her landlady that when she was finally released the landlady asked her to stay and see the war through in her house in safety and comfort.

The life of the women was naturally less regulated and disciplined than that of the men. They had to be punctual for their meals, they had nightly curfews, but there were no morning or evening roll-calls, no parades, no martinet Sergeant Majors. But they faced the same basic problems which the sudden transformation was throwing up for all internees, regardless of sex: how to tackle the void, how to organize a viable community and how to occupy themselves with work and leisure activities. They had the additional problems caused by the presence of a considerable number of children, from babies to teen-agers, problems of accommodation, occupation and education.

The men's camps were largely self-governing and self-disciplining communities with the military merely guarding them and exercising a limited degree of supervision. On the Rushen peninsula the Home

Office-appointed Commandant played a much more direct part. This was Dame Joanna Cruikshank, a former Matron-in-Chief of the British Red Cross Society, assisted by Miss Lockwood, her deputy. The *Sunday Express* described her as the 'ruler of this kingdom with wide arbitrary powers'.[12] Dame Joanna's task cannot have been an easy one. She had to reconcile the women's complaints – justified or otherwise – with the exigencies of the situation, arbitrate between the various disparate groups and interests, pacify the more militant amazons, help the less articulate ones, encourage some activities, discourage others. Comments on her from the inmates vary: some describe her as a rather formidable dragon, others were favourably impressed by her willingness to help wherever she could. But she certainly imposed the stamp of her personality on the camps in a way which by the nature of things, the military commandants did not in any of the men's camps. Dame Joanna resigned after a year and was replaced by a male Chief Inspector of Scotland Yard, who was also put in charge of the married camp, which by then had at last been established.

Once the internees had settled down in their boarding houses and had taken the measure of each other, they lost no time in organizing a community life. Two of the challenges with which they came to grips quickly and successfully were work and education; how to occupy themselves and how to occupy their children. To create work for themselves had a two-fold purpose: to beat boredom and, for those who had no money, to earn some. It could have had also another, more important purpose, namely to contribute to the war effort. Sylvia Pankhurst[13] urged the Government 'to put these women, many of whom desire to do something for this country which has given them asylum, to some useful war work', but somehow the various government departments who would have beeen concerned with this could never agree how such work could be organized within any of the internment camps.

But the internees, under the guidance of Mrs Borchardt, an enterprising young woman with lots of spunk and ideas, soon set to work.* There had been earlier isolated efforts to occupy the time usefully. One woman had made her own spinning wheel, then collected bits of fluff which straying sheep had left on fences and on the grass, spun it into wool, washed and woven it. Other women knitted with wool

---

* See Ruth Borchardt: *The Services Exchange in an Internment Camp*, Friends' Book Centre, 1943, in which she describes her work.

purchased in the shop. But, as Ruth Borchardt puts it – 'after we had used up all our savings and done all the knitting we ever wanted to do' – she set up a co-operative where everybody was encouraged to do what she knew best. Little workshops were established for sewing, dressmaking and shoe-repairing; a hairdressing salon and a laundry were set up; squads were formed for woodchopping and gardening. Tokens were issued in this 'Services Exchange' as payment for work done, which could then be exchanged for goods and services performed by others. The dressmaker could get her hair done that way, the laundress could get her shoes repaired. Community economics had reverted to a primitive barter stage. Later on the system became more sophisticated; the tokens could also be used to purchase tickets for the library, for concerts, for coffee and pastries in the '*Konditorei*'. For half a day's work each internee, regardless of her skill or her 'productivity', got two tokens. The scheme was announced on 19 September 1940: 1,200 women wanted to join immediately. There was never enough work for all of them and work had to be rationed to a maximum of six half days per week. Many women thus learnt new skills. There were occasional problems, particularly in respect of the sharing of tools, which were always in short supply, but on the whole Robert Owen would have approved.

The scheme worked well for over a year; at its height some five thousand tokens were in daily circulation, each worth about three pence. It only began to run down when releases started in earnest. It was discontinued in November 1941. Ruth Borchardt's epitaph was: 'Planned economy in a test tube'.

Schooling was organized for children of all ages. Fortunately there was no shortage of willing and qualified helpers. Two Frobel-trained nursery school teachers started a kindergarten. Minna Specht had been the head of a progressive school in Germany which after the advent of Hitler had transferred to North Wales. She had been interned in May and was now put in charge of the camp school. She ran it on the same advanced lines which she had pioneered in Germany, the teachers and pupils all being on first name terms, with a minimum of enforced discipline and a maximum of hoped-for co-operation from the pupils. Under the abnormal conditions under which the community was living, these methods did not always prove successful. Some of the older children began to run wild; others, however, profited and found it difficult afterwards to get used again to more conventional discipline and teaching methods in English schools.

For the older people there were the usual lectures on a variety of esoteric subjects as well as handicraft and art classes; there were concerts and amateur theatricals; there was the beach and there were walks along the seafront. Relations between the various groups were on the whole satisfactory. One of the internees belonged to a Judeo-Christian sect which aimed at combining the best of both religions. She did much to bring the two groups together, so much that in December a combined Christmas and Chanukkah play was staged, which meshed together the Christmas and the Maccabean story. It was a great success.*

Amongst the non-refugee women there were some who openly professed Nazi sympathies and were heard to indulge in snide anti-semitic remarks; they were a minority but they obviously caused problems. Mrs Corbett Ashby of the Quaker's Aliens' Protection Committee complained to Sir Herbert Emerson, the High Commissioner for Refugees, in January 1941, that some of these Nazi women were 'exercising terror over some middle class Jewesses who had led a sheltered existence before the Nazis had come to power'.[14] These Nazi women often shared rooms with the Jewesses; some were working in the camp administrative offices and thus could read the Jewish women's correspondence – and all because the authorities had refused to make a distinction. Emerson, however, denied all this; he had recently visited the Rushen camps and had seen no evidence of this, nor had Dame Joanna received any complaints. Eventually the non-refugee women were given the chance to move into a house of their own, away from Jewish 'contamination', but a surprisingly large number of them refused to live in an exclusively Nazi environment and preferred to stay put.

One of the better-known internees was Richard Wagner's twenty-one-year-old granddaughter, Friedelinde. On 12 December 1940, the *Daily Mail*, who called her Freda, quoted a statement by Osbert Peake that, although Miss Wagner had published several articles with an anti-Hitler tinge, she was known to have been a personal friend of Hitler, and that the reports from HM consuls in Switzerland, where the girl had previously lived, were not altogether favourable. But, like the grandson of the Kaiser, Wagner's granddaughter – who had fallen out with her British-born Nazi mother, Winifred – was opposed to

---

* The *Manchester Guardian* of 23 November 1940 has a graphic description of the camp and features an interview with Dame Joanna.

Nazism and did not associate with the Nazi elements in the camp and behaved with every propriety towards her fellow refugees.

So many women living together under such unusual conditions in such close proximity, created many problems on a personal level. Nerves often became frayed; ephemeral tiffs were blown up out of all proportions; envy, sloth, all the other deadly sins were bound to prosper. The absence of male company also did not help to smoothe personal relations. It may sound like male chauvinism, but it does appear as if, on the whole, a lot of men in an exclusively male environment can bear each other's company for longer and with less friction, than women can.

On the other hand, intense personal friendships were also formed. Some of these resulted in physical relationships, but lesbianism – as far as can be ascertained – existed only on a limited scale and – as with homosexuality in the men's camps – was accepted and tolerated by the others. It very occasionally led to triangular feuds. The women saw the Manxmen living in their enclave daily, but the only man to whom they could really talk was the local clergyman. One woman says he was mobbed whenever he passed down her street.

The married women whose husbands had also been interned had worries of their own. For those whose husbands had been deported overseas, it was a question of coming to terms with a long separation; it was different for those whose husbands were in camps not far away on the same island. They were at first not allowed to meet them; letters from one camp to another had to pass through the grossly overworked Central Censoring Office in Liverpool and it sometimes took weeks before a letter reached a recipient some thirty miles away.

From August 1940 onwards, regular monthly meetings were arranged. The married men from the various camps were brought to a hotel in Port Erin where they would be reunited with their wives and children, exchange gifts, often handmade by them, wander about and talk, laugh and cry with each other. There was of course no real privacy; the meetings were emotionally charged, as they usually are for prisoners; the women found it hard to overcome a mood of despondency once the husbands had left again. Almost from the outset the married couples inside, and their friends and patrons outside, were pressing the Home Office to set up a married camp where the family could once again function as a unit.

Typical of this agitation was a joint letter from E. M. Forster, the Duke of Newcastle and Ralph Vaughan Williams, printed in *The*

Times of 23 July 1940, in which they added their voice to the pleas for mixed camps.

Time and time again the Home Office spokesman confirmed that this was indeed the intention. But it was not until a year later, when the majority of the male and female internees had again been released, that the smaller of the two camps was finally converted into married quarters, where couples were able again to live as nearly-normal a life as the somewhat unusual conditions would permit.

Undoubtedly the two women's camps had their attractive features. They were situated in the best part of the island; the women were safe from bombing raids; inside their enclaves they had almost unlimited freedom; they had enough to eat and well-stocked shops to buy from, if they had the money. If they wanted to, there was enough to occupy their minds and hands. They had their beaches, their cinemas, their self-created entertainments. It sounds almost as if Beverley Nichols' description – notwithstanding his malicious intent – is correct. An interned woman in fact wrote a letter to the *News Chronicle* saying: 'We have been sent to the safest, most beautiful part of Britain. We will never forget what Britain has done for us refugees.'[15]

Yet these women were not really free. They had been forcefully separated from their husbands, from their families, from their normal environment; they were living in a wholly artificial atmosphere where nothing could be locked away, nothing was private, where one bore a stigma and resented it. None of them had asked to be 'cuddled' in relative safety and comfort. If there had been a psephologist amongst them and if she had taken a poll on who wanted to stay for the duration and who would accept the alternative of working all day on a lathe in a war factory in the East End of London or on a farm in the Shires, or of serving as an ATS amazon, there seems to be no doubt which of the two alternatives the great majority of the refugee women would have selected.

13 The Government Bows to the Storm

'Nothing shows more emphatically the essential democratic nature of our war time government than the debates about the internment of aliens, about the exercise of powers of arrest without trial, and the creation of special courts. These debates occurred in July and August 1940 when German guns were firing across the Channel, when invasion of these islands threatened, when German fighters and bombers were seeking supremacy in Britain's air and when two thirds of all broadcasting stations in Europe were prophesying the immediate downfall of the British Empire.'[1]

That is how a great British constitutional lawyer described the parliamentary debates held under siege conditions in a blacked-out chamber, at a moment when history was marking time, when citizens were bracing themselves for the ordeals ahead and government was making frantic efforts to replace what had been lost on the beaches of France, to husband what had been saved, particularly in the air, and to ward off whatever was in store. During those weeks, when the survival of the island literally hung in balance, when there were myriads of urgent and complex questions crowding in on government, at that very moment the innate sense of fairness of many public figures and private people of Britain, their feeling that a grave injustice had been done to a lot of hapless refugees, forced the government to devote time and effort to problems which were by no means intractable, but which were puny compared with the threat which the country was facing. As 'Argus' in the *Contemporary Review* of January 1941 puts it: 'these debates gave the lie to the old dictum *"inter arma silent leges"*.'

For the next few weeks there were not many sittings of either House of Parliament where ministers did not have to answer questions or make statements about general internment policy or individual cases. There were several adjournment debates at the opening of the new session of Parliament, a part of the debate on the King's Speech from the Throne was devoted to it. Three White Papers on release had to be issued in succession because of the growing criticism that not enough was being done.* A few members of the Commons, some peers and some proprietors of the popular press, were still firing warning shots across the bows of a more enlightened policy, but the great majority of parliamentarians, editorials and letter-writers were urging the Home Secretary to clean up what Victor Cazalet had called 'a bespattered page in our history'.

Hardly a day passed when the quality press did not publish an article or print a few letters on the subject of internment. Amongst the people who wrote letters to *The Times*, the *Manchester Guardian*, the *Spectator*, the *New Statesman and Nation*, and other publications, pleading for the interned refugees, were writers like E. M. Forster, H. G. Wells, J. B. Priestley, Storm Jameson, Osbert Sitwell and Eleanor Farjeon; artists like Clive Bell, Vanessa Bell, Duncan Grant, Muirhead Bone and James Bateman; actors like Sybil Thorndike and other prominent people like Gilbert Murray, Norman Angell, Lady Violet Bonham Carter and Maud Royden.

Almost as soon as indiscriminate internment began, many newspapers started to fire salvoes against it and public opinion once again began to swing round. On 10 and 11 July, whilst the first great Commons debate took place, *Mass Observation* found that fifty-five per cent of the sample still favoured internment and only twenty-seven per cent were in favour of a more discriminate policy. By the first week of August only thirty-three per cent approved of 'intern the lot'.[2]

The debate on the motion to adjourn the House,† concerned exclusively with internment, took place on 10 July 1940. It began at 5.42 in the afternoon; the House did not rise until 11.24, a total of five hours and forty-two minutes, devoted to the fate of some thirty thousand men and women put behind barbed wire in England, on the Isle of Man or *en route* to more distant shores. Victor Cazalet was the opener against the government, followed in batting order by Eleanor Rathbone, Graham White, Colonel Wedgwood, Colonel Evans, George Strauss, Wilfred Roberts, Sydney Silverman, Reginald Sorensen, Philip Noel Baker and Lord Wolmer.‡ The burden of their

---

* Details of these appear later in this chapter.

† The usual device for an MP to obtain time for a debate on a subject which he considers of urgent public importance.

‡ MPs for Chippenham (C); Combined English Universities (Ind); Birkenhead East (Lib); Newcastle-under-Lyme (Lab); Cardiff South (C); Lambeth North (Lab); Cumberland North (Lib); Nelson & Colne (Lab); Leyton West (Lab); Coventry (Lab) and Aldershot (C).

pleas was that whatever excuse might have existed initially for the panic decision to proceed with wholesale internment, it was unfair, wasteful for the war effort, and was giving the country a bad name. All the people about whose loyalty the Home Office had no doubt should be released as quickly as possible. Only two members dissented: Mavis Tate* said their concern should be above all for their own people; we should not be carried away by false sentimentality in the midst of appalling danger. David Logan† was even more direct. We should not waste our sympathy on any of these people and should reserve it for the hardships of our own kind. But the majority of the House was clearly on the side of justice and fairness. Osbert Peake admitted that on the whole the refugees had shown themselves worthy of our confidence, and that with one exception (he did not elaborate what that was), he knew of no serious hostile act to the state perpetrated by a refugee.

But he claimed that because of the swing of public opinion against the refugees after the German invasion of the Lowlands and of France, and the increasing difficulty of finding jobs for them, internment had become as much in the interest of the refugees themselves as for the security of the state. Both Peake and Sir Edward Grigg, who replied to the debate for the government, refused to be drawn on the likelihood of any early overall policy review or any large scale releases, but promised to pursue any suggestions for improvements in the camps. Lord Croft, the former Sir Henry Page Croft, whose own son-in-law, Fred Uhlman, had been interned as a 'C' class refugee sixteen days earlier, stated on the same day on behalf of the Government, that on grounds of military necessity they had accepted the principle of internment of large categories of enemy aliens. At that stage there was no hint that any change of that policy was under consideration.

But the Cabinet had taken notice of the growing disquiet and of the possible adverse effects of its policy of indiscriminate internment on public opinion abroad, particularly in the United States, whose Jewish population was almost solidly anglophile, despite their disapproval of Britain's Palestine policy. Although it was never formally announced, indiscriminate internment of enemy aliens was halted around 15 July and was never resumed again, except in specific individual cases. The official explanation later on was that it had been

---

* MP for Frome (C).
† MP for the Scotland Division of Liverpool (Lab).

suspended because of a shortage of accommodation, and that it could be resumed again once the camp population had been thinned out by deportations and releases. In fact public clamour had probably as much to do with this administrative decision as overcrowding. But the problems of what to do with the thousands already behind barbed wire remained.

The day after the great Commons debate, Churchill asked Clement Attlee, the Lord Privy Seal, to consider the whole problem as a matter of urgency. The emphasis was to be more on improvements in the camp conditions and on finding suitable employment for the internees, than on release; but when Attlee submitted his memorandum six days later, he had dealt with all aspects of the problem.[3] Cabinet considered his report the following day, 17 July.[4] The War Office and the Home Office, Attlee writes, 'are primarily interested in security but the situation poses a more far reaching problem. In a war of ideas every effort should be made to enlist on our side all those opposed to the Nazis and use their services to the fullest extent against the common enemy. But in cases of doubt bias must always be in favour of national security.'

It can be safely assumed that not many interned refugees would have disagreed with Attlee's summary, had they but known that their fate was being discussed at Cabinet level. The problem really was: had the right balance been struck between the two confronting considerations by abandoning the careful selection and winnowing process which had been practised between September 1939 and May 1940 and substituting indiscriminate internment in its place?

Attlee then put forward a number of practical suggestions about who should be released and how conditions in the camps could be improved. For the first time in an official document they are referred to by him under the odious name of 'concentration camps'. The Cabinet told him to revise some of his recommendations. He re-submitted his revised paper three days later; Cabinet approved it on 22 July.[5] Most of his suggestions were subsequently incorporated into the White Papers. They had been worked out in discussions with senior officials in Sir John Anderson's department. A Home Office principal officer at the time remembers the speed at which they had to work to produce their reports and recommendations. Everything had to be done in a top priority rush; the matters were considered that urgent.

Two other ministers were also concerned with enemy aliens' problems. On 18 July, Neville Chamberlain, Lord President of the

Council, reported that he had received a large number of complaints about conditions in the camps, which disturbed him greatly.[6] It seemed to take weeks to find out where a particular person was interned. Some members of the same family had been interned in the UK and others sent overseas. Many chronic invalids, suffering from tuberculosis and diabetes, had been taken; many in the camps were without soap or bedding. Chamberlain then challenged the suggestion, which had been made during the Cabinet meeting the day before, that the only people to be released should be those whose services to the state would outweigh the potential danger of their being at large. He suggested that the government should modify the principle of releasing only those whose services are essential. Chamberlain here highlighted a basic problem, which for weeks afterwards remained a principal topic of public discussion, namely: should the utility of an incarcerated refugee be the only, or the overriding, criterion for his release, or should it be innocence and loyalty? Surprisingly enough, at this early Cabinet meeting the consensus was that all class 'C' aliens who had been actively hostile to the present régimes in Germany, Austria and Italy, or whom it was undesirable to keep interned for other sufficient reasons, should be released. It took many months before that decision was implemented.

Two days later Cabinet considered a memorandum by Ernest Bevin, the Minister of Labour, on the best utilization of alien manpower. It decided to set up an International Labour Office to deal not only with friendly aliens, but also with all uninterned enemy aliens. Bevin also suggested that all aliens of military age should be required to enlist in special military units and that such conscription should also include the Pioneer Corps; but for this, consent of the various allied governments was required.

During its meeting on 22 July, Cabinet decided that the Home Secretary should make a statement in the House of Commons, broadly on the lines of Clement Attlee's recommendations. Sir John Anderson did so on the following day. Already on 11 July the Home Office had set up an entirely new department under Sir John Moylan. He now became the principal civil servant concerned with internment matters.[7] One of the people who had seen Attlee's memoranda in their draft form was Sir John Moylan's superior, Sir Alexander Maxwell, the permanent undersecretary. He commented on the situation with perception:

Will we keep in internment the great majority who are violently opposed to the common enemy or only those who are really dangerous? Most of us know personally some Germans and Austrians, whom we know not to be dangerous at all but find it difficult to believe that all those thousands of other Germans are like the ones we know.* Does the Cabinet accept or not accept the view of the Security Services that most of these people should remain interned? Supposing the Cabinet no longer accepts this view, on what principles should the sorting of them be based?

In his statement to the House on 23 July, Sir John Anderson only partially answered the questions of his undersecretary. Once again he reviewed past history, admitted that many mistakes had been made in the implementation of policy, stated that the Government was trying its best to remedy them and to improve conditions, but stressed that for the moment internment had to remain the rule rather than the exception. To help him with the problems he was appointing a small committee which was to review the whole principle of internment, to submit to him recommendations for any modifications of that policy, and to examine and make recommendations on individual cases and groups of cases. He also announced a major change in something which had already been a problem during the First World War – the duality between the War Office and the Home Office was to cease. In future his department would assume principal responsibility for internment.†

This change had also been suggested by Attlee who had rightly pointed out to Sir John that looking after civilian internees was really not the business of the army. He supported Sir Edward Grigg's remark during the Commons debate of 10 July, that the army should be relieved of this responsibility. Attlee suggested the setting-up of an entirely new organization under the Home Secretary, headed by a prominent civilian with adequate executive and administrative staff, to be concerned with conditions in the camps, with the treatment and employment of internees and with their transfer overseas. Questions of release should remain with the Home Secretary himself.

At a subsequent conference on 27 July between the War Office and Home Office officials under the chairmanship of Sir John Moylan, who had become the head designate of the new department, the vesting

---

* This brings to mind the bitter jest which made the rounds in pre-war Nazi Germany, that there must be at least sixty million Jews in Germany because every German knows at least one decent Jew.
† See Cab 200 (40) 15 and Cab 207 (40) 12 for details of Cabinet discussions on this matter.

date for the transfer was fixed for 5 August.[8] His department was to take over all functions hitherto exercised by the War Department, except for the provision of guards. The War Office would also continue to supply rations, clothing, motor transport, works services, as well as medical and dental officers, but interned doctors and dentists were in future to be used as much as possible. Only in camps reserved for category 'A' prisoners would the War Office continue to exercise all the same functions as before. In those camps the two-tier arrangements providing a superior service for the 4/6d prisoners would continue. In pursuit of this new policy, all Nazi sympathizers should be transferred before the vesting date to special camps. This in the end only happened much later. In fact, the whole transfer of responsibilities from one department of state to another never took place. Later on it led to a lot of acrimony between the two departments.*

Altogether five committees were appointed concerned with the problems arising from the internment of enemy aliens. One of these, under Sir Percy Lorraine, formerly Britain's ambassador in Rome, exclusively dealt with interned Italians. The other four were concerned with different aspects of the internment of Germans and Austrians.†

The first and probably most important one, was under the chairmanship of Mr Justice Asquith, aided by two members, both of whom had been engaged for some time in the welfare of refugees on an international scale, Sir Herbert Emerson and Major General Neill Malcolm. The committee's terms of reference were to examine the whole policy and suggest whatever changes it considered proper, and to examine all individual cases which were referred to it by the Home Secretary. In other words, it was to recommend to Sir John what sort of people could be released again and then to examine the *bona fides* of all those who applied for release. It was only an advisory committee, the ultimate decision on overall policy remained with the War Cabinet and on individual cases with the Home Secretary. From the

---

* Typical is a comment made in 1941 by the Permanent Undersecretary at the War Office, P. J. Grigg: 'We helped the Home Office out of the kindness of our heart but it is not our job to look after civilians (internees).' But the Home Office refused to take over saying they had no ex-policemen or ex-prison warders available to look after the internees. See letter dated 12 May 1941 from the Secretary of the Army Council to the Permanent Secretary at the Home Office and his reply dated 15 May in HO File 1/Gen 2/1/3.

† Ho. 1/Gen/2/1/3. See also Sir John Anderson's statement in the House on 20 November 1940 for full particulars.

beginning the committee adopted a humane and liberal attitude; not all its general as well as its individual recommendations were accepted. In any case, before the Home Secretary would sanction any release, he asked MI5 to comment on the case; their ideas were by no means always identical to those of the Asquith committee.

A *Council of Aliens* was also set up under the chairmanship of Lord Lytton, who, like Sir John Anderson, was a former governor of Bengal and for a short time had also acted as Viceroy of India. The original Cabinet recommendation had been that Lord Cranborne (heir to the Marquisate of Salisbury) should chair it, but he declined for reasons of health. Its membership varied from time to time. In November 1940 it consisted of Sir Herbert Emerson, Major-General Neill Malcolm, the Marchioness of Reading and the following parliamentary members: H. W. Butcher, E. Edwards, H. Graham White, G. Latham, P. J. Noel Baker, N. Maclean, and Eleanor Rathbone.

The Asquith Committee was primarily concerned with policy, particularly in respect of releases, whereas the Lytton Council's bailiwick was welfare inside the camps. Cabinet decided that the Council should report to the Foreign Secretary and nct, as all the other committees, to the Home Secretary, because of the great interest which other nations were showing in the conditions obtaining in the camps. It was not a very logical decision and led to a considerable amount of friction, resulting eventually in the resignation in a huff of Lord Lytton.

From the beginning there were personality problems. Because of the considerable number of interned socialists and trades unionists, the Cabinet was anxious that the TUC should be represented on the Council. The General Secretary, Sir Walter Citrine, was approached but he declined. [9] Churchill promised to explain to him the purpose of the Council and, if he was still unwilling, to ask him to suggest privately some other trades unionist. It was during that Cabinet meeting on 1 August that Churchill also said that the situation was now considerably more secure than it had been two months before, and that it was possible to take a somewhat less rigid attitude in regard to the internment of aliens.

Churchill's personal intervention with Citrine failed to sway him. Citrine refused to suggest anybody else. He told Churchill that the TUC should not be asked to nominate a representative to any committee affecting the working classes, in accordance with the undertaking given in October 1939 by Neville Chamberlain regarding consultations between government departments and the TUC. On the face of it this would have been an extraordinarily churlish refusal. There were hundreds of German and Austrian trades unionists incarcerated, many of them old colleagues of the TUC leadership; yet the TUC refused to help the government in any way to alleviate their lot because of some countervailing basic understanding between the two.

But Churchill's remark about the arrangement between his predecessor and the TUC is a puzzling one. According to the TUC annual report for 1940 there was indeed a meeting between Chamberlain and the General Council on 5 October 1939, during which it was arranged that consultations should always take place between the various ministries and the TUC on all matters in which the TUC or any of its affiliated members were concerned.[10] This seems to contradict Churchill's version and would make Citrine's refusal all the more strange. In any case, according to the TUC records, E. Edwards had been co-opted to the Council as their representative.[11] Later on Mary Sutherland, chief woman policy officer of the Labour Party, became a member of the Hurst Committee. The complaint by H. N. Brailsford in *Reynolds News* of 14 December, that not a single socialist or trades union official was on any of the tribunals dealing with internees, is obviously incorrect.

Whatever the official TUC attitude was, the refugee organizations were only too anxious to be represented on the Council as also on the Asquith Committee. On 30 July, the Board of Deputies suggested that, in view of the large number of Jews amongst the internees, two Jewish refugees with special knowledge of the problem and with impeccable credentials, should be co-opted to the committee.* Mr Justice Asquith privately intimated to Professor Selig Brodetsky, the President of the Board of Deputies, that he welcomed the suggestion. The Professor also approached Lord Lytton in a similar vein and once again the chairman was all in favour. But in both cases the suggestion was turned down. On behalf of the Foreign Office H. L. Baggaley told Lord Lytton that members of his Council were being appointed in a personal capacity and not as representatives of any particular organization. Nevertheless, Lord Lytton asked Professor Brodetsky on 7 August for practical suggestions on the sort of problems the Council should concern itself. Only Lady Reading can in any sense be

---

* In a memo to the Advisory Commission; at Bloomsbury House.

considered as a member of a Jewish Refugee Aid organization, but most of the members appointed to the panel had taken a great personal interest in the whole problem. As far as the Asquith Committee was concerned, it did unofficially consult from time to time both the Central Council for Jewish Refugees and also the Christian Council for Refugees.*

At the end of July the first White Paper (Cmd 6217) concerning 'Categories of Persons eligible for Release from Internment and Procedures to be followed in applying for Release' was published, setting out eighteen different categories under which people would be able to apply. Despite their apparently widely cast differentiation, these eighteen categories only covered a relatively limited number of refugees. The White Paper was therefore received with what Colonel Wedgwood on 1 August in the Commons, called 'universal reprobation'. He was so incensed that he wanted the House to adjourn and, when he failed, tried to introduce a vote of censure, but Attlee, as Leader of the House, refused to give him time. George Strauss' comment was that, under that White Paper, Einstein, Thomas Mann and Toscanini would have to remain interned.

The principal criticism was that the White Paper gave no help to political refugees, to outstanding artists and scientists, to students whose courses of study had been peremptorily cut off by internment, and to residents of long standing such as the elderly Austro–Poles who have been mentioned before. Disappointment was also expressed that for the ordinary refugee of no special skill essential for the war effort, and of no outstanding merit or who because of age or indifferent health could not join the Pioneer Corps, there seemed to be no chance to have his loyalty tested, let alone of release.

Once again the Foreign Office officials were at their most critical. Farquhar, head of the Southern Department, commented: 'The Home Secretary on his own authority and on the advice of our famous security services proceeds to lock up a lot of people.' When asked whether he can now release some of them again we are given evasive replies. Surely the Authority which has the power to lock up people also has the power to let them loose again.'[12] Another Civil Servant anotates in the margin: 'The continued delays and the persistent evidence of administrative ineptitude are very discreditable and

---

* See letter from Professor Brodetsky to Mr Justice Asquith, dated 31 August 1940 (at Bloomsbury House). Lady Violet Bonham Carter had been the go-between.

calculated not only to bring us into ridicule but also to make enemies of those who have been our friends.'

The correspondence columns of the press were also full of criticisms of the White Paper. Typical is a letter in *The Times* of 16 August 1940, from nine London correspondents of leading newspapers in neutral Europe: 'Our expectations that the White Paper will announce measures to repair the harm done to the traditional reputation of British fairness have not been fulfilled. The utilitarian principle is not a correct one.'

Resulting from all these criticisms and from suggestions made by the Asquith Committee, a second White Paper (Cmd 6223) was issued at the end of August which added a further category No 19; it covered people 'who by their writings or political activity had over a period of years taken a prominent part in opposition to the Nazi system and who were actively friendly towards the Allied cause'. To examine these cases Sir John Anderson convened a further committee chaired by Sir Cecil Barrington Hurst, a former president of the Permanent International Court of Justice at The Hague, assisted by Sir Andrew McFadyan, a prominent Liberal, who had lived in Berlin for a number of years, Professor Robert Seton Watson, the historian, and Ivonne Kirkpartrick, lately First Secretary at the Embassy in Berlin.

Ever since internment had begun, British people with intimate knowledge of Germany and of the refugees, as well as prominent refugees themselves, had been urging the authorities to consult the one group of people who were able to advise on the winnowing process and who could not be fooled by anybody pretending to be a refugee when he was really a Nazi agent in disguise – to wit, refugees whose own loyalty had been proved beyond a peradventure of doubt. Now at last the Home Secretary accepted that suggestion. He contacted W. Gilles, the head of the International Department of the Labour Party, and asked him to suggest a panel of prominent German and Austrian socialists and trade unionists, who could scrutinize applications made under category nineteen and make recommendations to the Hurst Committee.

A problem now arose over the composition of this panel, because emigré socialists were by no means a united body and could at first not agree who should be co-opted to it.* Their ideological differences not

---

* The following information is compiled partly from the unpublished papers of Willy Sander in the Friedrich Ebert archive in Bonn and from Werner Roeder's book: *Die Deutschen Sozialistischen Exilgruppen in Gross Britannien, 1940–1945,* Bonn, 1968.

only concerned the past – the nagging problem of why they had lost out so easily to Hitler and who was to blame for it – but also what sort of post-war future they envisaged for Germany. The official successor to the pre-Nazi Social Democratic Party was the SOPADE; but not all the former socialists had joined it, nor was there any unanimity within the party, whose headquarters had been moved, first to Prague, then to Paris and, in the wake of the French defeat, to London. A small minority amongst them were Vansittartists, arguing that the aggressive, nationalistic and pan-Germanistic spirit had been rampant in the old party just as everywhere else in Germany, and that only a break-up and total restructuring of the German lands would suffice. Gilles had put forward one of them as suitable panel member, but he declined because he was at loggerheads with the rest of the nominees. His name is Walter Loeb. For a time he had been a member of a Weimar *Reichsgovernment*; he left Germany as soon as the Nazis came to power. In August 1940 a long-time German resident in Britain reported to the International Solidarity Fund, a socialist charitable organization operating out of Bloomsbury House, that Loeb had told him that after the invasion of the Lowlands he had personally urged Attlee and Greenwood to intern everybody and not trust anybody claiming to be a refugee. When Willy Sander, the Secretary to the Fund, challenged Loeb, the latter tried to substantiate his advice in a long memorandum. Loeb himself, of course, was never interned; many of his colleagues were; some of them lost their lives on the *Arandora Star*.

The chairman of the advisory panel was Professor Kahn-Freund, later Sir Otto, assisted by the secretary and six further members. The Sander Papers clearly indicate that in making its recommendations on individual applications the panel was super-scrupulous. Every single statement by an applicant was thoroughly checked; if the applicant was not personally known to a panel member and there was no corroborative evidence from a reliable third party about a claim that he had been an active political opponent of the Nazi régime, the panel refused to recommend his release.

Eventually, after the panel had expressed its opinion, the Hurst Committee had made its recommendation and the Home Secretary had made his decision, a total of 1,502 people were released under category nineteen. About 1,900 people had their applications rejected because their cases were not considered to fall under that clause. No doubt, many of them were subsequently released under some other provision.

The second White Paper still left out the bulk of the internees and refugees, and criticism continued in the press and in Parliament. As a result, Churchill proposed during a Cabinet meeting on 2 September that he could make a statement in the House to the effect that at a time of the country's greatest danger, the War Cabinet had decided as an act of high policy that large numbers of aliens must be interned notwithstanding the great hardship involved. 'We are now in a stronger position and can release aliens again quickly even though this might involve some risk.'[13] But during another Cabinet meeting on 5 September, the Prime Minister stated that he did not after all propose to make on this occasion any reference to the question of aliens.[14]

One can only speculate what caused him to change his mind. Most probably the Security Services once again became alarmed at the prospect of large scale releases, 'involving some risk' and, through the Chiefs of Staff, exerted pressure on Churchill. This assumption is strengthened by a memorandum which the Home Secretary submitted to Cabinet on 26 November.[15] The previous week the Intelligence Sub-Committee had submitted recommendations to the Joint Chiefs of Staff which they in turn endorsed to the Home Defence Security Executive. They demanded that there should be no relaxation of the principles under which internment had originally been carried out and that due publicity should be given to the underlying reasons for the continued internment of a large number of aliens.

The new Home Secretary, Herbert Morrison, was clearly being pressured from both sides. In the memorandum to the Cabinet he mentioned that both Asquith and Lytton were recommending that everybody should be released who could convince him that they were friendlily disposed towards Britain. The military authorities clearly wanted release to be the exception rather than the rule. Morrison thought that the vocal element in favour of a more liberal policy was only a minority and that in times of public excitement, such as intensive bombing or a resumed threat of invasion, the pendulum might swing again the other way.

Nevertheless, a further and final White Paper Cmd 6233 was issued at the end of October adding three further clauses to the list of release categories. On 21 November Cabinet discussed the Home Secretary's memorandum and once again decided to widen the criteria, but on this occasion by a simple statement in the Commons without issuing yet another White Paper.[16]

Everybody who had reached their fiftieth year or who had applied to join the Auxiliary Military Pioneer Corps and had been rejected on medical grounds, could now be released provided he could convince the tribunal that he was actively friendly towards the allied cause.* At the same time the Home Secretary was to issue a statement that the Government did not contemplate any further enlargement of the release categories; on the contrary, a number of enemy aliens who could not be interned at the time because of a lack of accommodation in the camps, are now being sifted and some might still have to be interned. Critics saw in this statement yet another subtle, or not-so-subtle, attempt to induce able-bodied refugees to enlist in the Pioneer Corps. The ILP member McGovern, wanted to know how interned socialists would fare who were opposed to both imperialist causes.† Herbert Morrison pointed out that the exemption clause under the Military Service Act referred only to British citizens and could not be applied to enemy aliens.

In order to examine internees who were applying for release under categories eight and twenty, the Home Secretary appointed another eight *ad hoc* committees. These categories covered people of 'academic distinction' or those who had made outstanding contributions to Art, Science, Learning or Letters. Various bodies such as the Committee of Vice Chancellors and Principals of Universities, the Royal Society, the Royal Academy, Royal College of Music, the RIBA and the Pen Club, were asked to nominate committee members. Amongst the chairmen were the Vice Chancellor of Oxford University, Lord Justice Scott and Dr Ralph Vaughan Williams.‡

Only category 'C' people could be considered for release but there were, of course, still over 3,500 women interned in Rushen and several thousand men elsewhere on the Isle of Man, in Canada and Australia, all of whom were in category 'B'. There were also a number of class 'A', almost all of whom had by now been deported, who were genuine refugees and might be considered for release. Before any of them could apply under any of the twenty-two categories, they had first to be reclassified. The Home Secretary therefore appointed yet

---

* A confidential memorandum by Sir Herbert Emerson, dated 15 January 1941 (FO 371/29173) mentions a 'loyalty clause 23', but the last White Paper published (Cmd 6233) only lists twenty-two categories. Number twenty-three could therefore well cover the further provision mentioned here.
† This was during Question Time in the Commons on 26 November 1940, seven months before Hitler fell on Russia. For the faithful, Britain's cause then suddenly ceased to be imperialist!
‡ Herbert Morrison replying to Major Milner (Leeds Lab) on 5 December 1940.

another committee under the Chief Metropolitan Magistrate, Sir Robert Dummett, to review the classification of all those whose cases had not been previously heard by the Regional Advisory Committees who had had a brief life in April and May of 1940.* This committee sat in Bow Street Magistrate's Court; its hearings were much more formal and daunting, conducted rather on proper police court procedures.

For the internees in the UK, releases were naturally proceeding at much too slow a pace. The suspense was much worse for those in Canada and Australia, because it took many weeks before they knew that the government had not only halted internment but a policy was in the making under which they might have a chance to return home eventually as free men. Echoes of the frustration of these men could be heard in the press and in Parliament. During a debate in the Lords on 15 August, Lord Mancroft asked how one committee – the Asquith one – could possibly deal with thirty thousand cases. It would take years before everybody could get a hearing. We ought to have fifty such committees. Lord Newton asked whether it was true that twenty-seven people in the Home Office had the power to grant or to refuse liberation to the refugees? The Duke of Devonshire replied that there were in fact 320 officers in the Home Office concerned with internment. Their work was hampered, the Duke said, by the fact that due to mental strain some internees had asked as many as thirty different Peers and MPs to intercede on their behalf.

A letter writer in the *Manchester Guardian* calculated on 23 September that since the outbreak of the war, just over a year ago, the Government had appointed 137 tribunals and committees to deal with enemy aliens. Of this grand total 120 were original classification tribunals. Then came the Birkett Committee for category 'A' aliens; the twelve Regional Advisory Committees for appeals by 'B' aliens. Now there was Asquith, Lytton, Lorraine and Hurst. (The writer did not as yet know about Dummett and the eight *ad hoc* committees for eminent people.) He estimated that 494 people had been or are being employed in this work; very few of whom knew anything about Europe or about Hitler's policies.

Slowly releases were gathering speed. By 29 August only 616 people had been freed from UK camps; by 17 September the number had risen to 2,516; by 15 October to 5,200; by 18 January 1941 to 8,700 and by

---

* See Morrison's statement in the Commons on 20 November.

13 February to 10,112.* Only a few hundred had come back from Canada, none from Australia. It is to the camps in Canada and Australia that we will now turn our attention.

---

* According to statements made by Home Office representatives on the various dates in reply to questions by Eleanor Rathbone, Sir Richard Acland and Edmund Harvey.

14 *The New Canadians*

'When I look back
I see a row of lights
some dim, some blazing,
some steady,
while here and there
unfathomable darkness gazes into
nought.

These bygone weeks and months
behind an ever-present
stubborn wire fence
on which I now look back
as on a dream;
They are a row of lights,
some dim, some blazing,
some steady
while here and there
unfathomable darkness gazes into
nought.

I found my way
illuminated by these changing
lights,
But when the shadows came
I would have been alone
except for you.
For you and those
who knew the way or found it
when it led through depths,
through night and wilderness.
And thus I can with gratitude
and joy
look back upon that row of lights,
not only those which blaze,
those steady or those dim;
but also on the gaps of
unfathomable darkness gazing into
nought.'

A Bespattered Page?

THIS POEM was written by a seventeen-year-old boy after his return to the UK to a friend who was still interned in Canada. Alexander Paterson quoted it in his report.

The deported refugees had arrived in Canada during the month of July 1940. Bemused and bewildered they stood around the dockside in Quebec or Montreal, apprehensive as to how their new hosts were going to treat them. The initial reception was anything but friendly. This was not surprising. The Canadians had no idea what sort of people they were getting. Nobody had told them that in addition to some Nazi civilians, seamen, as well as *Luftwaffe* and army personnel, the three ships which had managed to complete the journey safely also contained over two thousand civilians who were all enemies of Nazi Germany and friends of Britain, interned and deported as a purely precautionary measure. Canada had willingly agreed to feed, house and guard all these supposedly dangerous characters in order to ease Britain's burden. She had no intention of doing more or of being particularly friendly towards them.

> As hotel porters blithely slap labels on tin trunks and it takes some persistence to scrape off these labels, so the Canadian Government has been told that these men and boys are all dangerous enemies. It has been very hard to disabuse them. They are treating these refugees with a greater degree of security and precaution than IRA convicts with long sentences are accorded in Dartmoor.

This is how Paterson summed up his impressions a few weeks after his arrival in Canada in November 1940, and after he had toured the various internment camps in the southern part of the country. As a Commissioner of Prisons he was certainly in a good position to compare. But he also added:

> Nobody is less entitled to criticize the treatment of these men and boys than the representative of a Government which at a time of great peril and acute haste pressed upon you (ie the Canadian Government) the task of their custody and unhappily misled you as to their degree of danger.

The whole operation of looking after internees and prisoners-of-war in Canada was under the control of Brigadier-General Panet, whom the Canadian Government had appointed Director General of Internment Operations as soon as they had agreed to the Home Office Request to receive and to guard these deportees.* Because the Canadians had no idea that they were getting any refugees, and knew nothing about the tribunals or the meaning of the various categories 'A', 'B' and 'C', they treated all the civilian internees as POWs Class 2 under the Canadian Defence Regulations.

But General Panet who, like Paterson, seems to have been a humane and perceptive individual, soon realized that the people whom he watched being disembarked and shifted into various camps, could not possibly be all dangerous characters; some of them at least must have been sent over by mistake. After dealing with the German soldiers, seamen and Nazi civilians, he wrote on 3 August 1940 to the War Office in London: 'The remainder are all refugees, including a large number of schoolboys, undergraduates, priests and rabbis.' Panet could not understand what they were doing there. To his own Government he suggested that rigid control arrangements for these people were quite inappropriate. The Defence Department should remove all the guards and convert the camps into self-governing republics. Not unnaturally, his superiors would not agree until the British Government confirmed that all these people were in fact not as dangerous as they had been led to believe. The Canadians therefore requested the Home Government to send out a responsible official to advise them on the degree of danger and the differences between the various categories. Sir John Anderson picked Alexander Paterson for the task. He could not have made a better choice. The warmth and wit which shines through every page of his report has been confirmed by every internee interviewed by me who talked to Paterson.

Canada had set aside a total of thirteen camps, into five of which the refugees were eventually concentrated; the remainder contained *Wehrmacht* officers, German other ranks, Italian civilians, and German merchant seamen and civilians, a grand total of 6,735 people. Of these, 2,290 were eventually considered non-dangerous, including 1,746 Jews.† But it took some time for the Canadians to ascertain these figures because the records which had accompanied the three transports were inaccurate and gave no clue to the classification of the

---

* For this and for most of what follows see the Paterson Report in the Home Office File Gen 200/117/163 op. cit.

† Figures mentioned in a report by Saul Hayes, National Executive Director of the United Jewish Refugee War Relief Association in Montreal, dated 8 August 1940 (at Bloomsbury House). This organization, and in particular its director, did a lot of good, charitable work for the internees, as did the Society of Friends.

individuals. In one camp alone, the Canadians found two hundred internees whose records had not been sent; on the other hand, they had been given particulars of a similar number of people of whom they could find no trace.

Paterson visited every one of these camps and spoke to every single internee who wished to see him. He listened patiently to everybody's complaints and wishes and promised to help them wherever he could. By then the White Papers had been issued and he explained to each individual under what category he might apply for release. He stressed that the step which was most likely to lead to success was to apply to join the Pioneer Corps, but he never pushed people to apply.

Materially, Paterson reported, the internees were well looked after; they were in fact overfed and, after some initial shortcomings, their sanitary facilities were 'more on the standards of American excellence than of British mediocrity'. But he considered that the military personnel was often unsuited to take care of these 'sensitive and temperamental human beings'. He was particularly shocked that in some camps the internees were forced to wear what he called 'a circus outfit' – 'professors dressed as clowns' – which consisted of a circular flat-topped hat, a jacket with a huge red circle on the back, and bright blue trousers, seamed with a broad red band. In other camps the prisoners were allowed to wear their own mufti. Paterson hints clearly at some anti-semitic bias amongst the officers and guards. He reported this to the Canadian Defence Department, who then issued an Order of the Day, posted outside all the camps: 'Canada is a free country where different races have contributed to make it a great nation. The practice to refer in a contemptuous way to those in your charge of Jewish faith is unworthy of a free Canadian and will cease forthwith.'

The straw which, as far as Paterson was concerned, finally broke the camel's back, was when one day he came across a lonely, shy seventeen-year-old boy, who had five months before broken his spectacles; the camp authorities had been quite insensitive to his plea for them to be mended. During all that time the boy had been unable to read and was in consequence very disturbed. On 26 April 1941, Paterson dashed off to the Canadian Government a highly critical report with practical suggestions as to how to improve matters. Within six days the Government accepted all his recommendations. They finally recognized that there was a distinct difference in the nature and treatment of hostile prisoners-of-war and of friendly refugees. Two separate departments were set up and a new Commissioner for Refugees was appointed, a former lawyer with whom Paterson got on well.*

The five camps into which the official refugees, that is to say, all the category 'B' and 'C' enemy aliens were concentrated were:

Camp 'I'   on the Ile aux Noix, P.Q. forty miles outside Montreal; an island fortress in the middle of the Richelieu River.

Camp 'S'   on St Helen's Island on the outskirts of Montreal, in the St Lawrence River.

Camp 'B'   At Fredericton, New Brunswick.

Camp 'A'   At Farnham P.Q.

Camp 'N'   At Sherbrooke P.Q.

Camp 'N' was the largest of these and gradually more and more internees were transferred to it from other camps. Of the remaining camps, camp 'R' at Red Rook near Nippigon in Ontario (but the nearest town of any size was Winnipeg in Manitoba) also contained a refugee element – the unfortunate, mislabelled 'A' Jews and the class 'C' schoolboys from Scotland.† Amongst them we meet again Eugen Spier, Alec Natan and the handicraft teacher. The camp leader, elected by the inmates, was Commodore Scharf; his deputy was Baron von Pillar, one of the early internees at Olympia. Another internee there was the obnoxious 'Putzi' Hanfstaengel. The camp contained 1,150 prisoners, of whom 850 were merchant seamen, 120 non-refugee civilians and 180 others, mostly Jews with a sprinkling of members of the International Seamen's Union and other 'politicals'; all of them had been *Duchess of York* shipmates.

It had taken a two days' train journey to transport the prisoners to this remote, totally isolated disused mining camp not far from the Nippigon Lake. As in all the other camps, no preparation had been made to receive the new guests and at first conditions were chaotic. Between 120 and 150 men had to sleep on the floor in small huts; there

---

* A Privy Council Order PC 4568 dated 25 June 1941, established two departments: a Commissioner of Internment Operations (POWs) and a Commissioner of Refugee Camps.
† All thirteen camps are enumerated in a report which the German Foreign Office received from the Swiss on 1 December 1940 (*Auswaertige* Amt RX II ZV 346). This list also contains the names of various camp leaders including the refugee ones, despite the repeated assurances in the Commons by the British Government that no names or particulars of interned refugees would be passed on to Germany via the Swiss.

was hardly any food; the guards were trigger happy. The eleven boys were put in the same hut as some rather rowdy and aggressive sailors and were mercilessly taunted by them. However, Commodore Scharf tried to deal fairly with all and living conditions rapidly improved. Food soon became plentiful; double deck bunks were provided for thirty men in each hut. Wood burning stoves gave warm, if somewhat smelly, comfort. The prisoners at first refused to put on what Paterson had called their circus outfit, with the big red circle, but when it started to get cold they changed their minds. The teacher recalls that there were thirty confessing Jews amongst them, who started immediately to hold regular religious services. On Yom Kippur 1940 the commandant asked the kitchen staff to prepare a special meal for them to break the fast after sundown. The cooks were all German sailors. When the Jews sat down, they brought in a big dish of fried bacon and nothing else.

Despite the Commodore's efforts, relations between the refugees and the Nazi element amongst the sailors never really improved. The camp had a small hospital staffed by two Jewish doctors and two male German nurses. They worked well together until one day some Nazi thugs rushed into the hospital hut and beat up the two doctors. This is how the refugees remember it. Scharf, in his report written after repatriation to Germany where he was under a cloud, says that the 'seamen were beaten up in hospital by the staff', and that 'everybody was punished by seven days arrest including the two Jewish doctors'. One can just picture the two Jewish doctors beating up a gang of hefty sailors. Scharf also complained that they were not allowed to hang up pictures of the Fuhrer nor nail up swastika flags. After the incident the refugees went on hunger strike until the commandant promised them that they would soon be sent to another camp exclusively reserved for refugees. But that did not happen for several months.

Spier's worst early impression of the camp was its utter isolation. The prisoners were not allowed to write any letters or send any telegrams; they had no idea what was happening in the outside world. The Germans decided to write a joint letter of protest to the nearest Swiss Consul to induce the German Government to retaliate against this breach of the Geneva Convention, but the refugees naturally refused to join in any such step. Spier was told by his Nazi hut-mates, who somehow had – or pretended to have – a conduit to the outside world that the Canadian papers were now openly discussing what was to happen to them in the event of the anticipated collapse of Great

Britain. The Nazis of course would be repatriated to the Fatherland, but what about the refugees? The Canadians had never bargained for the possibility that amongst the POWs whom they had agreed to accept there would be men who would be unwilling to go back to Germany. The Canadian Government had no intention of keeping them as permanent settlers and therefore willy-nilly would have to force them to return to Germany. Other Nazis told him that, according to letters which they had received from home, the authorities there were expecting that by 1 September at the latest, the war would be won and that 18 September had already been earmarked as the day on which all returned prisoners-of-war would be welcomed home in festive ceremonies.

The teacher remembers that whilst discipline amongst the seamen was rigidly enforced and the German civilians perforce had to conform, there was quite a lot of tension and bickering amongst the refugees. The Jews, the socialists, the communist seamen could endlessly argue not only about cherished political principles but about the vexing trifles of their everyday existence. The youngsters did not like it. There was no privacy for anybody; after dusk which as the winter approached came earlier and earlier, they were confined to their own cramped and smelly hut; they were liable to be shot if they as much as set a foot outside their door. According to the teacher many of the older ones started out as rational people but gradually began to go round the bend; a few ended up in a mental asylum. In his hut there was a homosexual couple in adjacent bunks; some of the older inmates complained about the noise which they were making at night. The 'female' partner of this union was a gifted, sensitive artist who painted pictures of naked women which one of the guards sold for him outside the camp on commission.

The eleven boys had a difficult time. Some of the adults took a fatherly interest in them and watched lest they succumb to homosexual practices. Others complained about their boisterousness. They got on best with the salty international seamen who taught them how to make ships in bottles and how to weave belts. Afterwards they traded these illegally with the guards for money or cigarettes.

Several people attempted escapes from the camp. None of the Nazis who tried got very far, but one of the political refugees who twice before had got away – once from a German concentration camp and then again from a Franco prison – almost succeeded for a third time. He managed to get across the forty-ninth parallel but was eventually picked up on a train, well inside the USA. The American authorities gave him the choice between being deported to Germany or Spain or being sent back to Canada. He chose the latter and after serving twenty-eight days in a Canadian glasshouse was put back again into Camp 'R'.

The Home Office still do not seem to have realized that there were some genuine refugees amongst the class 'A' prisoners, or if they did, they certainly failed to acquaint the Canadian authorities accordingly. The guards at Camp 'R' certainly never accepted that there were some fundamental differences between their wards. On 20 August 1940 Osbert Peake claimed that the Canadian Government had been fully briefed and that all the 'B' and 'C' internees had now been separated. Much later, on 17 September, all he could say was that 'considerable progress had been made in the segregation'. The eleven boys from Scotland had obviously been forgotten and so had Spier and his peers.

Only in January 1941 were they at last told that they would be moved into a camp in which they would be amongst their own sort. Scharf in his report to the German Foreign Office says that 'the removal of the Jews and other anti-German elements has created a much better atmosphere at the camp'. Well might it have done! The dislike had obviously been mutual. In bitterly cold weather the refugees, including the youngsters, spent two days and nights on a train before they reached their new home, Camp 'N'. For six months they had been in total isolation, seeing the same male faces every day. The teacher, then a teenager, remembers pangs of sadness when the train on the first evening passed slowly through a small town and through lighted kitchen windows he could see women preparing supper, a comforting home atmosphere which he had not been able to enjoy since the day in May of the previous year when the police had picked him up in far away Scotland.

The internees were disembarked in a railway siding, fell in for parade and were welcomed in a fashion by a fierce looking Regimental Sergeant Major who shouted at them to get moving and did not mince his words in telling them what he thought of them. He seems to have been a paradigm of his breed, ruling the roost with a rod of iron, a martinet who behind a rough exterior concealed a kindly, compassionate nature, and who did everything he could do for 'his' people in the camp.

The internees on the ss *Ettrick*, all of them class 'B' or 'C' internees, had been somewhat more fortunate than the class 'A' ones or the eleven boys. Once they had left the ship, they were separated from the German POWs and never saw them again. For a few weeks they were housed in old Army barracks on the Plains of Abraham, outside Quebec City. Sir Herman Bondi still recalls that the vista up there was one of the most beautiful he has ever seen. The barracks were situated high up on the mountain from which they had a glorious view of the broad river far below, sweeping majestically round a wide bend, with the lights of the town sparkling at night in the distance. He was almost sad to leave the camp, but the guards told him that the thin-walled huts were quite unsuitable for the harsh Canadian winter.

In mid-October they were transferred to the newly opened camp 'N' at Sherbrooke in Quebec Province.* The camp consisted of two railway sheds, one very big which served as a mass dormitory for six hundred internees and a smaller one which was used for messing and recreation. There was a big turntable in the bigger of the two sheds; the floors were pitted and greasy. The internees had at first only six lavatories and a very few showers between them, but within a few weeks the sanitary facilities were more than adequate. For the first few weeks they all slept on palliasses on the floor, but gradually double bunks were supplied; the tables and benches they fashioned in their own workshop. Canada had no shortage of timber; wood was also used for heating so that despite the onset of a bitter cold in the following month they were never really cold. They were well fed and warmly clothed so that the brisk, clear-cold winter presented no real hardship to most of them. Although there were of course older men amongst them, the average age of the Canadian deportees was quite a bit below those of the Isle of Man.

Cultural and educational activities which had already started at the transit camp on the Plains of Abraham, bloomed at Camp 'N' as they did in every single internment camp from the hot desert of Australia to 'boarding-house establishments' on the Isle of Man. Their inmates had their lectures and their discussion groups; education was available in almost every conceivable subject. They did physical exercises and had their regular card schools, their cafés and their cabarets. They wrote their own sketches and set them to music and they set up their own workshops. They even had their own Arbitration Court to settle

---

* The following report on the camps and on their inmates is partly based on personal interviews but also to some extent on an article by Barbara Moon in *Maclean's Magazine* of 10 February 1962. She must have interviewed a number of internees who settled in Canada.

internal disputes, often about trifling matters, headed by a lawyer who later became a QC. Another internee there later lost a leg in the war and is now one of Her Majesty's judges.

Like its sister camps on the three continents, Camp 'N' housed people of all shades of political opinions and like some of them had its own tightly controlled communist cell. In one of the Australian camps, the communists staged a vain attempt to take over the camp administration by coup. At Camp 'N' it was led by Hans Kahle, who had been a commander of the International Brigade in Spain. He is supposed to have served as the prototype for the hero of Hemmingway's: *For Whom the Bells Toll.* He became a Police President in East Germany after the war. Amongst the members of his cell was a young physics teacher, called Klaus Fuchs. His communist proclivities were well known, not only to the inmates, but also to the Army Intelligence Officers. Fuchs was one of the first to be released and returned to Britain to continue in nuclear research before being sent to America to join the 'Manhattan' project. An internee was quite shocked when years later, after the spy scandal had broken, Clement Attlee, by then Prime Minister, said in the House that during the war the Government had no inkling of Fuchs' communism. Quite clearly that was not so.

The camp was particularly rich in scientific talent. Apart from Fuchs, there was the future Sir Herman Bondi, now scientific adviser to Britain's Department of Energy; Thomas Gold, now Professor of Astronomy at Cornell University; Dr Max Perutz, a future Nobel Prize winner and head of the MRC unit in Cambridge; Professor Hans Kromberger, a theoretical physicist and later member of the Atomic Energy Commission; M. Heilbron, later Professor of Mathematics at Bristol University and F. G. Friedlaender of Trinity College, Cambridge. At that time Friedlaender was the only one of these scientists sufficiently well known for his case to be raised in Parliament. Shortly before the war he had obtained a starred First in his Tripos and whilst in internment completed his fellowship thesis on a mathematical problem of some relevance to the war effort.

Amongst this batch of refugees was Count Lingen, alias Prince Frederick of Prussia. Whilst they had been at their first camp, Camp 'L' on the Heights of Abraham, he had written a letter to the Governor-general's wife* which started: 'Dear Aunt Alice'. The IO stopped the

---

* Princess Alice, Countess of Athlone, a granddaughter of the old Queen.

letter, either because he did not know the true identity of the 'Count', or because he was unaware of the Hohenzollern connection with Queen Victoria's progeny. But soon afterwards the Earl of Athlone visited the camp and presented the inmates with a football. Thereafter Count Lingen was occasionally bidden to parties in the Governor-General's residence where he entertained the guests with his accordion. He would always bring back half-smoked cigarettes, which he had collected after the party was over and which he dished out to his fellow internees.

For the eleven boys from Camp 'R' life was significantly different from their old camp. Sullen, passive resistance to authority, which had been the hallmark of the Nazi dominated camp was replaced by an eagerness to co-operate. They could now engage in some productive work. They helped to make camouflage nets and ammunition boxes for the Canadian Army; their educational facilities were much improved amidst a galaxy of teaching talent; they were able to lead a much more active life. The handicraft teacher was able to fulfil a childhood ambition, to play ice-hockey in the country where that sport was king. With his first savings from his twenty cents-per-day wages in the workshop he bought himself a pair of skates. His major complaint about life in his new home was the lack of privacy, a characteristic which it shared with all other internment camps wherever they were, and the feeling that it was impossible ever to be alone with oneself and one's thoughts. But he emphasizes that whatever anybody else might say, the internment camp was not part of a Gulag Archipelago, nor was it like Colditz; it was an adventure, which, viewed in retrospect, helped to develop one's character and an ability to persevere in adversity.

The last consignment of internees from the ss *Sobieski* landed at Quebec the day after the *Ettrick* had discharged her human cargo. After separation from the POWs' the internees were taken two hundred miles up country until the train stopped in an open field. They were disembarked, surrounded by soldiers mounting machine guns. The Canadian guards had been told that they were all Nazi soldiers captured in battle and were puzzled that they should wear civilian clothes and that some of the older ones looked distinctly unmilitary. After a short bus ride they were taken by barge into the middle of the Richelieu River to their new home, the eighteenth-century fortress on the Île de Noix. They had to leave their luggage behind. When they recovered it the next morning they found themselves minus some of

H

their personal belongings which had disappeared. All that one internee collected from the soldiers was the handle of his suitcase with his name tag still on it.

The camp had all the usual educational and artistic activities and a good workshop in which a variety of skills were taught. An internee, then seventeen, who eventually settled in Canada writes:

> I spent half a day working and half a day card playing and sleeping. I was taught carpentry and since I had left school at an early age, I obtained all my higher education in the camps. Internment was a break for me. Where else could I have spent my time in such close proximity with such a variety of intellectuals, all of whom were bored and only too anxious to talk and teach us.

This boy's chance came when, much later, a Colonel in the Canadian Army engaged in some private, profitable enterprise. In a suburb of Montreal he opened up a workshop for the repair of vital machinery, in which he employed skilled internees. They were freed from virtually all restrictions; all they had to do was to report to the 'Mounties' once a month.

From the outset efforts were made, both in Britain and in Canada to arrange for release in Canada and integration into the Canadian war effort of all the refugees who wanted to stay, and whom the Home Office considered eligible for release. Similar requests were also made in respect of the refugees shipped to Australia. But the Home Office resolutely refused to approach the Dominion governments on these lines. As Herbert Morrison said in the Commons on 17 October, 'The two Governments have only agreed to take these people into safe custody on the express understanding that they would eventually be returned to the United Kingdom. Neither of them can be expected to accept any as immigrants.' Internees whose release he was able to authorize would have to be brought back to Britain or to emigrate to another country.

For most of the refugees that 'other country' meant the United States, for the internees in Canada so near, yet quite unattainable. There were several thousand refugees who had entered Britain as transmigrants, waiting only for the day when, under the strict American quota regulations, their registration number would come up and they could be examined for a visa. Many of them were now in internment on all three continents. But even when that day finally dawned, the would-be immigrants were confronted with a seemingly insurmountable problem in that US immigration regulations stipulated that visas could only be granted to free people and not to prisoners or internees. In Britain that problem had been overcome by bringing an internee to London once he had been notified by the US Consulate that his visa was available and setting him free so that he could collect it. But for a considerable time the Australian and Canadian governments were not prepared to allow any of their custodial prisoners liberty, not even in order to pay a visit to a US Consulate. Moreover, in the case of the Canadian internees, a further difficulty existed in that an alien wishing to immigrate into the US from a contiguous territory had to prove that he had paid his own fare to the American continent. The internees, however, had been ferried across free of charge. Some of the people, with good connections outside, overcame the legal impediment by securing visas to Cuba and then immigrating into the US from that 'non-contiguous' island.

In addition to those registered under the quota system, there were in Canada others with parents or other close relatives in the USA, who were anxious to join them. This was one of the many problems to which Alexander Paterson set his mind. A scheme to take these internees to Newfoundland, set them free, so that they could then immigrate into the US as free people, came to nothing because of opposition by the American Legion. Three times Paterson journeyed to Washington to enlist the help of the US administration, but he was faced with a further problem. The Allan Bill before Congress stipulated that nobody could be admitted to the USA during the war who had relatives in Germany or in German occupied Europe, and that no alien could enter the country who had not been a free man for at least one year. Paterson's efforts were finally abortive. In the face of determined right-wing opposition the sympathetic State Department could do nothing to help him.

By then the British Government had issued its three White Papers setting out the grounds on which people could be released. Under Paterson's guidance, applications were forwarded to London for consideration by the Home Office and its various advisory committees. Most of those who applied wanted to join the Pioneer Corps. The first transport of 287 internees left for Britain on 26 December 1940, a further 274 left on 24 February 1941 and another batch of 330 on 26 June.

The internees were taken to Halifax and housed in army barracks. They were allowed their freedom on parole and had to wait until a ship became available to take them back to either Glasgow or Liverpool. For many the return trip was sheer luxury compared with their outward journey. Those who joined the army were sworn in on arrival, given their King's shilling and sent home on leave. Those who were to be released on other grounds were taken for a short while to the Isle of Man until all formalities had been completed.

Amongst the first batch returning from Canada was Walter Wallich, then a young man, now a senior BBC producer. He had been at King's College, Cambridge for eighteen months, collecting research material for a combined PhD and Fellowship thesis. He had been arrested in May and taken to Bury St Edmunds to join some two or three hundred other internees, many of them from the University. He remembers that one of them was Professor Lauterpacht, Professor of International Law. Whilst they were in Bury St Edmunds, there was a sudden flap because papers which the professor had set for the tripos examinations could not be found and the exams had to be postponed until he could tell them where he had locked the questions away.

Wallich had known Alexander Paterson as a family friend for many years and fully confirms the humanitarianism which shows through every page of the Paterson Report. The young man had volunteered to join the army and was one of the first to be accepted. On arrival in Halifax he and his batch met Paterson but found no boat to take them home. The steamer which had been earmarked for them was a flat-bottomed Belgian vessel which had been plying along the Congo River. It had sailed across the South Atlantic and up along the American coast, but its mixed crew had now refused to take the ill-suited ship across the North Atlantic. Paterson persuaded her captain, a salty Welshman, to use his human cargo as a makeshift crew. None of them had so much as sailed a yacht, but enough volunteers were found to act as stokers, engineers, sailors and stewards, and, in January 1941, they sailed the ship safely through icebergs and submarine-infested waters to Liverpool.

As soon as Walter Wallich had been given army leave he hurried to see his old landlady in Cambridge. She had kept his rooms scrupulously clean; everything was in its proper place, but he was not able to find any of his research papers. Somewhat apprehensively he asked the landlady who replied: 'After you had been taken I got to thinking. What if that nice young man is really a spy? These papers might incriminate him and he might swing for it. So I lit a big fire in the boiler. It took me two days to burn them all.' 'She was such a nice woman,' Wallich comments, 'I could not even be cross with her.' After a distinguished war record he never went back to academia.

By the spring of 1942 only 972 out of 2,541 refugees whom Ottowa had reclassified as 'Interned Refugees (Friendly Aliens)' were left. By then both Canada and Australia had at last come to realize that these people might be able to play a part in their own war effort and that they could safely be released in the Dominion. Just what contribution they would ultimately make to post-war life in these countries, nobody realized at the time.

Barbara Moon, in the *Maclean's* article, lists a number of people by name, some of whom became well known in Canada and all of whom have contributed to the richness and diversity of their new homeland. Amongst the people whom she mentions are what she describes as a television pioneer in the marriage between serious music and show business, a jazz pianist and composer, an opera producer, a piano accompanist, an *avant-garde* painter, the owner of a modern art gallery, a TV scriptwriter (son of the German–Jewish author Jakob Wasserman), an impresario, an historian of Canadian Jewry, an Augustinian Father who is a baptized Jew and has become prominent in the Judeo-Christian reconciliation movement, a professor of English and author of several novels, professors of sociology and economics, a barrister, a stockbroker, a dambuilder, an airport controller, a Ju-Jitsu instructor to the police, a banquet manager and a vendor of hot dogs at a baseball stadium. Surely, no other group of immigrants so small and compact can have contributed in quite the same extent to the variety of Canadian life.

A song, composed by the jazz pianist whilst he was interned became a very popular hit in later years. It was called: 'You'll get used to it'. For public consumption he altered the words slightly. The original version was:

> You can scream and you can shout.
> They'll never let you out.
> It serves you right, you so-and-so.
> Why weren't you a naturalized Eskimo?

15 *Down Under*

THE TRAIN was churning through the arid, endless prairies. Occasionally wallabies and kangaroos with youngsters peeping out of their pouches could be seen hopping alongside the railway tracks; low brushwood, clumps of trees and much more rarely a farmstead – these were the first impressions which the internees, recently disgorged from the good ship *Dunera*, gathered of their new homeland, Australia. They were on their way 450 miles across country to their new home in New South Wales. Before boarding the train everyone had been given a luscious luncheon box, in such succulent contrast to the ship's 'grub' that all those interviewed still remember the boxes thirty-eight years later. Their escorts were elderly soldiers, many of them veterans of Gallipoli, who were relieved to hear their prisoners speak English and to find that they were not the Nazi parachutists whom they had been led to expect. In stark contrast to the recent shipboard experiences they soon established such a chummy atmosphere that one internee was not particularly surprised when one of the diggers said to him: 'Hey, mate, hold my rifle, whilst I roll a cigarette.' He had his first lesson in rolling his own cigarettes that night.*

After a day's and a night's journey the train eventually ground to a halt in a field, not far from a middle-sized town, called Hay. In the distance the internees could see some huts, surrounded by the inevitable barbed wire fence. They disembarked and were told by a Sergeant Major to line up for the usual counting of heads. After weeks of weary experiences and a long, cooped-up train ride, the internees showed no more discipline than in any other camp anywhere. They would not stand still. Eventually the RSM gave up and reported to the commandant: 'Approximately 2,000 men all present and correct, Sir.' After inspection and an address by their new commandant each man was issued with a mug of tea and a jumbo beef sandwich. One internee, the owner of a London vegetarian restaurant, surreptitiously

---

* The account of the life at Hay is partly based on the recollections of various internees and also on the article by Cyril Pearl in the Australian *Reader's Digest* of December 1973, op. cit.

tried to pass his sandwich to his neighbour. An officer saw it and asked sharply whether prime Australian beef was not good enough for him. The internee explained his vegetarian principles; the officer grumbled and left the parade ground. Shortly afterwards he returned with an equally large tomato sandwich in his hand. This little incident, if nothing else, jolted the men back again into a world where warmth and compassion still existed.

Hay consisted of two separate camps in the bush, numbers seven and eight. For the first few days all the internees were herded into camp eight as the other one was not ready. The two camps were about two hundred yards from each other, divided by a barbed wire fence and tightly segregated. Strictly speaking, any written communication between inmates of one camp to another had to be routed via the Chief Censor in Liverpool, but the internees were soon able to establish a more direct conduit of communication through their outside working parties.

On the morning following their arrival, some internees suddenly spotted the well-hated Major Scott, erstwhile overlord of the *Dunera*, approaching the fence, together with some Australian officers. Spontaneous jeering and cat-calling broke out, stones were tossed against the fence and the Major and his escort withdrew in haste. The internees' spokesman was summoned by the Commandant and was read the riot act, but when he explained some of the background to their violent reaction, nothing further was heard of the incident.

Each of the two camps eventually housed one thousand internees in thirty-six huts equipped with the standard double bunks, with additional huts for messing, recreation and ablutions. Food was soon available in abundance, but was at first not well balanced, at least not in the way to which Europeans had been used. Their standard ration was two and a half pounds of meat every single day of the week, mostly lamb. Amongst them were a number of vegetarians and Jews, strictly obeying their dietary laws, so that the individual ration for the carnivorous non-kosher internees was in fact even bigger. Anything which had not been consumed at the end of the day had to be burnt. These were the standard Australian Army rations and, as in Canada, prisoners received the same scale of food as members of the armed forces. By contrast they did not have enough green vegetables and hardly any fresh fruit. But, as the internees became their own market gardeners, this soon changed. Temperatures in the summer often rose to 110 degrees fahrenheit, with little shade anywhere and the growing of produce required skills different from those acquired on a London allotment. But those with 'green fingers' were soon successful.

Within a few days the internees at Hay had built up an internal administration and activities blossomed as in all the other camps in Britain and Canada. They received no guidance from the authorities; there was of course, no intercommunication between a camp on the Isle of Man, one in Ontario and another in New South Wales; yet it is astonishing to what extent similar objectives were pursued, along similar lines with the same degree of success. They elected their hut leaders, their row leader and a camp leader; they appointed a civil service responsible for everything from cleaning the latrines to staffing the library. Within days of their arrival a camp university started its activities. Boys were prepared for the summer Matric with the help of twelve teachers and were later transferred to a camp in Victoria so that they could sit for the examination under the auspices of Melbourne University. They had their cafés and art exhibitions, their debating societies and their camp newspapers (one of them called the *Boomerang*), their religious services, their bridge tournaments and their chess clubs, their workshops and their football matches. They even appointed their own cabinet for such departments as Social Services, Labour, Culture, and Justice. Their 'Minister of Justice' in later years became a real Minister of the Interior in one of the post-war German *Laender*.

However, each internment camp also had its special features resulting from the unique talents of one inmate or another. Camp Seven at Hay soon boasted its own vegetarian kitchen. In Camp Eight the financial arrangements were much more sophisticated than in any other. Its canteen began by selling toothpaste and razor blades but within a few months not only contained almost everything that the inmates wanted for their basic needs, but had also become an agent for a Sydney Mail Order house from whose catalogue the internees could freely choose provided they were able to pay. They had three possible sources of income: private means, assistance from relatives or charitable organizations, and wages for work done inside or outside the camp. As in all other camps their means of exchange were at first crude chits of paper or iou's, which were debited to their camp account (coins or notes of the realm were not allowed to circulate in any internment camp). But Camp Eight numbered amongst its inmates a former director of the Austrian State Bank and designer of some Austrian Schilling notes. This man, later a director of a merchant bank in the city, designed three elaborate notes, worth 6d, 1/– and 2/– respectively, which were submitted for approval to the Commonwealth Bank of Australia, who had the monopoly of note issue. The currency was duly approved for internal circulation only, with one objection: the internees were not allowed to fill the centre escutcheon with the Commonwealth coat-of-arms. They therefore substituted a sheep – symbolic of their own status as well as of the continent's chief source of wealth; supported by a kangeroo and an emu. The border of the notes consisted of a web of barbed wire entanglements into which the designer had cleverly woven the words: we are here, because we are here, because we are here.* A local firm in Hay printed the notes in three different colours. They were issued and the internees' camp account debited; they became the camp's only trading currency. But not for long; one day the Commandant received a wire from the Commonwealth Bank that their original approval had been wrong; money could not be printed, not even for internal circulation. The notes were all called in and put on a bonfire except for a few which internees managed to keep. The camp had to revert again to scraps of paper.

Amongst the internees was Peter Stadlen, whose energy and enthusiasm seems to have been boundless. He was one of several unfortunate people whose release had been authorized by the Home Secretary before he was deported, but by the time the order reached Huyton he was already on the high seas. His sponsors for release had been Thomas Mann, Yehudi Menuhin and Eleanor Roosevelt. It took over a year for him to come home.† The only musical instrument in the camp was a violin belonging to one of the inmates. Later on the Quakers donated an upright piano, but before that happened Stadlen was occasionally taken out under escort to the local church for him to practise on its harmonium. He had managed to bring out with him the Novello piano score of Handel's 'Israel in Egypt' and from this he transcribed on lavatory paper the scores for the violin and for the various voices. He built up a choir of seventy-five internees; the first performance of the Handel oratorio was given in front of the whole camp and its officers. Thereafter he rehearsed them in Mozart's C Major Mass, a mass by Palestrina and madrigals by Orlando Lasso.

---

* See illustration section.
† After he had landed at Liverpool he heard the tannoy boom out his name. The message was: 'Dr Vaughan Williams wants you to get in touch with him urgently.' The news rather pleased him.

A Bespattered Page?

Some of the purest voices belonged to a group of young Jews who, under the supervision of an orthodox rabbi, lived a strictly religious life, very much on their own. The rabbi refused at first to let them take part in these secular performances, but eventually relented on condition that whenever the words 'God' or 'Jesus' appeared in the text, they had to mouth just 'la, la, la'. Freddy Fisher, interned in the adjacent camp, and now the editor of another national newspaper, remembers a performance of the prisoners' chorus in Beethoven's Fidelio, a most appropriate piece of music for the occasion.

Some of the orthodox boys were amongst the first to be released, at very short notice, for onward migration to Palestine. They refused to leave camp as it would have meant having to travel on the Sabbath if they did not wish to miss their ship at Sydney. The rabbi had ruled that travel on the Sabbath was only permitted in cases of grave illness or under compulsion. The commandant refused to issue an order to that effect, saying that he had already had enough troubles with the religiously orthodox, but the Sergeant Major, appealed to by the camp father, told the boys 'you either pack up and go, or else. . . .' The boys were only too happy that the problem had been solved for them; they travelled on the Sabbath, reached their ship in time and duly went to a new life on a kibbutz in the Holy Land.

The internees in Australia received a lot of moral and material help, not only from Jewish charitable organizations, who did everything possible, but also from the Society of Friends, and, after some initial hesitation, from the Church of England. Soon after their arrival a protestant internee wrote to the Anglican Bishop of Sydney, Pilcher, asking for his help. The Right Reverend replied on these lines: 'What nasty trick are you trying to play on us? Are you not ashamed pretending to be refugees when in fact you have all been interned because you are dangerous Nazis? When I got your letter, I made enquiries in London and they have confirmed this.' By then the Bishop of Chichester had already uttered his outspoken criticisms in the Upper House against indiscriminate internment and several government spokesmen had repeatedly declared that the Australians had been put fully in the picture as to who these internees really were. Yet here was a senior clergyman still in total ignorance. However, he agreed to visit the camp and after he had spoken to many internees and in particular had seen the young Jews with their skull caps and prayer shawls engaged in devotional exercises in their hut, his attitude changed completely and he became a good friend of the internees.

As in Canada, the internees in Australia were designated at first as prisoners-of-war and treated as such. Soon after their arrival the representative of the protecting power, a Swiss consul, arrived and offered them his assistance. Again quite spontaneously – as in every other camp – the camp leaders refused to have any parley with him; they had no wish to be 'protected' by a representative of their mortal enemies against their friends. The consul was puzzled; the Commandant impressed. This also helped to revise his initial attitude towards his charges. But for a while they had to continue to write their letters on the official forms bearing the imprimature of POW mail.

Censoring was done initially by the camp Intelligence Officer. A week or two after their arrival this officer called in the camp leader and told him that he was a worried man. There seemed to be an internee in the camp whose name was being mentioned in a number of letters which internees were writing home, yet they had no trace of him in their records. Had they missed him out and if so where was he hiding? Apparently petty thieving on a small scale was still occurring in the camp, though on nothing like the extent of the *Dunera*, and some people mentioned in their correspondence that 'Herr Gannef is still with us', *Gannef* being the Yiddish word for thief. The camp leader explained the mystery; the IO laughed and told him that they could write quite freely about life in the camp.

With financial backing from the Australian Jewish Welfare Society, and the support of the military, the internees organized their market gardening, fodder growing, poultry and dairy farming. They carried out their own irrigation works and established workshops for tailoring, bootmaking, carpentry and joinery. The interned doctors and dentists assisted the Medical Officer in the care of the sick and, together with trained nurses, staffed the camp hospitals. The 196 members of the Jewish orthodox group were allowed to send their own butcher into a nearby knacker's yard for the ritual killing. One man started his own private zoo by collecting lizards and other indigenous animals whilst outside on working parties. A search for an alleged baby dinosaur proved fruitless.

One of the internees was to be a post-war Austrian ambassador to the Court of St James; he was a man of great physical strength and whilst on the *Dunera* he cracked open a precious tin of sardines with his bare hands after the key had been lost. Other internees were a Viennese actor, who later became a principal interpreter at the Nuremberg trials, a future judge, a former chief PT instructor to the Bavarian police and two members of well-known banking families, the Erlangers and the Bleichroeders, one of whom was later killed as a glider pilot at Arnhem.

In January 1941 HM Government, under persistent pressure from its critics, sent an emissary to Australia, some months after they had dispatched Paterson to Canada. This was Major (later Lieutenant-Colonel) Julian Layton, who had previously been in charge of Richborough Camp and had been acting as a liaison officer between the War Office and Bloomsbury House. His brief was to dispel the misunderstandings which had arisen about the whole internment policy and the nature of the internees, to contact the refugees in their camps, look after their welfare and explain to them what chances existed for their release, particularly if they were to join the Pioneer Corps. Eventually over four hundred men enlisted.

Others applied to be released. But by June 1941 – eleven months after their departure – only eighty-two people had actually returned; a further fifty-one were on the high seas and another 310 were waiting in Australia for shipping accommodation.* By December 1941 the great majority of the internees were still stuck in Australia. During an adjournment debate on his own motion in the House of Lords, the Bishop of Chichester stated that he did not believe the constant excuses about the lack of shipping. The *Sterling Castle* had recently returned to Britain from the Antipodes with 1,500 empty berths. Surely if we had been able to ship out over 2,500 internees on one boat it should not be outside the bounds of possibility to bring back a somewhat smaller number in several ships.

During the middle of 1941 the two camps at Hay were gradually being emptied; some of the internees were taken to a smaller camp at Orange, much nearer to Sydney, awaiting their return to Britain; others were transported to Tatura, a camp in Victoria. The transfers had been arranged by Major Layton who had considered the sand-swept, arid Hay a quite unsuitable location for Europeans. At Orange the Hay internees met up again with the *Arandora Star* survivors who had been taken directly from Melbourne to Tatura Camp, one hundred miles to the north. It will be remembered that amongst these survivors there had been a number of genuine refugees, two of whom, the London antiquarian bookseller and Peter Jacobsohn the Harvard staff

---

* See the report to the London Board of Deputies, dated 20 November 1940 at Bloomsbury House.

member, we now meet again at Tatura. The Italians, including our toilet roll diarist, were also there, but in a separate cluster of huts. All of them report the initial suspiciousness and brusqueness of their Australian guards which soon turned into friendliness. They, too, remember the very generous food rations and adequate housing and clothing.

At Orange the refugees were at first put together with class 'A' and Nazi prisoners. This was the Hay contingent's first experience of living together with these people. They did not have a pleasant time. After constant protests they were put into a separate cantonment, divided from the others by a wire fence. One day a singing contest took place across the fence, but unlike the one between Beckmesser and Walter. The Nazis were bellowing out their marching songs, the refugees replying in equal decibel strength with such patriotic songs as *Rule, Britannia* and *We will hang out our washing on the Siegfried Line*. By then the refugee section of Tatura housed some two hundred Pioneer Corps recruits who were taken out for rudimentary drilling.

The religious bookseller, who had been classified as category 'A', and had endured both the *Arandora Star* and the *Dunera*, all because he had tried to take his hard-earned money out of Germany illegally, suffered a further sad testing of his faith. On Yom Kippur day 1940 he received a telegram that his house in North London had been bombed; his parents, his sister, his brother and sister-in-law had all been killed; his own wife and four children had escaped because they had been interned on the Isle of Man. His wife was brought back to London for a few days and lodged at Holloway so that she could attend the funeral under escort, but nothing could be done for him. He was not released until March 1942, well over two years after he had been first interned.

As berths became available the internees due to be released in the UK, particularly those accepted for the Pioneer Corps, were returned home, mostly across the Pacific and then through the Panama Canal. One man tells that they shared their ship with some rough-and-ready members of the Australian Timber Corps who called the refugees 'limeys' with good humoured contempt: a pleasant reincarnation from their previous existences, first as Jews and then as Nazis. After being battered by severe storms off Greenland which forced their convoy to scatter, they landed in Liverpool in October 1941 at the same berth where eighteen months before they had been driven aboard the *Dunera*. Huyton had by then ceased to be used as an internment camp and was now a Western Command depot. It was there that they were sworn in as members of HM Forces and were given their King's shilling. They were joined by other Pioneer Corps recruits. One of them had no English and spoke only Yiddish, instead of taking his oath of allegiance to 'King George, his heirs and successors', he swore fealty to the '*melech und seine Mishpochah*'.*

As in Canada, many of the Australian internees were anxious to move on to the United States but they faced the same problem: they were not free people; the Commonwealth Government refused to set them free even for a day and the Americans would only grant visas to free people.† It was a vicious circle. Others would have liked to settle in Australia but here again, as in Canada, the Australians considered themselves mere custodial guardians of prisoners or internees for the British Government. It took the Australian authorities a considerable time before they finally realized that many of the people whom they were keeping behind barbed wire could be of use to them in their own war effort. In August 1941 Robert Menzies, the Prime Minister, announced that some internees had been released to do work of national importance.

Gradually more and more were absorbed in the war effort. Two optical glass experts were set up in a factory to make lenses for searchlights. Eventually the Australian Labour Corps was opened for the enlistment of interned refugees. 512 men volunteered for the Eighth Employment Company stationed near Melbourne. A number of them in their off-duty time enrolled at the night school of Melbourne University; of these forty graduated.

Altogether 915 men, mainly bachelors, stayed in Australia, a figure surprisingly close to the Canadian one. Amongst them are professors of philosophy and theoretical physics at the Australian National University in Canberra, a former Secretary of the Department of Territories, an expert in the artificial insemination of cattle (formerly a bank manager in Germany), a Dean of a School of Social Sciences, the Head of the Department of Metereology of Melbourne University, a composer and musical critic, a university adviser on athletics and a theatre director.

The men who stayed in Canada and Australia probably found it simpler to integrate and become wholly accepted than those who returned and settled in Britain because it is much easier to do so in

---

* Yiddish for 'King and his relatives'.
† According to Herbert Morrison in reply to a question in the House on 16 June 1941, there were three hundred such cases.

new and evolving societies than in old established and relatively closed ones; but, wherever the internees returned again to freedom and settled down they played – with the inevitable exceptions – a useful part and spiced the variety of national life.

16   *Release*

WE MUST NOW RETURN to the late summer and autumn of 1940, and to the bulk of the 'loyal enemy aliens'; those who had not been deported and who, with a few exceptions, had by now been concentrated into the Isle of Man camps, sorted out, and separated from the not so loyal ones.

Towards the end of August 1940, many of them had settled down to some sort of fruitful routine. The initial reactions of heartache or hysteria, resentment or recalcitrancy among the older, and of adventure or mischief amongst the younger, had gradually become subdued and had been replaced by either listless resignation or by active participation in the multifarious activities which creative inmates had organized. Relations with the military had become much more relaxed and friendly. The war situation outside seemed to be steadily improving; Britain was holding her own. The biggest morale booster of all was the gradually accelerating, though still intermittent, flow of correspondence with relations and friends. Though releases had not yet started in earnest, many people were moderately optimistic that their ordeal might not last too long and hoped to be free again. Cultural and educational activities were at their most intensive phase, before the talents started to be drained off again into the outside world.

The internees no longer felt like forgotten people. They heard about the various parliamentary debates; they read some of the articles and letters in the newspapers; now for the first time important people came to listen to their grievances. Pastor Hildebrandt, one of the interned members of the German Confessional Church, has described a visit which the Bishop of Chichester had paid to his camp.[1]

> We were all drawn up to receive him. When he at last appeared, accompanied by the Bishop of Sodor and Man, and the Mayor of Douglas, he could scarce reply to our cheers and at first could only stammer and stutter. It was an unforgettable moment. The sight of these refugees in their new captivity was just too much for him.

The Bishop was told of the internees' principal complaint. As soon as he got back to Liverpool he went straight to the Central Postal Censorship Office, saw all the hundreds of unsorted mailbags which had accumulated, and with all the aura and wrath of a prince of the church, stirred up the officials there. Three days later the camp post office was inundated with letters. Hildebrandt says: 'We all knew whom to thank.'

But the views expressed by the Bishop during his visit were not universally welcome. The *Isle of Man Examiner* called him 'that self-appointed champion of captive Nazis and Fascists' and there were demands in the House of Keys that he should in future be barred from entering the island.[2] After the war the refugees did not forget their patron saint. In the Church of St Michael and All Angels in Harrow Weald stands a statue of St Michael, created by a refugee sculptor in his honour as a 'thanks offering of men and women who found in Britain a refuge from tyranny'.

Once the first White Paper had been published and release became a possibility, increased tension crept into the camps' atmosphere. The eighteen categories were scrutinized and analysed and became the principal topic of conversation. No matter how tenuous the connection was, almost everybody put in an application, sometimes under more than one category. Relatives, friends, solicitors and Members of Parliament were bombarded with letters and telegrams; only those who had nobody outside or who preferred the security of internment to the uncertainties of unfettered freedom in war-time Britain, remained unaffected.

The most promising way to freedom, and the one which the government favoured, was enlistment in the unarmed alien companies of the Auxiliary Military Pioneer Corps. Altogether some five thousand men joined the Corps straight from various internment camps.* The War Office dispatched a special recruiting officer to the island whose methods sometimes smacked of high pressure salesmanship. In one camp he invited all able-bodied men to meet him. He then had the doors

---

* For more about the alien companies of the Pioneer Corps, see Norman Bentwich: *I Understand the Risks – the story of the refugees from Nazi oppression who fought in the British Forces during the War*. London 1950. He says that altogether seven thousand men served in the fifteen alien companies. Of these more than half were eventually transferred into various combatant units and of those, as far as could be ascertained, 150 died on active service. The remainder either stayed in the AMPC for the duration or were discharged, either on medical grounds or because their special skills could be better used elsewhere.

locked and said that nobody would be allowed to leave until he had told him why he did not want to join up. This rather hamfisted approach discouraged some who had originally intended to enlist. The whole recruiting approach had been unnecessary; most of the refugees were only too anxious to join. During my own medical at Hutchinsons, one of the elderly refugees who was suffering from a mild form of diabetes, was anxiously trying to induce another recruit to let him have some of his urine so that he could pass the test. Whoever passed his medical and a subsequent security check was eventually called to the Commandanture where the Commanding Officer administered the oath of loyalty, handed over the King's shilling, and warned the recruit that he had now become a member of His Majesty's Forces, subject to the full rigours of military law. When it came to my turn, I and my fellow recruits were told somewhat sheepishly by the Commandant that we could only leave by next morning's steamer. There was no outside accommodation available for us and although we were now free men, would we mind spending another night behind barbed wire? We gladly returned to our old billet to celebrate farewell with our housemates. Next morning we were marched under armed escort to the pier and put aboard the steamer.

As the steamer pulled into the open sea we stood at the railing and watched the island disappear into the morning mist. Our feelings were mixed. We were obviously happy that at last we were free people again. We delighted in the prospect of an early reunion with our wives and children. We were slightly sad that we had to leave behind such an interesting, heterodox community, and we were apprehensive as to how we would fit into army life, yet at the same time we were looking forward to it.

As soon as we arrived in Liverpool we were taken to the nearest barracks and kitted out with the same battle dress uniforms that our 'jailers' had worn. Suspected poachers had been turned overnight into apprentice gamekeepers.

The first people to leave the camps were the very old and the sick – all those who, under the original instructions to the Chief Constables, should never have been interned at all. They were followed by all those bizarre characters, who through ignorance or neglect were regarded as Germans or Austrians, but could speak no German and who had been in Britain uninterruptedly since early childhood. Then came those whose work was considered vital for the war effort, the factory owners on the industrial estates in Cardiff and on Tyneside, the technicians and the scientists.★ During October the exodus into the Pioneer Corps began. There followed a frustrating worrying pause for the majority, for all those who did not qualify under any of the eighteen clauses of the first White Paper and who had to wait until the categories were eventually cast somewhat wider.

As the first batches of released internees began to return to the mainland and to freedom, interviews with some of them appeared in various newspapers. Some of the liberated refugees not only expressed their understanding of the critical situation during the summer in which indiscriminate internment had become inevitable, but also spoke in glowing terms about the good time which they had enjoyed in their camps.† It had really been more like a holiday at government expense. However, other papers challenged the veracity of these roseate accounts. They alleged that before release the refugees had been made to sign statements promising that they would not disclose to outsiders, not even to their own families, details of life inside the camps, and that they were warned that if they broke that solemn undertaking they would be liable to immediate reinternment. When on arrival at Liverpool they were waylaid by reporters, some feared that the newsmen were really MI5 people in disguise, sent to trip them up; others were just too scared to tell the truth; thus they all painted false pictures. A letter in the *Spectator* of 30 August 1940, alleges that an internee was told to sign such an undertaking without even being given a chance to read it properly, and that on reporting his return at the local police station, he was again cautioned to keep silent about his internment experiences. During a press conference in August Lord Lytton, on behalf of HM Government, denied all these stories.[3] The only document which the internees was asked to sign was a receipt for the return of whatever valuables and papers had been confiscated from them on first internment. That in fact is the correct story, but it may just be possible that one or the other camp officer had issued a verbal *caveat* to the released refugees not to talk about their experiences.

At the beginning of 1941 the majority of the refugees were still

---

★ In the nineteen thirties HM Government had created factory and trading estates in the high unemployment areas of Tyneside and South Wales and had encouraged refugee industrialists by offering financial incentives to start up factories there. Many of them, as well as some of their key personnel, had been interned, although most of these factories were now on war work.

† See, for instance, the letter by F. Eisner in *The Times* of 13 December 1940 and also the letter by Isaac Puch, a 'retired master tailor of Salford' in the *Daily Mail* of 13 August 1940.

behind barbed wire. On the whole they were by now much better off than those interned in Canada and Australia. They had all been separated from the more obnoxious Nazi elements. Through the gates they had seen some of their camp mates leave for freedom and had attended many farewell parties. These were often upsetting occasions for those left behind, but at least the exodus continued day by day and there was always the hope that one's own turn would come soon. Unlike those interned overseas they could anticipate their own release.

Unbeknown to them, and to the British public at large, the military authorities once again became alarmed during the early weeks of 1941 about the possibility of a German invasion attempt. On 23 January the recently constituted interdepartmental Aliens Advisory Committee met, chaired by Sir Frank Newsam – Sir Alexander Maxwell's deputy and eventual successor at the Home Office – , and attended by representatives from MI5, the Admiralty and from the Refugee Section of the Foreign Office.[4]

The members agreed that the security services should immediately compile a list of all aliens, particularly those living in coastal and dock areas, who in the event of an imminent German invasion should be arrested and, as long as transport was still available, be moved to camps. According to the Foreign Office man there was a long wrangle between Newsam and the MI5 representative during which Newsam pointed out the inconsistency of once again contemplating mass internment while continuing releases from the camps. It was the FO representative's impression that 'MI5 would like to intern everybody who spoke with a guttural voice'. R. E. Latham as usual added his own biting marginal comments to the report. Such a policy, he said, would dismantle everything which had been done to clear up the whole question of refugees, and all the problems created by the inefficient security services. If invasion should occur, Latham considered the military on the spot had ample powers under existing martial law to deal with everybody, alien or Britisher.

In February the Home Office advised the Chief Constables that the Government was not considering general internment, either now or at the moment of any invasion, but that it might authorize arrest of selected aliens. Meanwhile Chief Constables should, after consultation with Regional Security Offices, prepare lists of suspects. Latham's comment, in a memo to Newsam, was that the habitual xenophobia of Chief Constables was well known, 'Last June,' he wrote, 'it resulted in many people being interned who should never have been arrested.' He urged Newsam that the Home Secretary should exercise a much firmer control over his police chiefs.

By that time any possibility of reviving Operation *Seelöwe* had been abandoned. Hitler was concentrating on preparing *Barbarossa*, the invasion of Soviet Russia. Britain remained inviolate from invasion threats and no further large scale internment of enemy aliens took place.

But the criticisms of the security services by other government officials continued unabated. Lord Beaverbrook, who as Minister for Aircraft Production was at that time concentrating everything on replacing the aircraft losses sustained during the Battle of Britain, and bringing production up to maximum peak, wrote to Churchill on 24 January:

Dear Prime Minister,

Here is the story of the children of Israel and of our effort to rescue them from the land of Egypt and the house of bondage. On the seventh of October 1940, I wrote to the Home Secretary asking his permission to recruit mechanics and technicians from the concentration camps for our MAP factories. On the fourth of December Morrison gave his consent to our project of sending two reputable Jews, Dr Alexander and Mr Blauhorn, to the camps for the purpose of examining and selecting suitable internees. The Jewish mission to the Jews set off. They brought back a most admirable report containing careful records of 639 internees, 446 Jews and 193 gentiles. On the fourth of January I sent a list to the Home Secretary and asked for the release of all but thirteen of them. I emphasized the need for their labour. On 24 January we still await our Jews. I am told that they are being investigated by MI5. But already they have been examined carefully not only by Dr A and Mr B but also by Morrison's representatives in the camps. Will you therefore please give an order discharging MI5 from any further responsibility in relation to these Jews.

Yours sincerely

Beaverbrook[5]

The letter brought about prompt and positive action. Complaints about MI5 had also come from another noble Lord, the chairman of the Advisory Council on Aliens, who felt so frustrated in his work that he decided to resign. Early in January the BBC had asked Lord Lytton to explain on their Overseas Services, beamed to the USA, why the refugees had been interned. The original draft of his speech had been so highly critical of the panic decision, that at the urging of the Home Secretary and the suggestion of R. E. Latham who was acting as

Secretary to the Aliens Council, he agreed to tone it down, but his disenchantment continued to grow.

Finally he wrote on 21 January to the Foreign Secretary:

Dear Anthony,

The attitude of the Security people (which I suppose means in fact MI5) is, I think, responsible for all that I criticize most in the internment policy of the Government. They persist in saying that they know nothing about the large body of refugees who have been quite senselessly interned; although in fact, if only they had taken the trouble, they should know everything about each one of them. The intelligence service is so bad that a number of people have been released who are notoriously dangerous. It adds immensely to the bitterness of all those refugees who are our friends and who are imprisoned without any hope of release since they are humble people who don't come into any of the categories of the White Paper. I have very great doubts whether men who did these things, which I have seen done, are capable of defeating the gangsters of Europe.

Latham, asked by Eden to comment, wrote on 24 January: 'I am in full agreement with the substance of Lord Lytton's complaints about the irresponsibility of MI5 and the fact that the cause of their irresponsibility is their own incompetence.' Eden tried hard to dissuade Lytton from resigning. He promised to examine the whole question and to see what could be done to remove the difficulties which Lytton claimed were obstructing his work, but Lord Lytton remained adamant. He resigned, officially for health reasons, and was eventually succeeded by Sir Herbert Emerson.★

As a result of the complaints by both Beaverbrook and Lytton, Churchill sent a memo to Eden and Morrison:

I have heard from various quarters that the witch-finding activities of MI5 are becoming an actual impediment to the more important work of the Department. I am carefully considering certain changes not only in MI5 but also in the control of Intelligence and the Secret Services. . . . I have no doubt that there is a certain amount of risk that some bad people might get loose but our dangers are much less now than they were in May or June. The whole organization of the country, the Home Guard and so forth are much more efficient against fifth column activities that I am sure a more rapid process of release from internment should be adopted.[6]

★ According to Latham on 21 January (FO 371/29180), what had incensed Lord Lytton in particular was that he had personally sponsored the release of a man in whom he had complete confidence; yet the Home Secretary had refused the application as the result of an adverse MI5 report.

The Prime Minister's recommendation to speed up releases was issued two days after the meeting at the Home Office at which MI5 had advocated resumption of internment in view of a possible invasion!

Lord Lytton's Council was not the only body concerned with refugees and with internment which felt frustrated. On 15 January, Sir Herbert Emerson, on behalf of the Advisory Committee, sent a confidential memo[7] to Herbert Morrison complaining that the rate of releases was much too slow, mainly due to the inadequacy of the Intelligence Services on the Isle of Man. Not enough liaison existed between MI5 and Scotland Yard, whose job it was to vet applicants, and the camp commandants who knew a lot about their charges but little about their previous record. Once the categories had been exhausted, what was to happen to the rest of the internees? The longer they were kept interned, Sir Herbert pointed out, the more people outside would think that a black mark existed against them and the more difficult it would become for these refugees, once they were released, to be accepted by their neighbours and get jobs.

The American press and public – and to some extent also the US authorities – had been rather critical of British policy towards refugees.* But in June 1941 – six months before they were forced into the war – the US Government issued instructions which, as Sir Herbert Emerson pointed out in a letter to a State Department official in Washington, went far beyond Britain's cautious attitude. In future visas to enter the USA would be denied to anybody who had close relatives living in territories controlled by either Germany, Italy or Russia. The official justification by the US Assistant Solicitor General was that such immigrants might become spies through threats or through actual torture of close relatives. However, Lord Halifax, now British Ambassador in Washington, in a cable to the Foreign Office, voiced his suspicion. What certain sections of the State Department really wanted to achieve, he said, was to restrict the flood of immigrants from Central Europe. They would rather see them accommodated elsewhere, perhaps in some parts of the British Empire. It is of course an old story, from biblical days to Vietnam; it made it even more difficult for refugees interned in Britain to obtain US quota visas.

---

* The US Government's attitude towards a substantial group of their enemy aliens, namely the Japanese, was much harsher than that of the British Government towards the German refugees. They transported a large number of whole families from the West Coast to the interior, where they were kept under unpleasant conditions. Included in this mass deportation were many native Americans of Japanese origin – the so-called 'Nisei'.

A Bespattered Page?

The *Dunera* court martial in the summer of 1941 and the slow return of internees from Canada and Australia, all with their own stories, kept up public interest for a while, but gradually the topic faded from the press and from Commons' question time. Very occasionally the few xenophobic members of the House uttered warnings. Major Petherick* accused the Home Office of being weak.

> It was so easy for an enemy alien to claim that he was an anti-Nazi because his daughter had once been insulted by a *Gauleiter*. Have the results on the continent not shown what dangerous consequences such incredible weakness can have? Anybody who says he hates Hess (who had just landed in Scotland) is regarded as a gift from Germany and Austria, but a British subject of unmixed British blood for many centuries is automatically suspect.

But the Major was now very much in a minority.

One of the questions which exercised some of the MPs was naturalization of serving soldiers of enemy nationality. In most other allied countries, notably in the USA, members of the Armed Forces were preferentially naturalized. On 23 January Colonel Wedgwood demanded that the same privilege should be extended to refugees who had volunteered for Britain but Morrison declared that this would be impossible under war-time conditions. On 31 July Aneurin Bevan avowed that people who were prepared to serve our country and risk their lives in doing so were surely particularly desirous citizens but he got the same dusty answer.

Gradually releases were gathering speed. By 22 January 1941 9,816 people had been freed; some ten thousand men and women remained interned in the UK and another six thousand men in the two dominions. By 13 February the number of releases had risen to 10,112.⁹ By October 1941 6,928 were still interned in the UK† of whom 3,091 were in category 'C', victims of 'Nazi oppression' behind barbed wire. A month later the total had been reduced to 6,598 men and women.

Releases continued throughout 1942 and beyond on a diminishing scale but a hardcore of people remained interned until the end of the war. They were people who either had no wish to be repatriated to Nazi Germany and whom the Home Office, on the advice of the security services, did not consider safe enough to be left at large, or a

---

* Member for Penryn and Falmouth (C).
† Herbert Morrison to Geoffrey Mander, House of Commons 9 October.

very small number of refugees who simply refused to apply for release. They had not applied to be interned, why should they now apply to be set free again?

One such reluctant refugee was a painter who was happy with his brushes and his canvas. The camp gave him shelter, food, security and plenty of leisure to paint. What more did he want? He became such an embarrassment to the authorities that they asked his friend, who had recently been released from the same camp, to return to the Isle of Man and persuade the painter to apply for release. He was eventually successful.

Gradually, one by one, the internees left their temporary homes behind barbed wire, to pick up again their old threads or to start weaving new ones; to resume where they had left off many months before or to embark on altogether new careers, new challenges and new adventures. The schoolboys went back to finish off their secondary education; some of the undergraduates returned to their universities; others joined the Army. The factory owners, their foremen and technicians, the scientists and engineers, the university and school teachers, all those engaged in essential work, resumed their old tasks. The journalists, writers and trades unionists were absorbed by the BBC, by the press and by the various overt and clandestine government agencies concerned with publicity and propaganda; at last their experiences and their expertise became part of Britain's effort to reach and to soften the mind of the Germans. The elderly and the invalids went back to their families or became again wards of charitable organizations. All those thousands who had no special skills and who for one reason or another could not or would not join the Armed Forces took on humble, hum-drum jobs as fire fighters, air raid wardens, postmen, unskilled factory hands and agricultural workers, becoming very small cogs in the vast war effort machine. Most of the fit and active women, released from Rushen, whether single or married with family responsibilities, also played their part in hospitals, nurseries, schools, factories, in the Land Army and in the ATS.

But the biggest challenge came to the internees who joined the alien companies of the Auxiliary Military Pioneer Corps. For the next three years they helped to build roads, camps and airfields, to shovel coal, to load and unload railway trucks with coils of barbed wire, pit props and all manner of warlike stores, to act as unskilled handymen to the armed forces of the Crown, until at last the authorities yielded to their pleas that they were being wasted and allowed them to transfer to combatant units. The majority of them then became troopers, riflemen, sappers or gunners with a sprinkling of aircraftmen and able seamen. A number of them joined special units such as the Commandos or the Parachute Brigade. They went in due course to the Middle East, to India and into Europe and into establishments so secret that even today they cannot talk about what they did. A fair number were commissioned and some of these assisted in the interrogation of prisoners-of-war and later in Allied Military Government as town majors and other officers engaged in the administration and denazification of post-war Germany. The story of all these pioneers still remains to be told.

When, some time after the end of the war, they were demobilized, they faced problems similar to those of many of their British comrades-in-arms in reintegrating into civilian life. Only a minority of them were able to resume where they had left off before the outbreak of war, the majority had not been long enough in England or had been too young to have become established in a career.

But on the whole they prospered. With their war gratuities some established their own workshops, later to become substantial factories, their export trading concerns, art galleries and publishing houses. Some became bankers, stockbrokers, accountants, librarians, civil servants and shop assistants. Others went under government schemes to universities and colleges to become doctors, lawyers, teachers and engineers. Of those who had originally meant to stay in Britain only temporarily whilst waiting for onward emigration some now moved on to more distant shores, particularly to the USA and to the Dominions, where on the whole they were equally successful in establishing themselves. Not many went back to Germany; those who did were either politically motivated people, anxious to help in rebuilding a democratic Germany, or were elderly men and women who had been unable to acclimatize themselves to a strange language and to unfamiliar customs. Not many of the thirty thousand interned refugees were able to climb up to the pinnacle of public acclaim or commercial success, but even fewer probably could be rated as failures or as having disgraced themselves.

Most of those who served in HM Forces anglicized their names (to fox the Germans should they be captured).* If it were not for their

---

* A Moses became a Montgomery; a Kohn became a Cunninghame; a Schlesinger a Sheridan; a Pomeranzenbaum turned into a Delamare-Pomeroy – and a Stensch into a Stent.

ineradicable accents they would have disappeared long ago as an identifiable group. But that has already happened with most of their children.

For the great majority of them the months which they spent in internment camps have become a distant and blurred memory which long ago lost all relevance to their present life. Whatever grudges and resentments they bore at the time, have left no trace and that is of course as it should be. They mostly only remember the comic and tragicomic incidents of a now somewhat unreal, no longer tangible interlude in their lives.

Aliens Registration Book, stamped with release permit

17   *The Phantom Fifth Column*

WHENEVER – particularly during the early days – the internees puzzled over the rationale of their incarceration and discussed the possible reasons that had prompted the authorities to put thousands of avowed victims and enemies of Nazi Germany into barbed wire stockades, they usually agreed that it had been the result of panic, misconception and muddle, which however harsh and unfair it may have been, was excusable in a dire emergency. Few speculated on anything more sinister.

Research for this book, begun thirty-six years later, was undertaken with the same presumption in mind. In the early stages of the investigation it became clear that the prime propagator of wholesale internment, the authority which was ultimately responsible for it, was not the Cabinet, nor any of the major departments of state, nor the police, not even the Chiefs of Staff, but the department of Military Intelligence responsible for internal security and for the detection of espionage and other subversive activities – MI5. It was they who alerted and alarmed all the other government departments and it was their persistent, urgent requests which in the end could not be ignored.

The British Security Services, in peace and war, used to have a reputation second to none; the stories of successful exploits during the two world wars by both MI5 and MI6 are legion. Brilliant ruses and deceptions constantly misled the enemy, and, with a very few exceptions such as the 'Cicero' or the Best affairs, aborted every major German attempt at espionage. Why should they therefore have resorted to this crude and unsophisticated operation of indiscriminate internment and continued to insist on it in the face of mounting criticism and of all the obvious disadvantages?

As the research progressed, it became clear that the high opinion of the efficacy and subtlety of MI5 held by many outsiders, including fiction writers, was not at the time shared by all insiders. At least one senior official in the Foreign Office went further and suspected something more sinister behind the stance of the security services. The minute by R. E. Latham, mentioned on page 75 seems a clear enough indication that he thought that the security services were not only inefficient, but also that somewhere in the higher echelons there were people who were part of the real fifth column in this country, people who were deliberately focusing public unease on the hapless refugees, the better to carry on their own dirty work in the shadows. Some press columnists, such as Kingsley Martin, and R. H. Crossman, as well as H. G. Wells seem to have harboured similar suspicions. Was wholesale internment in fact part of an overall conspiracy, of a fifth column master plan, which would not only allow the real traitors to carry on their work unhindered, but would also concentrate the foes of Germany, all those on the proscribed Gestapo List, where they could all be captured with the minimum of effort?

For many years public concern concentrated on the degree of effectiveness of Soviet penetration into our security services, but hardly any attention was paid to the question whether German 'moles' had also been active within the intelligence departments before and during the war.

This question leads to the more fundamental one: was there in fact an effective fifth column in existence in Britain organized from Berlin, waiting in the wings for invasion day to help the enemy to conquer and later to administer the country?

Whoever has researched into this question has come to the same conclusion, namely that no such fifth column existed in Britain, nor was it really an effective force in any of the countries which Nazi Germany occupied during the war. A senior official in the German Foreign Office gave me his private opinion that Germany not only had no really effective network of agents, foreign nationals or German residents, in any European country, but that the degree of co-operation which they received from the indigenous population, compared with the resistance which they encountered in Western Europe, was insignificant, with the exception of France. Even there little if anything had been organized beforehand; people like Laval and his ilk were simply opportunists who collaborated only after France had given up. For the rest, the Quislings, Musserts and Degrelles and their followers were often more of an embarrassment or of a nuisance than of any real help to the German occupation authorities.

A Dutch historian, Louis de Jong, Director of the Netherlands State Institute for War Documents, on the whole supports that view.[1] He is primarily concerned with the German conquest of Holland, but has also investigated alleged fifth column activities in other countries, including Britain. In the light of all the lurid, frightening accounts which flooded across the Channel in May 1940, and which were given additional credence by the British ambassador at The Hague, his comments on the Dutch situation are particularly interesting.

> There is no evidence that Germans who lived in Holland or even Dutch nationals have in any way worth mentioning aided the invasion forces. In none of the German documents concerned with the offensive in the Lowlands is there any mention of a fifth column. There is no confirmed case of any German parachutists landing disguised as policemen, postmen, priests, or nurses. The fact that Holland could be overrun in five days seemed so unbelievable that many thought it must have been due to internal treachery. As to the reports that German refugees also lent support to the invading forces, which resulted later in the internment of thousands of them in England and France, there is again not a single case of such help which has been proven.

De Jong does not think that there were many people in England who would have co-operated with the Nazis in the event of a successful invasion. He quotes Hitler at a *Führer* Conference on 21 July 1940, as saying: 'We cannot count that there would be much support at our disposal in England.' In other *Führer* Conferences on 16 July and 26 August, Hitler asked how his paratroopers could operate in a hostile Britain – and again there is no mention of any fifth column waiting for them. De Jong's view is that the fear of a fifth column throughout Europe is understandable, but it was greatly exaggerated. It hit the refugees particularly hard. Britain tried hard to be fair and at great expense and inconvenience sorted them all out. Then at the moment of crisis they threw it all out again and decided to intern everybody. It is easy for the historian, he says, to condemn the panic measures with hindsight, but in the circumstances they were understandable.

According to the American historian David Kahn, Hitler was, until 1937, still dreaming of carving up the world in partnership with Britain and therefore forbade any serious *Abwehr* work in England lest it jeopardize his friendly approaches.[2] Thereafter attempts began to be made to infiltrate Britain with agents and to set up an espionage network but it was never particularly successful. Unbeknown to the Germans all their agents in the UK had been smoked out before the war and had been turned round by British Intelligence. The same happened to some foreign nationals such as Poles, Spaniards etc, who were smuggled into Britain in 1939–40, were captured or deliberately gave themselves up soon after landing. Thereafter they fed their German paymasters only such intelligence as MI5 provided for them.

Dr Jong reports that in the spring of 1940 the *Abwehr* made contact with Welsh nationalists and asked them to sabotage essential installations, later in 1940 they made similar approaches to some Scottish nationalists, but had no success with either of them. Kahn mentions a Welsh nationalist whom the *Abwehr* had enlisted some time before the war and who did organize a network of subagents, but soon they also began to work for MI5. It was only with the IRA in Dublin that Germany maintained regular contact, says Kahn, until their liaison officer was expelled by the Irish Government.

Support for the assumption that no organized fifth column of agents existed in England, is also given in a top secret document published by the Nazi political police, for the benefit of the Army, which I found in the German Archives.[3] It gives a potted, inaccurate and highly prejudiced history of the United Kingdom, lists important buildings in London such as museums, with the private addresses of the museum directors, who, it says, might well have hidden their more important art treasures at home; it shows a detailed table of organization of Scotland Yard, somewhat out of date; lists the names (and some photographs) of members of the British Security Forces, and enumerates details of various Jewish and Freemason bodies, the two groups which would have to be neutralized first. Nowhere is there any mention of any German agents or British sympathizers whose help could be enlisted. Surely if they existed, it would have been essential to mention them in a document of this nature.

Another document, supposed to have been printed in Leipzig in 1941, was published after the war in German and English in Lancing, Sussex, under the title: 'German-Occupied Britain'. It contains detailed instructions to the German Armed Forces as to how to proceed with the administration of Britain.* Again there is no mention of any readily available collaborators, whether British or foreign.

Another indication that German intelligence about Britain was poor is the list of prominent people – British as well as refugees – which the political police had issued, with instructions that after invasion they were to be arrested immediately they had been located.[4] It contains 2,300 names and is an amazingly heterogenous – and inaccurate – 'roll

* Published by 'Scott and Ford'. The original is at the Institute for Contemporary History in Munich. But Dr Roeder – one of their senior staff members – thinks it is a fake. He may well be right.

of honour'. Amongst foreigners are the Polish pianist and the first President of his newly constituted country, Paderewski, who had never lived in England and had died that year in America; the physicist Leo Szillard who by then also lived in America (it was he who, via Einstein, had alerted Roosevelt to atomic research in Germany); Sigmund Freud, described simply as *'Jude'*, who died just before the war; Heinrich Bruening, the former Reichschancellor whose address is given correctly as Harvard University, Cambridge – the compiler obviously did not know that there was more than one Cambridge in the world; Heinrich Mann – the brother of Thomas – living in California and, interestingly enough, the former Berlin Police Commissioner Weiss, the man who had been amongst the first ten people interned in Britain. In fact there are a number of people on this Gestapo list of enemies who spent some time in British internment camps.

The British names are an even odder assortment, ranging from Noel Coward, Lytton Strachey, Vera Brittain (Shirley Williams' mother) and Leonard and Virginia Woolf to – not unreasonably – Winston Churchill and Harold Laski. The list also contains the names of the newspaper proprietor Lord Camrose, and of Lady Astor of Cliveden, generally considered to have been appeasers and thus wrongly suspected of Nazi sympathies. On the other hand the list omits names of many prominent, politically engaged people who had been active in the fight against fascism and nazism. Whoever compiled the list could not have had the benefit of accurate advice from well-informed agents on the spot.

Another piece of evidence of how poorly Germany was informed on conditions in Britain is surely the clumsy attempt by Schellenberg, Himmler's emissary, to persuade the Duke of Windsor to return to occupied France from Lisbon and hold himself in readiness to become Hitler's Regent in a conquered Britain.

Members of the Nazi Party living abroad had been organized and were tightly controlled by the *'Auslandsorganisation'* – the foreign branch of the NSDAP. Churchill had called them the 'Nazimintern' (paraphrasing the 'Comintern') and before the war had asked for an investigation of their activities by Parliament. In the spring of 1939 Britain and France proscribed the local branches and Britain expelled twelve members including the leader Otto Karlowa.

Many of these Nazis living in Britain – waiters, chefs, salesmen and technicians – were lower middle class or working class, with a sprinkling of journalists and teachers. Some of them were certainly spying on the more prominent refugees and reporting on general conditions in their locality, but there is no evidence that those who overtly belonged to the Party engaged in espionage or had any treasonable contacts with British subjects in positions of authority. In any case, by the time war broke out, they had been expelled, had returned home by choice or were interned immediately.*

In the light of all the evidence it can therefore be reasonably assumed that there was no significant number of German agents in Britain, pretending refugees, neutral foreigners or British subjects – engaged in intelligence or sabotage work. Also it would seem that there existed no fifth column under direct orders from Germany which had penetrated any of the centres of power, in particular not British Intelligence.

Yet there was at least one senior Foreign Office official, R. E. Latham, who clearly thought otherwise. One does not know on what evidence his suspicions were based; perhaps he wrote in sheer exasperation at the ineptness of Military Intelligence, or perhaps he had in mind one or other of the fringe organizations on the extreme political right.

A number of organizations had existed before the war to promote Anglo-German friendship. The oldest one was the *Anglo-German Association*, a post-World War One organization under the patronage of Lord D'Abernon who had been British ambassador in Berlin during the critical years of the Weimar Republic. He had been an advocate of a better treatment of Germany at a time when this was still a laudable objective, which, if implemented, could have militated against the popular appeal of Nazism. With the advent of Hitler, the Association dissolved itself.† In October 1935 – the year in which Britain signed a Naval Treaty with Hitler's Germany and made Nazi Germany 'respectable' again – it was restarted as the Anglo-German Fellowship under Lord Mount Temple, a very right-wing peer. In the following year Ribbentrop founded a sister organization, the *Deutsche-Englische Gesellschaft*, which was active in disseminating German propaganda. But the most outspoken pro-Nazi organization in Britain was the 'Link', started in 1937 under the leadership of Admiral Sir Barrie Domville. It was a most active propagandist for Nazi ideas and an

---

* For these and other details of Nazi party organization see Donald M. Mckale: *The Swastika Outside Germany*, Kent State University Press, 1977.

† For more details see: Dietrich Aigner: *Das Ringen um England*, Bechtle Verlag, 1969.

apologist for every act of internal and external aggression perpetrated by the Nazi régime. At its height it claimed 4,325 members.[5] They were organized in thirty-five branches and apart from the gallant Admiral included at least two peers of the realm and two well-known university professors. The Link was the distribution channel for a propaganda broadsheet, *News from Germany* which emanated from a Herr H. R. Hoffmann who operated from a private house on the Starnberg Lake in Bavaria and who seems to have been the main unofficial link between Goebbels' ministry in Berlin and various British sympathizers.* But to what extent the Link ever received direct financial aid from Germany has never been established.

Apart from these organizations exclusively concerned with Anglo-German relations, there were a number of fringe political parties propagating fascist and national-socialist ideas as the panacea for Britain's problems. The biggest and best known was the British Union of Fascists under the leadership of Sir Oswald Mosley, but there were also other, much smaller, splinter groups such as the Imperial Fascist League, the Nordic League, the British People's Party and the National-Socialist League, led by William Joyce, who was to achieve notoriety as Lord Haw-Haw. They were all overtly anti-semitic, anti-democratic fascist organizations, which had for years been warning the government against the admission of the refugees. As is inevitable amongst extreme splinter groups at either end of the political spectrum, they quarrelled with each other. A letter from A. S. Leese, the *Führer* of the Imperial Fascist League to Herr Hoffmann in Bavaria, dated 3 March 1934† describes the Mosleyites as 'kosher Fascists'. He hoped that they would not deceive Herr Hitler.

The German link-man in London with all these various groups was a Dr R. G. Rosel, who officially ran an Anglo-German information service and was also the Nazi *Gauleiter*‡ for Britain. His closest connection was with the Link. He was expelled in June 1939 and his information service closed down.

It is generally considered that neither Hitler nor Goebbels placed much faith in the strength and the efficacy of these extreme right-wing

---

* For much of the following see: John Baker White: *The Big Lie*, London 1955.
† The Microfilm records MA 1291 Reel 34 folder 670 at the Institute in Munich contain for example a letter from a Professor of Music in Edgware (Middlesex), dated 24 August 1939, just a few days before the outbreak of war, in which this British patriot writes: 'If I had any money I would come to Germany and broadcast to my countrymen, many of whom are admiring Hitler.'
‡ Regional chief.

groups and Anglo-German propaganda associations in Britain. Even that simpleton Ribbentrop, who had been convinced when he came to Britain as ambassador that, with his champagne connections with British high society, he could swing the British establishment over to Germany, had lost his illusions by 1939. The *Führer* had obviously believed, as the Kaiser had done twenty-five years earlier, that he could get away with more and more aggressive acts and that a Britain softened up by appeasement would never stand and fight; but whatever ideas he had once had of forging a criminal partnership with Britain, he knew by 1939 that fascist or national-socialist Britain was a non-starter. It seems most unlikely that any of the political splinter groups or Anglo-German associations were part of a German financed conspiracy responsible for the internment of the refugees, or in fact for anything at all. It just did not exist.

There were no doubt individuals in Britain, some of them probably in influential positions and wielding some political clout, who during the phony war period were still hoping that Britain could eventually come to an accommodation with Hitler, allowing him then to pounce on his temporary ally Stalin and thus rid Britain of the communist menace. After all, the *Führer* himself, in a speech made after the conquest of Poland, had waved a spurious olive branch in Britain's direction. For such people the presence of all these German refugees at large was something of a nuisance. Kenneth de Courcy, on the extreme right of the Tory party, told a refugee lady some weeks before she was taken to the Isle of Man herself: 'Sooner or later England must come to terms with Germany. You refugees will obviously agitate against any peace with the Nazis. We have therefore no alternative but to intern you all to prevent you from interfering.' However it is unlikely that in this particular instance he spoke for any influential body of opinion or that neutralizing the refugees to stop them from interfering with the whipping up of a popular peace movement played any part in the internment decision.

But it is undeniable that military intelligence early in 1940 initiated a concerted campaign casting suspicions on thousands of mainly Jewish refugees and advocating wholesale internment, a campaign which certain newspapers eagerly took up. The question remains: why did they do it?

The absence of any conspiratorial or sinister motivation predicates that some senior officers in the Security Services genuinely believed that the unrestricted presence of some seventy-six thousand enemy aliens on an island threatened by hostile invasion, presented a real danger and that only wholesale incarceration could minimize the risk. Old fashioned, public school type prejudices may have played their part in arriving at such a conclusion – prejudices against foreigners in general, laced with a good dose of bias against 'dagos' and Jews in particular. There may also have been some concern that tribunals who had ordered the internment of only 569 Germans and Austrians could not have done their job properly; they must have been too superficial or too lenient and the situation was much too critical to wait until every individual case could be re-examined once again. Perhaps they even doubted the thoroughness and accuracy of their own investigations and records. They realized that in Sir John Anderson they had a determined opponent to wholesale internment and that it would be necessary to rouse public opinion in order to force government to adopt the tough measures which Military Intelligence considered vital for the welfare of the country.

In this they found willing helpers in certain press Lords and journalists. Once again it can be ruled out that any of them were involved in any traitorous conspiracy. But no doubt they suffered from acute embarrassment, if not from a bad conscience. They must have been anxious to obliterate in the public mind their own immediate political past; hoping that if they were '*plus royaliste que le roi*' people would forget their pre-war pro-Nazi propaganda. Prejudices against liberals, Jews, refugees and people on the Left, undoubtedly played a part, prejudices which certain popular organs of the press have never been slow to exploit. Lurid stories about spies and saboteurs make good copy. The concerted anti-refugee campaign in the spring of 1940 was reprehensible but it was not treasonable.

In the course of the various debates in Parliament, arguments other than national security were also advanced by government spokesmen to justify indiscriminate internment, but none of these were really valid. It was said that it was being done in the interests of the refugees themselves, to protect them from public wrath and violence. 'The inflamed eye of the man in the street' would not be able to distinguish between a refugee and a Nazi German. But although some refugees were no doubt treated by their neighbours with some degree of suspicion and aloofness, there is no evidence that any of them ever suffered any real hardship or physical violence. No German-speaking couples were ever assaulted on a Clapham omnibus. On the contrary, there is plenty of evidence of sympathy and understanding shown by ordinary British people for the refugee men, women and children who lived amongst them or shared the same air-raid shelters with them.

It is also claimed that many refugees would find themselves unemployed and without means because British working men and women would refuse to work alongside them. Internment was therefore in their own best interests. Once again there is no evidence that this ever happened. On the contrary, all those who were released or who had escaped internment had no difficulty in integrating themselves into the war effort once the restrictions on the employment of aliens were lifted; yet the stigma of internment should have, if anything, raised the level of suspicion.

Another claim was that, in the event of invasion, refugees might, because of their own precarious situation, add alarm to a confused situation and so depress public morale. It is difficult to refute that argument because, fortunately, it was never put to the test, but it remains unconvincing.

Finally it was argued by some that whilst the refugees were behind barbed wire it would be much easier to interrogate them and to extract from them any special knowledge useful to the war effort. But the refugees were only too anxious to put whatever information they had at the government's disposal; many had been saddened during the early months of the war when their offers of help had been spurned. Surely internment and the resentment which it caused, could only make them less and not more willing to assist.

Post-war research has clearly shown that the tales of fifth column activities in the occupied countries, of treachery and sabotage by native Quislings or disguised German agents were largely figments of a fanciful imagination. It was superior force, the element of surprise and the brutality, coupled in some cases with a lack of moral fibre and with political weakness, which had given Germany so many quick victories; sedition played only a minor part, if any at all. It is therefore clear that the internment of some thirty thousand Germans and Austrians, of whom the great majority were Jews, victims of Nazi persecution, passionate enemies of Hitler and all he stood for, was unnecessary, wasteful, counterproductive and a blot on a page of history.

But that is the judgement of hindsight. From Churchill to the ordinary man in the street, the lurid tales of deceit and treachery, of agents planted in the guise of refugees, were genuinely believed in 1940. The months of May and June of that year were months of supreme crisis and if there had been even a handful of real saboteurs or traitors amongst these thirty thousand men and women, then justification for their indiscriminate internment cannot be gainsaid; and at the time it was accepted as such by most of the refugees.

It is therefore not indiscriminate internment as such which can be criticized, but the ham-fisted, unimaginative, arbitrary way in which it was started, carried out and then stopped again; the petty restrictions; the insensitive news blackout; the delays in family correspondence; the slow progress of the release machine; the confusion of the overseas deportations; the herding together of refugees and Nazis; the inability to organize useful work inside or outside any of the camps, and the incarceration of so many who, under the original Home Office instructions, should never have been interned at all.

It is a tale full of muddle, misunderstandings and maladroitness. As has been shown, time and time again the officers in charge of the camps, whether in Britain, Canada or Australia, were totally unaware that the people whom they were to guard were not dangerous parachutists or Nazi agents, but mainly Jewish refugees about whom nothing particularly adverse was known individually, but who had been arrested as a purely precautionary measure. It would have been simple to notify the officials correctly all along the lines of communication. Yet nowhere was it done properly; in the case of the Dominions, not even after the matter had been clarified in the House of Commons.

Not only were the dominion governments not properly informed, but it seems clear that the officials concerned in the War Office and Intelligence did not correctly brief even their own Government. Some of the replies to questions in the House in the early days of internment are clear evidence of this.

It really seems inconceivable that, even in the confused crisis of the summer of 1940, all this was just an administrative slip-up; one cannot help presuming that the information was deliberately not passed on by people who were prejudiced and very suspicious of all foreigners.

Internment never became a party-political issue. Although many of the xenophobic advocates of 'interning them all' were on the right of the Tory Party, there were also some left-wing members of the Labour Party who were equally suspicious of all aliens. On the other hand, amongst the parliamentary paladins of the internees there were as many Conservatives as there were Liberals, Socialists and Independent members. It was a Conservative MP who called indiscriminate internment a 'bespattered page' in British history. His was an emotive reaction to a situation which for a few months became a catalyst of opinions, similar, though to nothing like the same extent of course, to the Dreyfus affair. The blots which Victor Cazalet castigated have long since faded and been forgotten; the page of history was soon wiped clean by the protests of so many enlightened politicians, journalists, academics and artists, by the humane response of so many civil servants and soldiers (once they knew with what sort of people they were dealing); by the way the British public allowed the refugees to integrate themselves into war-time Britain once they had regained their freedom.

*   *   *

In the autumn of 1944 I was sitting on the terrace of the Gymkhana Club in New Delhi, sipping my gin and tonic, looking, I thought, like the pukkah captain Sahib that the servants obviously thought me to be, even if my accent could not fool fellow officers.

I had just come off the tennis court where in a mixed doubles my partner had been the wife of my brigadier. As we were returning to the clubhouse she looked at my set of 'whiter than white' molars and remarked: 'I say young man, are those teeth your own?'

I thought, 'have I at last arrived? Have I become a member of the establishment now?' And then I thought back to how just four years before I had been gazing wistfully at the barbed wire strands of Hutchinsons Camp and at the deep blue sea beyond. Life certainly had changed since then. Those five months of internment had been a strange experience, harsh, testing, stimulating, not a bad preparation for what came afterwards. The memory of the unpleasant aspects and experiences had already faded; what remained was the awareness that it had also meant a stretching of stamina and intellect and memories of the people and the challenges that had been met. It had, after all, not been a wasted period, not a bad time. That was the perspective in 1944. It is still the same in 1980.

Notes

CHAPTER I

1 Case of Wells *v*. Williams.
2 33 Geo III Cap. 4. also 30 Geo III Cap. 50.
3 14/18/13.
4 For further elaboration, see Professor G. Leibholz: *Völkerrechtliche Stellung der Refugees im Kriege*, in '*Archiv des Völkerrechtes*', 2.
5 Cab. 27(33)2.
6 Cab. 23(35)5.
7 Cab. 23(33)2.
8 Cab. 27(33)8. and C.P. 96(33)7.
9 MP for Wolverhampton East (Lib).
10 Cab. 16/193 Report of the Sub-Committee on the Employment of Aliens in Secret Munitions Work (of the Committee Imperial Defence).
11 Police War Instructions, Section 6. PWIG.
12 Report of German Jewish Aid Committee, August 1939, in Bloomsbury House.
13 Statistical Survey: Movement for the Care of Children from Germany.
14 Cab. 14(38)6.
15 Home Office File 7004 63/11.
16 Home Office File 7004 63/12.
17 Cab. 16/211.
18 CAW 21; 252nd Meeting of Committee of Imperial Defence.
19 G. Dixon (Home Office) Memorandum, 6 April 1939. File 7004 63/25.
20 File 7004 63/39.
21 John Wheeler Bennett: *John Anderson, Viscount Waverley*, London 1962, pp 238 ff.
22 Letters dated 2 March and 26 March 1940, op. cit. above.
23 Cabinet Conclusion Cab. 37/(39)/11 and Interim Report CP 151 (39).
24 Cabinet Minutes W Mn 112(39) and Committee Report WP(G)(39)138.

CHAPTER 2

1 Eugen Spier: *The Protecting Power*, London 1951.
2 Memorandum on the Control of Aliens, op. cit.
3 Archive of the *Auswaertige Amt*, Bonn RX 11 Zv 175. Memo is dated 12/2/1940.
4 Judex (a pseudonym): *Anderson's Prisoners*, a pamphlet published by Gollancz in 1940.
5 Sir John Anderson, House of Commons, 4 April 1940.

Notes

CHAPTER 3
1 *Evening Standard*, 17 July 1940.
2 *Daily Herald*, 27 July 1940 and *News Chronicle* 29 July 1940.
3 HPC (40)92.

CHAPTER 4
1 Sir John Anderson, in reply to Colonel Burton (Sudbury C).
2 13th meeting held on 21 March 1940 WP(G)(40)115.
3 Cab. 123(4)15.
4 WP(G)(40)131.
5 FO 371/25244.
6 Judex: *Anderson's Prisoners*, op. cit.
7 National Council for Civil Liberties pamphlet '*Internment and Treatment of Aliens*', May 1941.
8 FO 371/25244.
9 In the Oxford University Press series: 'History of England', footnote on page 491.
10 See Sir Henry Tizard's Papers at the Imperial War Museum. Also, Dr R. V. Jones' book: *The Most Secret War*, London 1978.
11 *New Statesman and Nation*, 25 May.
12 Cab. 128(40).
13 Cab. 137(40)11.
14 FO 371/25244.
15 Ibid.
16 Ibid.
17 FO 371/29185.
18 Minutes in Bloomsbury House archives.
19 File C 15/1/3 at Bloomsbury House.

CHAPTER 5
1 Cab. 141(40) Appendix containing WP(40)168.
2 Report No. 18 in WP(R) 40/170.
3 CAB 79 (40) 4 and 5.
4 CAB 161(40)6.
5 CAB 137(40)11 and CAB 174(40)13.
6 CAB 175(40)13.
7 CAB 175(40)12.
8 CAB 260(40)1 and WP(G) 40 187.
9 WP(40)213. For the meeting of 27 May see CAB 141(40) Appendix and WP(40)168.
10 FO File Gen 200/6/72.
11 CAB 174(40)13.
12 R. E. Latham minute and memorandum in FO 371/25253.

13 Loewenstein Papers at the Institut für Zeitgeschichte, Munich 9a. Fol. 1.
14 FO 371/25253 dated 27 June 1940.
15 Ronald Jasper: *George Bell, Bishop of Chichester*, London 1967, page 147.

CHAPTER 6

1 Swiss Report No 23 in *Auswaertige Amt* Archive (RX 11 Zv 57).
2 Report by Rabbi Robinow, dated 6 May, to the Board of Deputies after visiting both Paignton and Seaton.
3 RX 11 Zv 57, dated 23 May 1940.
4 RX 11 Zv 175, letter dated 17 March 1941.
5 On 26 April 1940. Both letters are at Bloomsbury House.
6 Report by Otto Voelger to the German Foreign Office, dated 7 November 1941. (RX 11 Zv 58).
7 Tristan Busch (real name A. Schuetz): *Secret Service Unmasked*, London. Translated from German, introduction by Wickham Steed.
8 Dated 6 March 1941 (WO File 79/Internees 296).
9 RX 11 Zv 90.
10 RX 11 Zv 175.

CHAPTER 7

1 Home Office File Gen 200/117/163.
2 WP(40)432.
3 WP(G)(40)170.
4 CAB 298(40)5.
5 Eugen Spier: *The Protecting Power*, op. cit. pp 131 ff.
6 *Auswaertige Amt* Archive RX 11 Zv 59.
7 *New York Times*, 7 July 1940.
8 Details contained in a letter sent to his parents. *Auswaertige Amt* RV 11 Zv 58.
9 In the House of Lords on 8 August 1940.
10 FO 371/25210.
11 CAB 224(40)5.
12 WP(40)432.
13 CAB 284(40)6.
14 *Auswaertige Amt* Archive RX 11 Zv 58.
15 Bundesarchiv Koblenz Saenger Papers. Zs.g.102122.
16 *Auswaertige Amt* RV 11 Zv 58.
17 Paterson Report op. cit.
18 For this account see the internal memo from Sir John Moylan, Head of Section B3 at the Home Office (Gen 29/3/438), dated 8 August 1941.
19 See the article by Barbara Moon in the Canadian magazine *MacCleans* of 10 February 1962. Also a personal interview.
20 Sir John Moylan, op. cit.
21 See the *MacCleans* article, op. cit.

Notes

CHAPTER 8

1 Memo by the Lord President of the Council on 'Internees and Prisoners of War'. WP(G)(40)170.
2 R. E. Latham, 19 July 1940. FO 371/25210.
3 Captain Margesson replying to Colonel Wedgwood, House of Commons, 3 September 1941.

CHAPTER 9

1 FO 371/29221.
2 Chaim Raphael: *Memoirs of a Special Case*, London 1962.
3 CAB 224(40)5.
4 CAB 284(40)6.
5 Alfred Lomnitz: *Never Mind Mister Lom*, London 1941.
6 Dated 5 August 1940, at Bloomsbury House.
7 Sir John Moylan to the Secretary of the Board of Deputies.
8 Richard Friedenthal: *Die Welt in der Nusschale*, Munich 1965.
9 Dated 30 July 1940, at Bloomsbury House.

CHAPTER 10

1 *Spectator*, 28 March 1941.
2 Fred Uhlman: '*The Making of an Englishman*', Victor Gollancz, 1960.
3 Command Papers 6217 of July 1940, 6233 of August 1940 and 6233 (revised) of October 1940.

CHAPTER 11

1 *Jack Bilbo: An Autobiography*. The Modern Art Gallery, King Charles Street, London.
2 Printed in Issue Forty-Seven of the *Onchan Pioneer*.
3 Published in the issue of 28 September 1940.
4 Letter in the *Manchester Guardian*, 26 August 1940.

CHAPTER 12

1 In her monograph *A Tale of Internment*, Allen & Unwin 1942.
2 According to a report in the *Daily Sketch* dated 26 May.
3 Letter to the Secretary of the Board of Deputies – at Bloomsbury House.
4 Legationsrat Kundt, head of department KULT E of the *Auswaertige Amt*. Report dated 18 January 1940 (RX 11 Zv 346).
5 Letter from a repatriated in *Auswaertige Amt* archive RX 11 Zv 175.

6 *Sunday Chronicle*, 11 May 1941.
7 Laffitte: *The Internment of Enemy Aliens*, op. cit.
8 Harry Schnur's letter in the issue of 17 May 1941.
9 6 June 1940.
10 WP(G)(40)309.
11 *Manchester Guardian*, 21 February 1941. Article by Bertha Bracey of the Society of Friends.
12 On 23 December 1940.
13 In a letter in the *Manchester Guardian* on 6 June 1940.
14 FO 371/29173.
15 Issue dated 31 October 1940.

CHAPTER 13

1 W. Ivor Jennings: *The British Constitution*, Cambridge 1941.
2 Judex: *Anderson's Prisoners*, op. cit.
3 WP(G)(40)187.
4 Cab 206(40)1.
5 WP(G)(40)195 and Cab 209(40)13.
6 Cab 207(40)12.
7 HO File Gen. 230/1/1.
8 HO File Gen. 230/1/1.
9 Cab 217(40)3 and Cab 218(40)2.
10 Section K(140) page 166.
11 Section J(120) page 150.
12 FO 371/25210.
13 Cab 239(40)15.
14 Cab 240(40)10.
15 WP(G)(40)309.
16 Cab 293(40)9.

CHAPTER 16

1 Ronald Jasper: *George Bell*, op. cit.
2 The *Daily Mail*, 19 November 1940.
3 The *Daily Telegraph*, 23 August 1940.
4 FO 371/29173. This file contains all the documents mentioned in this context.
5 FO 371/29180.
6 Memo dated 25 January 1941. FO 371/29180.
7 FO 371/29173.
8 Letter dated 17 June 1941. FO 371/29221.
9 HO File Gen 29/3/4381.

Notes

CHAPTER 17

1 Louis de Jong: *De Duitse Vijfde Colonne in de Tweede Wereldoorlog*, Amsterdam 1953.
2 David Kahn: *Hitler's Spies*, op. cit.
3 *'Informationsheft Grossbritannien'* DCM.04. Published by the Sicherheitshauptamt (at the Bundesarchiv in Koblenz).
4 *Sonderfahndungslists G.B.* issued by the Reichssicherheitshauptamt in Koblenz, DC 15,31 5404/75.
5 Wiener Library Bulletin in May 1939.

A Note on Sources and Index

A Note on Sources

Primary Sources
Personal interviews with people listed under 'Acknowledgments', also mementoes kept by them.
Taped interviews at Imperial War Museum
Public Record Office:
  a) Foreign Office Files.
  b) War Office Files.
  c) Cabinet Records.
Home Office: General Files.
  Patterson Report.
  White Papers.
Hansard.
British Library, Colindale: Newspaper and Periodicals' Files.
Wiener Library: Depositions of former internees and Camp Papers.
Bloomsbury House: Correspondence between Jewish bodies and official authorities.
Imperial War Museum: Sir Henry Tizard Papers.
Auswaertige Amt, Bonn: Internment Files.
Friedrich Ebert Institute, Bonn: Sanders Papers.
Bundesarchiv, Koblenz: Saenger Papers.
Institut fur Zeitgeschichte, Munich: Loewenstein and Natan Papers and other original documents relevant to internment.

Secondary sources
Aigner, Dietrich: *Das Ringen um England*, 1969
Baker White, John: *The Big Lie*, 1955
Bennett, John Wheeler: *John Anderson, Viscount Waverley*, 1962
Bentwich, Norman: *I Understand the Risks*, 1950
Bilbo, Jack: *An Autobiography*
Borchardt, Ruth: *The Services Exchange in an Internment Camp*, 1943
Busch, Tristan: *Secret Service*
Friedenthal, Richard: *Die Welt in der Nusschale*, 1965
  Hitler's Table Talk, 1953
Jasper, Ronald: *George Bell, Bishop of Chichester*, 1967
Jennings, W. Ivor: *The British Constitution*, 1941
Jones, Dr R. V: *The Most Secret War*, 1978
Jong, Louis de: *De Duitse Vigfde Colonne in de Twede Wereldoorlig*, 1953
'Judex': *Anderson's Prisoners*, 1940
Kahn, David: *Hitler's Spies*, 1978
Lafitte, Francis: *The Internment of Enemy Aliens*, 1941
Laurent, Livia: *A Tale of Internment*, 1942
Lomnitz, Alfred: *Never Mind Mister Lum*, 1941

A Note on Sources

McKale, Donald: *The Swastika outside Germany*, 1977

Moon, Barbara, Article in *Mcleans* Magazine, 1962

National Council for Civil Liberties: *Internment and Treatment of Aliens*, 1941

Raphael, Chaim: *Memoirs of a Special Case*, 1962

Roeder, Werner: *Die Deutschen Sozialistischen Exilgruppen in Gros Britannien*, 1968

Sharf, Andrew: *Nazi Racialism and the British Press*, 1963

Sievers, Leo: *Juden in Deutschland*, 1977

Spier, Eugen: *The Protecting Power*, 1951

Spier, Eugen: *Focus. A Footnote to the History of the Thirties*, 1963

Stokes, Mary: *Eleanor Rathbone*, 1949

Taylor, A. J. P: *History of England*, 1918–1945

Index

Index

Index